Spatial Policing

Spatial Policing

The Influence of Time, Space, and Geography on Law Enforcement Practices

SECOND EDITION

Edited by

Charles E. Crawford
Western Michigan University

Carolina Academic Press
Durham, North Carolina

Library of Congress Cataloging-in-Publication Data

Names: Crawford, Charles E., 1967- editor.
Title: Spatial policing : the influence of time, space, and geography on law enforcement practices / edited by Charles E. Crawford.
Description: Second edition. | Durham, North Carolina : Carolina Academic Press, [2018] | Includes bibliographical references and index.
Identifiers: LCCN 2017052807 | ISBN 9781611638349 (alk. paper)
Subjects: LCSH: Police. | Spatial behavior. | Spatial analysis (Statistics) | Crime prevention.
Classification: LCC HV7921 .S656 2018 | DDC 363.23--dc22
LC record available at https://lccn.loc.gov/2017052807

eISBN 978-1-53100-428-6

Carolina Academic Press
700 Kent Street
Durham, North Carolina 27701
Telephone (919) 489-7486
Fax (919) 493-5668
www.cap-press.com

Printed in the United States of America

To Raeshell, Ryan, and Devin

Contents

Acknowledgments

I would like to thank all of my contributors for taking the time to share your expertise. Without you this project would not have been possible. I cannot express enough gratitude to Beth Hall at Carolina Academic Press for your encouragement and to Susan Trimble for your assistance in bringing this project to life.

Introduction

Several high-profile incidents over the last few years in America have highlighted the need to understand policing actions in context. Citizens across the nation and in some cases the world have witnessed police use of force and tactics in some cities that were deeply disturbing. When a local or national news agency reports on a police-involved shooting, or we watch videos on social media of mistreatment and differential practices in minority neighborhoods that may only be a few blocks away, we may ask ourselves: how can policing actions be so different in that space or location? For example, are the differential practices simply a result of the group of people the police encounter? What is it about an area of the city that makes it a hot spot for crime at night? Why do the police act, speak, and patrol so differently across segments of the city? At their core, the questions all show an awareness of the influence of space, time, and geography on law enforcement.

Researchers have also begun to realize the importance of the situational context of police actions. Imagine a police officer apprehending a suspect. The officer may choose many different courses of action and options for the use of force if warranted. These choices do not exist in a vacuum and are conditioned by when and where the arrest takes place. Consider for a moment how the following dichotomies of spatial context can vary for an arrest: a public area versus private residence, night time versus early morning, and a high-risk patrol area versus a relatively safe suburban neighborhood. Clearly there are other spatial and temporal contexts that are much more complex, and all can greatly enhance the understanding of law enforcement practices.

Spatial Policing pulls together some of the leading researchers in policing, and those with research interests on the impact of spatial, cultural, and technological issues on criminal justice practices, to explore how widely varying contexts can influence police actions. My own interest in this topic began through studying the situational framework of police use of force. The most significant findings tended to revolve around the actions of the citizen or arrestee in response to the officer's attempt to make the arrest. Nonetheless, there were some intriguing, significant results connected to space and time. For example, the dichotomy of a public space versus a private space may appear simple at first. However, a resident's home or apartment versus a public street or parking lot has a great deal of meaning.

Reflect on the spatial context of your own home. You have a sense of authority in this context; it is private and you have ownership. Now consider a police officer in your home ordering you to comply with various commands. This represents a challenge to the authority you believe exists in your own residence. Disobeying the commands, or resisting the arrest, is more likely to happen in this private spatial context. Imagine the same scenario, but this time the officer has asked you to step outside or walk with them a few feet to the patrol car, essentially bringing you into their world or the public space. Your basic rights and protections are still in place, but the feeling or sense of authority is greatly reduced, and compliance is more likely given this public context. This action capitalizes on the officer's knowledge of the shift in the spatial environment.

The previous example of public versus private space demonstrates one context. Imagine how the scenario would be complicated if the exchange took place on a college campus. Does a dormitory occupant have the same sense of ownership and authority to control the space in the presence of a campus police officer? Now change the geographic location to an inner city low-income area. Would the officer's attitude be different, or use of authority greater in the personal space than if it were only a few miles away in an upper middle class suburb? What if the space is now an area of a national border crossing; how would the officer's authority be impacted? If the officer was wearing a body camera or if the interaction was being streamed live on social media would the introduction of this surveillance technology change the outcome? Would the officer's and citizen's race or ethnicity further influence the actions taken during this encounter? How do police mark and define actions in cyberspace? These are challenging questions with many facets that will be explored within this text.

The issue of space in policing is probably something many practitioners and citizens are aware of, but may not have given this topic more than a passing thought other than noticing that an area looks more dangerous, or a person looks out of place at a particular location or time. Throughout its ten chapters *Spatial Policing* will investigate many of these spatial, geographic, and technological contexts to reveal how these changing environments shape policing practices.

Chapter 1: Space and Policing by Charles E. Crawford. In this chapter, I briefly review the debate over defining space and place, the theoretical contributions of the Chicago School of Criminology, and environmental criminology. In addition, I focus on two developments from the criminology of place that have had the most direct impact on policing: defensible space, and the "broken windows" thesis. This chapter also reviews how cities and police departments have come to terms with battles over space between various counterpublics. Furthermore, the chapter explores key theoretical contributions to understanding how police mark and respond to unique spatial contexts. It is only when police departments recognize the importance of the spatial context they patrol and the people contained within its boundaries that are they able to resolve conflict. In the end, space provides an important framework for understanding police operations in our society.

Chapter 2: Remapping the City: Public Identity, Cultural Space, and Social Justice by Jeff Ferrell. In this reprint of Ferrell's classic article, he takes a fascinating look at the complexities and conflicts over public space. Ferrell illustrates that there are multiple groups engaged in battles over what may appear to be mundane public spaces: parks, parking lots, shopping areas, and sidewalks. As Ferrell points out, the conflict between these groups revolves around cultural space or the deep meanings groups attach to these locations. As space is redefined through conflict there must also be control of those who are deemed foreign in these recreated locations, bringing marginal groups into a direct confrontation with city officials and the criminal justice system.

Chapter 3: Policing Cyberspace: Mass Surveillance and the Expansion of the State by Frank Tridico. In this chapter, Frank Tridico explores the complexities and legalities of investigations and law enforcement actions in cyberspace. Increasingly our world relies on digital communications for critical parts of global economies and networks. As state powers increased after the terrorist attacks of September 11, 2001, a host of new laws were passed that directly impacted how evidence would be seized and how information would be gathered, creating numerous challenges and legal questions in the face of cyberpolicing at each level of government.

Chapter 4: Minorities, Space, and Policing by Charles E. Crawford. In this chapter, I explore the police-minority relationship through a spatial framework. Many of America's most violent urban disturbances have revolved around hostile police contact in Black communities or spaces. To gain some insight into how these events may unfold, I offer a review of recent high-profile cases, leading theories, and critical research on what may be one of most enduring and serious problems in law enforcement—policing the minority space. Policing the minority space contains many challenges, as there is a rich detailed history of how these spaces were created and their relationships with law enforcement. By recognizing the distinctiveness of the minority space, possible improvements in police-citizen relationships and patrol practices may be revealed. Policy implications are discussed.

Chapter 5: Policing Borders: Immigration, Criminalization, and Militarization in the Era of Social Control Profitability by Martin Guevara Urbina and Ilse Aglaé Peña. In this chapter, Urbina and Peña explore in great detail one of the most contentious issues in recent American politics: that is, policing the border between the United States and Mexico. This unique spatial context of the border poses numerous challenges for policing in the face of globalization, immigration, and the increased militarization of law enforcement. Issues of citizenship, the Constitution, fighting terrorism, and the war on drugs are all discussed.

Chapter 6: Rural Law Enforcement: Real Police Work? by Robert Hartmann McNamara. In this chapter, McNamara explores the often-misunderstood policing context of rural space. The chapter offers a rich discussion of the definitional issues of rural locations. Many of the traditional crimes that are associated with urban areas such as gangs, drugs, and DUIs occur in the rural setting and represent distinctive challenges for police departments operating in this framework. Furthermore, policing rural areas can entail some unusual issues such as dealing with agricultural and wildlife crimes, and patrol officers having to cover sizeable distances to provide service.

Chapter 7: Policing Urban Spaces by Kim M. Lersch. In this chapter, Lersch offers a comprehensive account of policing in the urban environment. When citizens think about a law enforcement agency they typically envision the departments in our nation's largest cities. This is partly due to the considerable amount of research attention given to urban crime, police practices, and popular culture portrayals of these departments. Policing in the urban spatial context can be difficult, as the concept of neighborhood and community can vary dramatically across the city, resulting in differential treatment, patrol practices, and crime types.

Chapter 8: Policing Educational Spaces: Status, Practices, and Challenges by Emmanuel P. Barthe. In this chapter, Barthe describe the complexities of providing law enforcement service in the campus context. Perceptions of the safe and structured environment of a college or high school campus have been shattered in the last decade with a series of high-profile mass episodes of violence. The mandates of traditional law enforcement to protect lives and valuable property of both the school and students are at odds with campus law enforcement's service roots. Furthermore, the educational space raises difficult questions, such as where exactly does the campus end and how should various crimes be handled both in and around the school?

Chapter 9: The Meaning of Surveillance in Public Space by Gregory J. Howard and Elizabeth P. Bradshaw. In this chapter, Howard and Bradshaw explore contemporary surveillance practices, technologies, and their implications for policing, and the capacity of each to structure the use and experience of public space. Furthermore, the authors review not only concepts and implications of surveillance and information gathering, but also the resistance to such efforts and predictions for the future use of ever-increasing technology.

Chapter 10: Spatial Crime Prevention: Traditional Versus Non-Traditional Perspectives by Ronald G. Burns and Brie Diamond. In this final chapter, Burns and Diamond review the changing nature of law enforcement in the United States and the importance of crime prevention. Both practitioners and theorists since the Chicago School have realized that crime occurs in specific physical locations and environments. This knowledge has led to several developments to address the spatial context of crime prevention, including both physical and cyberspace. This spatial awareness of deterrence can be found in crime prevention through environmental design (CPTED), defensible space, and the technological innovations of Geographic Information Systems (GIS) applications. As Burns states, controlling space and preventing crime is at the heart of policing.

One of the goals I have for *Spatial Policing* is that it may serve as a starting point and resource for critically assessing how space and location impact law enforcement practices. The space in which we all interact either in public or private is a powerful influence on our lives. The space we occupy can enhance our feelings of ownership and authority, or it may give visual and cultural cues that show how powerless and unsafe we are in a given location. City planners, architects, and security agencies are well aware of the influence of space and location on behavior, and increasingly how the use of powerful technological tools may be used to both monitor and regulate space. This awareness is seen in criminology and in our nation's police departments today. After reading *Spatial Policing*, I hope that you will never look at any given space quite the same, and that you take the time to examine the design elements, visual cues, cameras, and other technologies that may be present and how each of these respond to the demands placed on a given location from various groups, and most importantly how the police operate in that spatial context.

Spatial Policing

1

Space and Policing

Charles E. Crawford

Imagine that you have just joined the police force in a large urban department and have been given a patrol assignment in one of the toughest sections of the city. This may be a location you have passed many times as a citizen, or you were aware of the spatial and cultural cues that told you this space was different, perhaps unsafe. However, this is now a space that you must learn to navigate as a part of your assignment. This assigned space has a history and community; it is a neighborhood in which people live, work, and grow, and some commit crime. As you begin your patrol you feel the tension as you pass groups of young men on the sidewalk, and your attempts to greet citizens in the neighborhood are at times rebuffed or met with cold stares, as no one wants to be seen talking to an officer in uniform. As the night progresses and you answer calls for service, a few people are thankful and supportive, yet you find that many citizens, suspects, and victims in this space challenge your authority, legitimacy, and character.

You can easily visualize the difficulties of working in such an environment. You may also doubt whether you can return the next day after such a reception. As you drive your patrol car back to the station and reflect over the day's events, several questions may run through your mind. How can the police effectively work in such a challenging environment? How do other officers in my department view the space of the city in which they provide service and enforce the law? What forces have created the animosity citizens have towards the police in this part of the city? What is it about this space that makes it so different from the rest of the city?

Attempting to answer these questions is of the utmost importance in policing, and at the root of designing a better police response is the recognition that policing must be sensitive to space. As the introductory thought exercise illustrates, officers are aware of space and notice and feel the changes as they move throughout the city, yet the literature on police actions tends to focus on other contexts of police-citizen interactions, such as sociological and psychological forces, while neglecting the space in which crime, police, and citizens come together.

The literature that does exist on police and the importance of the space in which they operate supports what many in policing and the community intuitively know—space and location matter. The perception of space, whether it is Ferguson, Chicago, Baltimore, or a small town, conditions officer actions, responses, and ultimately how citizens react to the police. Many areas within these cities are communities truly in need. While they may be resilient and culturally rich, in some of these spaces crime and violence are simply a part of everyday life and a well-planned, space-sensitive police response is needed the most.

Space

Space remains a contested issue among social scientists and professionals. Consider for a moment the professional groups that work with space: architects, urban planners, and interior and landscape designers. As these professionals employ their craft, they shape the ways we engage in commerce, visit, and reside. Each of these professionals may have their own agendas and ideas on how and where these various activities should take place. Even the term *space* is not without conflicting meanings and interpretations. For example, some define it as abstract geometries, such as distance, direction, and shape (Hillier & Hanson, 1984). For others, space is what place becomes when things of meaning and value are removed (de Certeau, 1984; Harvey, 1996).

Although we often used these terms interchangeably, *place*, *location*, and *neighborhood* have distinct meanings for sociologists and researchers of space. For example, Gieryn (2000) observes that place is not space, space becomes a place when it is filled with people, objects, and practices. Nor should space be confused with geographic boundaries, nor can it be found in the virtual world of cyberspace. One way to conceptualize place is to think of it as a distinct location in our world. A place may be your favorite armchair, your village, your neighborhood, a seaside, or a mountaintop (Entrikin, 1989, 1991; Gieryn, 2000).

Clearly, space is at the heart of this book, and the term is used at many points by several of the contributing authors. We assume that our meaning of *space* is apparent to the reader, but as the previous discussion illustrates, there is still a need for clarity. By no means is this chapter intended to solve the space/place debate. For this text, I follow the advice of Herbert Gans (2002), who suggests that sociologists of place (or those new to the decades-long debate) avoid reifying space and studies that posit all social life exist in space. Taking Gans's advice, this chapter and the subsequent contributions best fit with his "use-centered view of space." This definition of space allows us to examine how individuals, police departments, and society transform natural space into social space and what forces (economic, political, and legal) come into play in the uses and exchanges within these spaces.

Space and the Public

In addition to the controversy surrounding the definitions of *space* and *place*, there is conflict over what is truly a public space. For example, political philosopher Habermas (1989) views public space as an arena of discourse open and accessible to all, where private citizens would come to discuss "public matters." This egalitarian view of the public space is best reflected in the golden ages and golden sites, such as the early modern coffeehouses of Paris and London, and the New England town square, where open public dialogue may have occurred. Researchers of place and space such as Margaret Crawford (1995) and Nancy Fraser (1993) illustrate how history challenges this notion of inclusion and shared space. Public space is not uncontested space. A variety of groups compete for access, recognition, and even ownership. Space may be used to claim, or form, social identities and culture, and it is necessary to understand the unique roll that it plays in society. However, if we were to reflect on world history, it does not take long to find groups that were not a part of the "public" and therefore did not have rights or access to these spaces.

For example, the status of being a slave in many nations of the world, such as ancient Greece, Rome, and the antebellum South in the United States, restricted the use of public space and engaging in any type of debate over public matters. This status differentiation can also be found with gender and class. Middle-class American women during the nineteenth and twentieth centuries formed philanthropic and activist groups based on their definition of motherhood, often excluding less privileged women, who had to find access to the public space through work or other avenues (Crawford, 1995). Democracy and access to the public arena is constantly changing as different groups both defend and challenge the state. The concept of multiple publics or counterpublics that challenge and redefine public space (Fraser,

Figure 1.1: Counterpublics and the Demands on Public Space

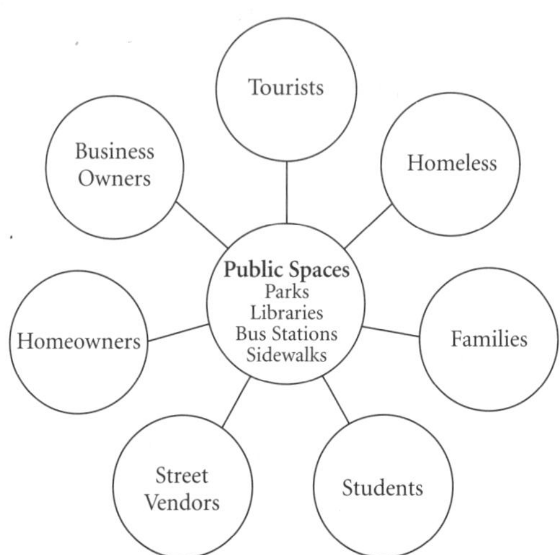

1993) is of key interest for law enforcement. As new demands and challenges over space arise, police departments are often called to settle the dispute.

Challenging Space

The use of public space may be challenged in several ways. Consider, for example, a park that you may frequent in your city. You may view the park as a place to relax, read, or take young children to play. More than likely, your perceived use of the space aligns with the intent of the city planners and designers. The next time you visit a public space such as the park or library, sit back and take note of the various publics that are there and what claims or challenges they impose. Figure 1.1 may help illustrate the complex nature of spatial boundaries and the public.

Each group views the space differently based on their needs and desired uses. Frequently, the uses are at odds with each other, creating conflict. Further complicating the use of space is the role time of day can play in this challenge. City sidewalks, for example, are needed by citizens to pass safely from building to building, and business owners need the public to have access to their establishments during regular operating hours. Contemplate for a moment the conflict that can arise over the use of a sidewalk based on the time of day. During regular operating hours, a business owner may challenge a street artist's use of the sidewalk and may call the police to remove a panhandler or a homeless person's belongings. However, at night the sidewalk may be trans-

Figure 1.2: Defining Public Space from the Top and Bottom

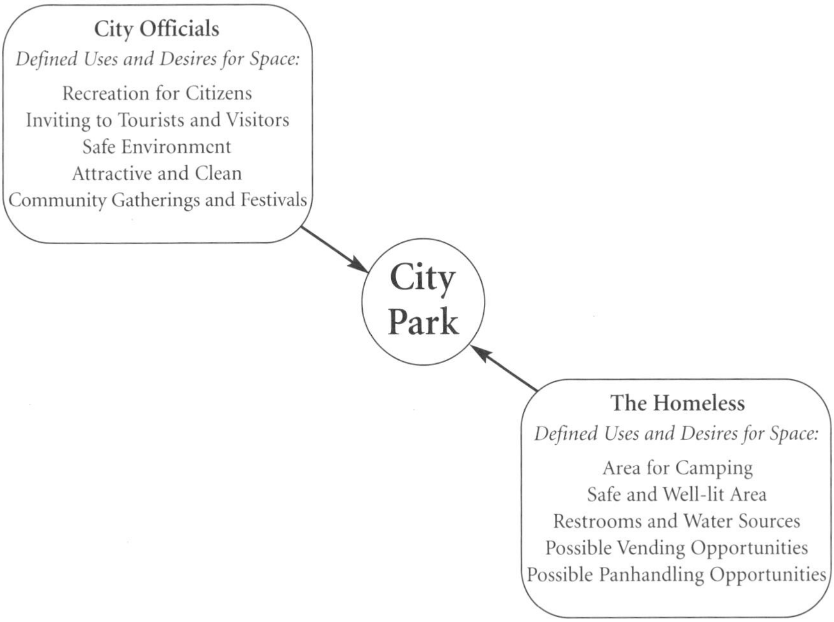

formed into a gallery by the artist, a portable storefront by a peddler, and lodging by the homeless. These acts essentially push the boundaries of space in unique ways by redefining them from a bottom-up perspective.

We are left facing the fact that no single public space can be all-inclusive at all times. The challenges may be imposed not only from the bottom up, as the previous examples show, but also from the top down, as city planners, architects, and security design firms introduce their vision of safety, use of space, and flow of pedestrians. Returning to the park example, consider how two very different groups may challenge the use of this recreational space: the homeless and city officials. Figure 1.2 illustrates the possible definitions and uses each group may try to force on the space.

These competing uses of space can lead to direct conflict in many cases. On one level, there are just differing needs of each competing group. The homeless may view the park as a safe haven and attempt to create an area of survival. City officials often respond to the demands of other publics and attempt to create a safe and attractive recreational area for families. On another level, there is a blurring of the line between public and private space as the homeless engage in private activities such as sleeping or bathing in a public setting, further challenging the legitimate use of that space. This conflict often escalates and can result in new laws that restrict activities and access to public spaces for some groups. Because of the contested usage from various marginalized groups, James Holston (1995) describes a place like this park as a space of insurgent citizenship. This conflict and insurgency can turn cities, parks, and other public spaces into war zones, as police departments engage in bum sweeps and citizens abandon the public sphere and retreat into suburban and more controlled enclaves.

Theories of Space and Crime

The connection of crime and space has received renewed research interest in criminology, perhaps to the delight of the field of geography, which has much to offer. This renewed interest has been met with enthusiasm as universities and the National Institute of Justice have begun offering courses in crime mapping and analysis. In addition, there are millions of state and federal grant dollars to be had by police departments and researchers willing to conduct spatial crime analysis. The use of computers to analyze the space-crime connection is one of the innovations pushing this trend. One example is the CompStat (Computer Statistics) program that began as a model to manage patrol operations by using timely and accurate crime statistics in the New York City Police Department under Commissioner William J. Bratton in 1994. The importance of this program in terms of this discussion is that it focuses on hot spots and the geographic location of crime. The program was hailed as a success in reducing crime in New York City and was replicated in many larger police departments. Because of the research attention and reported success, smaller departments have begun to implement similar programs.

After receiving a $15,000 grant from the Maryland governor's office, the rural St. Mary's sheriff's department implemented the big-city crime-fighting strategy of CompStat. The outcome has been positive. Sheriff Timothy Cameron reported that in the past the deputies were not communicating. Through regular meetings and analysis of crime incidents (although there are few in this rural area), there has been a reduction in overall crime and praise for the program. At one meeting, the sheriff reported that commanders reviewed a report of a man looking at child pornography on a computer in his car. The department contacted the FBI and learned that the man had molested a three-year-old girl. Cameron stated, "If it hadn't been for that conversation, that [report] would've been filed, and that would've continued to happen" (Zapotosky, 2008).

Despite the appearance of a new trend, the space-crime connection has long been recognized in the field of criminology. Crime mapping as a concept dates back to France in 1829, when geographer Adriano Balbi partnered with Andre-Michel Guerry to create some of the first crime maps. Using crime statistics from 1825 to 1829 along with census information, they were able to map out property and personal crimes, as well as education levels in various French provinces. Through map comparison, Balbi and Guerry discovered that areas with high levels of property crime had fewer crimes against persons, and areas with higher levels of education had more property crimes (Weisburd & McEwen, 1998).

Despite the groundbreaking work of Balbi and Guerry and the subsequent contributions of Lambert-Adolphe Quetelet to the study of crime and space, these results were disregarded. In part, there was a push from the nineteenth century's positivist school of criminology to search for empirical facts to confirm the idea that multiple features within the individual determined crime (Lily, Cullen, & Ball, 2003). Weisburd and McEwen (1998) offer a more practical explanation of why research interest may have turned away from the use of maps and crime statistics: It was time-consuming, maps of interest were not developed regularly, crime theories were not as developed, and the analysis was cumbersome work (p. 8).

By contrast, the United States was years away from collecting accurate crime and demographic data. The theoretical connections to crime and space remained undeveloped until unique circumstances in Chicago during the 1920s led observers and researchers to ask the question, Is the city to blame for the nation's crime problem? Researchers from the University of Chicago, Robert Park and Ernest Burgess, developed what came to be known as social ecology, or the ecological school of criminology. This was an attempt to apply the work of biologists, who studied how organisms interacted with their environment, to better understand how human communities interacted with their localized environments (Haggett, 1977).

Park and Burgess viewed cities in concentric zones or rings of increasing size, like on a target, with each zone having unique characteristics and populations with certain behaviors. Clifford Shaw and Henry McKay applied this concentric zone model to study juvenile delinquency. These early ecological theories, with their focus on space or location, became known as area studies, and because of the researchers' study of Chicago they were collectively referred to as the Chicago School of Criminology. There were several notable contributions from the Chicago School, such as the use of official statistics, ethnographic data, and the demonstration that community has an influence on behavior.

Perhaps the most relevant influence from the ecological approach is the modern application of environmental criminology or the criminology of place. This emergent perspective emphasizes crime prevention and the importance of the geographic location of crime, whether it is a street corner, apartment building, or an entire neighborhood. Rodney Stark, for example, in his classic 1987 article, posed a series of thought-provoking questions: How is it that neighborhoods can remain sites of high crime despite a complete turnover in their populations? If the neighborhood was tough because certain groups lived in them, why did it remain tough after the groups departed? Finally, why didn't the neighborhoods these groups departed to not become tough? The answer is at the heart of the environmental approach; "there must be something about places as such that sustains crime" (Stark, 1987, p. 893).

This theoretical movement is a departure from previous major attempts to explain crime in that it focuses on the crime event, not the criminality of the individual or group. Crime is a complex event and in many ways is more complex than traditional unicausal theories suggest (e.g., biological explanations, hedonism, or capitalist structure). Brantingham and Brantingham (1993) illustrate this complexity with the following statement on the perspectives that may be broadly considered under the framework of environmental criminology: "the movement has assumed that crimes can be no more easily explained than headaches or backaches. Such classes of events will never be attributable to any single cause or understood through any single explanation ... patterns in events can point towards different etiologies or clusters of etiologies under different conditions" (p. 260).

The theories and perspective that recognize the connection of crime and space have a variety of different names: rational choice theory, routine activities, and strategic analysis. The application of these theoretical approaches may be found in crime prevention through environmental design (CPTED), hot spot analysis, and, of key interest for this chapter, the broken windows thesis. In sum, the criminology of place views location as just as predictive of crime as the criminality of the offender, the lifestyle of the victim, or the demographics of the victimized residence.

Theory into Practice

The most direct connection of spatial awareness to police practices may be found in two notable applications of theories from the criminology of place: defensible space, and the broken windows thesis of Wilson and Kelling (1982). The concept of defensible space comes from architect Oscar Newman's seminal text *Defensible Space* (1972). Newman states that defensible space is a simple and down-to-earth concept that may be defined as the reassignment of physical areas and responsibility (Newman, 1996). Defensible space is about empowering law-abiding citizens and giving them the necessary tools to combat crime. By subdividing public spaces, Newman hopes that individual citizens and small groups are able to control their reassigned areas, thereby leaving the criminal ineffective and isolated.

Newman has reflected back on his work and states that after reviewing the literature of CPTED, he is surprised how his concept of defensible space has been misconstrued and misused. For example, Newman tells of being taken on tours of newly constructed housing projects that were ringed with fences and contained purposely positioned phone booths, all claiming to be based on his defensible space concept. He was faced with telling the designers they essentially lacked the underlying theory and philosophy of defensible space. Adding insult to injury, designers claimed the defensible space concept to be invalid when there was no accompanying reduction in crime (Newman, 1996). As he states on these misunderstandings of his work, "I have tried to avoid mystery and mumbo jumbo ... yet a whole cult has sprung up around these misunderstandings with its own pseudo language, misbegotten concepts, and rituals" (Newman, 1996, p. 3).

Newman suggests that he is more concerned with what people do and has chosen not to respond to his critics in academia or those in government who cannot defend their own past policy failures. He recalls visiting various housing projects where developers and designers had spent hundreds of thousands of dollars to modify public areas in the name of defensible space, all for naught because they failed to grasp his relatively simple concept. He stated he was mortified and concluded that too many professionals have limited themselves to only reading *Defensible Space* (1972) (which was at the beginning of his career), and did not read his follow-up works: *Design Guidelines for Achieving Defensible Space* (1976) or *Community of Interest* (1981) (Newman, 1996, pp. 3–4). Newman's contributions to the understanding of crime and space are substantial, and the impact of his work is still seen today despite some valid criticisms (e.g., Steventon, 1996; Taylor, Gottfredson, & Brower, 1980).

As important as Newman's contributions are to the criminology of place, perhaps the most influential article to connect space, crime, and policing is the 1982 article by James Q. Wilson and George L. Kelling titled "Broken Windows: The Police and Neighborhood Safety." The essay was based on the results of the Newark Foot Patrol Experiment conducted during the mid-1970s as well as their own observations and interviews with officers assigned to the experiment. The now-famous analogy from the article used a broken window to describe the relationship between crime and public disorder. If a window is broken and not repaired, others soon follow, and this becomes a signal that no one cares and breaking other windows costs nothing. This is true in both desirable and undesirable neighborhoods. Essentially, once the sense of mutual respect and regard for others has been removed, vandalism may flourish.

Although not unavoidable, the initial broken window may lead to serious crime or at the very least an increase in fear of crime among the residents with subsequent changes in activities. The change in space has a powerful impact on citizen behavior and the opportunity for crime, as the authors state:

> They will use the streets less often, and when on the streets will stay apart from their fellows, moving with averted eyes, silent lips, and hurried steps. "Don't get involved." For some residents, this growing atomization will matter little, because the neighborhood is not their "home" but "the place where they live." … Such an area is vulnerable to criminal invasion. Though it is not inevitable, it is more likely that here, rather than in places where people are confident they can regulate public behavior by informal controls, drugs will change hands, prostitutes will solicit, and cars will be stripped. That the drunks will be robbed by boys who do it as a lark and the prostitutes' customers will be robbed by men who do it purposefully and perhaps violently. (Wilson & Kelling, 1982, p. 3)

Interestingly, results from the evaluation of the foot patrol experiment by the Police Foundation showed that maintaining public order according to neighborhood standards did not always result in a reduction in crime (Wilson & Kelling, 1982).

Instead of defining order with high arrest statistics or a reduction in the crime rate, order was viewed on a typical beat by enforcing the neighborhood rules that conditioned the interaction between "regulars" and "strangers." The foot patrol officers got a chance to know the regulars, who included decent folks as well as drunks and addicts who knew their place. Strangers were often viewed suspiciously, and if they loitered the officer would ask them what business they had in the neighborhood and if they had any means of support. If the answer was not to the officer's satisfaction, the stranger was asked to leave. These rules were defined with the collaboration of "regulars" in the neighborhood who often assisted the officer's enforcement efforts. The rules varied from neighborhood to neighborhood, showing the sensitivity that was needed to address each population's unique space.

The broken windows thesis led to an increase in order maintenance policing, a concept that according to the authors was lost during the 1960s and 1970s as the mandates of policing changed to reflect the fear over the increasing crime rate of the time. This return to order maintenance led to a focus on quality of life nuisances, such as panhandling, vagrancy, and prostitution. Perhaps the most famous and controversial example of the implementation of this thesis was in New York City under former mayor Rudolph Giuliani during the mid-1990s. The New York City Police Department operated the Quality of Life Campaign, which listed 25 specific offenses that would be targeted, including squeegee men, turnstile jumpers, and the homeless sleeping in public (Erzen, 2001). In the past, enforcement efforts for these minor violations typically resulted in a court appearance ticket. Under the revised efforts, these offenders were detained to verify names and discover if any outstanding warrants were present. Guiliani's administration received much acclaim and reported great success with these policies with more than a 60% reduction in homicides between 1993 and 1997 (Greene, 1999).

As Erzen (2001) points out, the Quality of Life Campaign may have increased feelings of safety and surface-level order that are often reduced as a consequence of living in a large city. However, the operations of campaign did not go without criticism. The program may have been successful at removing disorderly people, but the claims of the Guiliani administration that targeting these misdemeanors led to reductions in robbery, rape, and murder are flimsy at best. Perhaps the most serious critique of the Quality of Life Campaign was the greater discretion given to police in defining order and solving the problem by any means they chose.

The broken windows thesis is fascinating and was clearly the framework for the Quality of Life Campaign. Yet the thesis itself is not without criticism. Perhaps the most stinging review is offered by Samuel Walker, who believes that the concept of broken windows is based on a romanticized albeit false interpretation of the early watchman-style of policing, and the supposed crime control orientation of the police may be exaggerated. Nonetheless, Walker is clear that we should not throw the proverbial baby out with the bath water, as the broken windows thesis accurately assessed the policing research of the time, and achieving feelings of public safety is something evidently within reach of the police (Walker, 1984).

The broken windows thesis is provocative, and its impact on policing and cities across the nation is undeniable. Despite criticisms, there has been some support for Wilson and Kelling's thesis, such as Wesley Skogan's text *Disorder and Decline: Crime and the Spiral of Decay in American Neighborhoods* (1992), in which he found disorder was related to vandalism, graffiti, feelings of safety, and urban decline. Kelling and Coles (1998) responded to some of the critics of broken windows and opponents of order maintenance policing who believed the thesis was essentially about street sweeps of undesirables:

> In fact, the ideas presented in "Broken Windows" were antithetical to the use of "street sweeping" tactics targeted on "undesirables" rather, they advocated close collaboration between police and citizens, including street people, in the development of neighborhood standards. Moreover, neighborhood rules were to be enforced for the most part through non-arrests approaches—education, persuasion, counseling, and ordering—so that arrest would only be resorted to when other approaches failed. (pp. 22–23)

Basically, the implementation of order maintenance programs, such as the Quality of Life Campaign in New York City, may not have comprised the order maintenance envisioned in broken windows or Kelling's Newark Foot Patrol Experiment.

The strongest connection of broken windows to this text, I believe, is the awareness of the distinctiveness of space at the neighborhood level. This awareness is reflected in the thought-provoking question Wilson and Kelling (1982) pose: "Should police activity on the street be shaped in important ways, by the standards of the neighborhood rather than by the rules of the state?" (p. 6). This question should be taken seriously; not unlike Newman's defensible space concept, the concept of maintaining order for some can mean order at any cost. Even Wilson and Kelling (1982) admit that some of the things the patrol officers did would not hold up to legal scrutiny.

The difficulty that lies here is that we must recognize (as the authors did) that there may not be a universal standard of neighborhood order, and police run the risk of violating our senses of equity and fairness. There are certain behaviors that most neighborhoods would view as undesirable in their spaces, and the police may be called in to deal with the offensive person. There is a risk that for some, desirability may be based on race, ethnicity, or nationality. At their core, the applications of the criminology of place are powerful tools for police departments as well as citizens to shape space in ways to create safety and order that may ultimately reduce certain crimes.

Policing Space

At its core, policing has always been about regulating and controlling space. Social power and control is derived from directing and restricting people's movement within a territory, which by extension controls the actions of residents. Whether it is asking a motorist to exit a vehicle, a resident to step outside of their home into public space, or a helicopter assisting patrol vehicles in a high-speed pursuit, police actions set boundaries and move citizens around, in, and out of spaces. There have been numerous groundbreaking examinations of ecology and crime that have opened new vistas for research and supplying theoretical connections on policing and space that may have been missing in the past.

David Klinger (1997) offers an ecological explanation of police behavior that accounts for the amount of vigor with which police applied their formal authority. Essentially, the neighborhood context impacts what officers define as "normal" crime, and that police applied less effort in areas where deviance was prominent. Furthermore, as Klinger and others have noted (e.g., Niederhoffer, 1967), it is not simply that the neighborhood is economically disadvantaged or has higher levels of deviance that affects policing actions, but a multitude of factors such as officer workload, victim worthiness, and seriousness of the crime. Additionally, Klinger's theory points out the nuance of the nesting of neighborhoods in patrol districts, which may directly impact not only the actions of the police assigned to them but also how crime affects the space. For example, officers assigned to low-crime neighborhoods nested in low-crime districts will respond vigorously to crime, which in turn, inhibits crime from gaining a foothold and changing the space into a high-crime area. Essentially, Klinger's theory suggests that the criminality a neighborhood experiences is substantially influenced by the level of deviance in the patrol district in which they are situated (1997, p. 300).

The importance of understanding the use and awareness of space by police officers is also illustrated by Steve Herbert's research on the Los Angeles Police Department in which he states, "Police officers so fundamentally embed their powers in the boundaries they create and enforce that analysis of their practices must attend to the means by which they make and mark space" (Herbert, 1997, p. 21). Herbert further demonstrates the complexities of police making and marking boundaries by showing how other aspects of law enforcement contextualize police actions, such as the bureaucracy of the department, concerns over safety, race, and competence in the field. For example, despite a great deal of autonomy and discretion, police are constrained by bureaucratic controls. Departments have bureaucratic rules and units that may shape the spatial range of an officer's focus. As Herbert details, a narcotics officer's concerns cover a wide range of space, but a smaller range of offenses as compared to patrol officers. Bureaucracy also creates a clear chain of command with spatial ramifications to improve efficiency and provide knowledge of who controls the scene (1997, p. 574). Another key factor that is highly relevant today is the issue of race and space. Officers may be likely to view a minority space as dangerous (melding race and space with the concern for safety) and view the people within the space as being a potential threat. This in turn impacts the officer's imposition of order and aggressive actions. An interesting loop may also be created as citizen complaints mount in minority spaces and subsequent pressures are placed on police administrators who respond through bureaucratic policy changes that are spatial aware and possibly impact an officer's actions.

The police focus and response to space may also result in interesting and practical applications. Sherman, Gartin, and Buerger (1989) provided research evidence for what many police administrators have experienced, that crime is not distributed evenly throughout the city and there are "hot spots" for crime and police activity. The analysis revealed that 50% of the calls for service were generated by 3.3% of all addresses and intersections. This concentration of crime is not random and even within such crime-prone spaces there may be small safe havens that remain free from crime, revealing an even deeper level of spatial context. This realization of spatial variance in crime has led to innovative responses in policing, particularly the use of problem-oriented policing (POP), which was first described by Goldstein (1979).

Goldstein expressed that the police should address the underlying problems of a space that lead to areas of high crime and disorder. Eck and Spelman (1987) would further expand POP with addition of the SARA model, which was an acronym for scan, analysis, response, and assess. POP essentially outlined a process for police and interested parties to address law enforcement needs in hot spots. Although POP has shown some effectiveness and allowed departments to identify problems and responses, the process is not without flaws. For example, Koper (2014) notes several shortcomings of the approach in practice, such as differing definitions and geographic spaces (city blocks vs. entire neighborhoods), limited community input, differing amounts of vigor in program application, short-term focus, and different forms of assessing success. Although they may often receive lower priority due to traditional policing practices, each of these developments represents a breakthrough in police recognition and operations that are spatial aware.

To further advance a practical spatial policing approach Lum and Koper (2012) proposed applying the technique of investigative case processing to places instead of individuals. Under this model, police would use the same end strategy of "arresting" a suspect or in this approach the place, in an effort to stop or reduce crime through a planned intervention. Furthermore, the conceptualization of traditional investigative elements may change according to Koper, Egg, and Lum (2015). Victims may be citizens, businesses, or properties, and witnesses may be residents or even surveillance technology. The investigative team may include detectives, patrol officers, and research analysts who review the information gathered, such as crime patterns, affected properties, and environmental conditions that may facilitate crime. The authors further suggest that the familiarity with this investigative process may enable its acceptance by police departments and may convince those new to the perspective of place-based investigation that the efforts should receive the same priority and resources as traditional investigations of crimes against people.

While space- and place-based policing has received research attention it is not the primary focus of many departments or research evaluations of policing efforts. When these strategies are employed they are aimed at specific crimes such as gun violence, illicit drug markets, and gang activity. These are serious crimes that have unique space, class, and in some cases racial connections that require innovative solutions, and I urge the reader to review the theoretical and evaluation literature referenced in this section to gain a deeper understanding of what agencies across the country have done. Although gangs and gun violence often take center stage in policing and space research, there is a population that frequently challenges traditional policing solutions and addressing their issues may assist in dealing with the larger problems of a neighborhood or district, and that population is the homeless.

The Homeless

Possibly the most difficult challenges over the use of space comes from the multifaceted population of the homeless. With nearly 600,000 homeless people on any given night in the United States (Housing & Urban Development, 2015), this large population places numerous demands on public space that may run counter to the intentions of developers, residents, and city officials. As Margret Crawford (1995) points out, for the homeless, the lines between public and private space are practically nonexistent. The homeless may occupy parks, streets, sidewalks, and other public spaces they deem necessary for their personal and economic survival. Often under the veil of broken windows or an attempt to deal with the disorder described by Skogan (1992), cities began to pass ordinances that targeted the associated activities of the homeless. For example, some cities have ordinances and limits on food sharing (e.g., free public feeding of the homeless), public sleeping, panhandling, and loitering. The effect of these ordinances is that they criminalize the activities associated with the status of being homeless or of those who have unstable housing. Police departments, in turn, must enforce these laws and address neighborhood or city concerns over the use of public space.

Crawford (2008) details the laws and police actions in numerous cities across the United States that have attempted to regulate the homeless population's use of public space. Of the various laws that have been passed, the prohibition of public sleeping is most relevant to policing space and the homeless. While there are many cities in the United States that deal with large populations of the homeless, San Francisco is representative of the complexities involved in policing contested spaces. In San Francisco, the estimated homeless population is 6,000 people, and only a fraction can be housed in shelters (Fuller, 2016). This sizable homeless population often turns to alternative forms of shelter, such as the numerous tent encampments around the city that seemingly appear overnight, and has turned these areas into unique battlegrounds over space.

The impact of homeless encampments on public space is undeniable. Mid-year 2016, the city had received nearly 7,000 tent encampment complaints, which was an increase of nearly 55% from the previous year (Alexander, 2016). The sidewalks near these encampments become zones where illicit drug use, alcohol consumption, and improper sanitation waste disposal are common issues and factors behind the numerous complaints to city authorities. This essentially placed city officials, residents, police, and the homeless on a collision course. City officials enacted a plan to clear the tent encampments through the use of an Encampment Resolution Team that informs the tent residents that the space has been target for removal, but there is help available (Fagan, 2016). It is an attempt to solve a complex problem, but there is still an enforcement component, as earlier during the year of 2016 the police dismantled a 250-person homeless encampment (Alexander, 2016). This contested space of the sidewalks of the city and creation of tent communities is frustrating for each of the parties involved.

Enforcing anti-public sleeping laws along with sweeps of homeless encampments are probably the most physical and direct confrontation to be found over public space. If the issue is conflict over space and order, how can the police recognize this challenge and demonstrate an understanding of the reality that the public sphere may not be welcoming to all citizens at all times? The solutions to the issues surrounding homelessness may be well beyond the services that police can provide, but given the unique challenges posed to accessing public space, order, and the intersections of public health and safety, departments across the country may do well to consider the investigative case of place-based approach.

Conclusion

The use of space as a tool to understand crime has a long and rich history. From the early work of Balbi and Guerry to the collective works of the Chicago School of Criminology there has been a fascination with how space and geography impact human behavior. This rich history ultimately led to the field of environmental criminology and some of the most important direct practical applications in design and policing. The subsequent influence of these applications on police practices over the past 25 years has been significant, as they have offered new ways of conceptualizing how law enforcement operates in space and how departments may increase feelings of safety, reduce crime, and best serve the multiple publics that exist.

How space is used, viewed, and defined will probably remain an area of conflict and in some extreme cases there may be mini-war zones in public spaces. The police are not immune from the influence of space and are frequently called on to bring order into areas of conflict. This is not to suggest that a hard spatial determinism or a simple stimulus-and-response relationship between environment and citizens exists. Volumes have been written about the various factors that influence human behavior and crime. Yet it is hard to deny that space holds some power over our actions and reactions.

Consider the visual cues of a space that tell us if an area is safe or unsafe, controlled or uncontrolled, whether there are constraints on our behavior or none exist. Individuals may decode this spatial information differently and behave accordingly. For those that have a stake in crime prevention or improving police practices, understanding the push and pull of the environment is key. Whether it is securing order, reducing gun violence, improving feelings of community safety and police legitimacy, or assisting homeless populations, to paraphrase Stark, there must be something about places (Stark, 1987, p. 893). I hope that this chapter begins the journey to understanding the influence of space on policing that is explored through the remaining contributions to this book.

References

Alexander, K. (2016, June 26). Enforcing laws, changing attitudes: Would stronger enforcement of laws against street camping and petty crime reduce homelessness? *San Francisco Chronicle*. Retrieved from http://projects.sfchronicle.com/sf-homeless/encampments/.

Brantingham, P. L., & Brantingham, P. J. (1993). Environment, routine, and situation: Toward a pattern theory of crime. In R. Clarke & M. Felson (Eds.), *Routine activity and rational choice* (pp. 259–294). Edison, NJ: Transaction Publishers.

Crawford, C. (2008). The criminalization of homelessness. In R. McNamara (Ed.), *Homelessness in America* (Vol. 3) (pp. 47–60). Westport: Greenwood Publishing.

Crawford, M. (1995). Contesting the public realm: Struggles over public space in Los Angeles. *Journal of Architectural Education, 49*(1), 4–9.

de Certeau, M. (1984). *The practice of everyday life.* Berkeley: University of California Press.

Eck, J. E., & Spelman, W. (1987). *Problem-solving: Problem-oriented policing in Newport News.* Washington, DC: Police Executive Research Forum.

Entrikin, J. (1989). Place, region and modernity. In J. Agnew & J. Duncan (Eds.), *The power of place: Bringing together geographical and sociological imaginations* (pp. 30–43). Boston: Unwin Hyman.

Entrikin, J. (1991). *The betweeness of place: Towards a geography of modernity.* London: Macmillan.

Erzen, T. (2001). Turnstile jumpers and broken windows. In A. McArdle & T. Erzen (Eds.), *Zero tolerance: Quality of life and the new police brutality in New York City* (pp. 19–49). New York: New York University Press.

Fagan, K. (2006, April 15). L.A.'s homeless law ruled unconstitutional. *San Francisco Chronicle.* Retrieved from http://www.sfgate.com/cgibin/article.cgi?f=/c/a/2006/04/15/homeless.tmp.

Fraser, N. (1993). Rethinking the public sphere: A contribution to the critique of actually existing democracy. In B. Robbins (Ed.), *The phantom public sphere* (pp. 108–142). Minneapolis: University of Minnesota Press.

Fuller, T. (2016). San Francisco wants homeless to leave tent camp, but some vow to fight. *The New York Times.* Retrieved from http://www.nytimes.com/2016/02/27/us/san-francisco-wants-homeless-to-leave-tent-camp-but-some-vow-to-fight.html?_r=0.

Gans, H. (2002). The sociology of space: A use-centered view. *City & Community, 1*(4), 329–339.

Gieryn, T. F. (2000). A place for space. *Annual Review of Sociology, 26*, 463–496.

Goldstein, H. (1979). Improving policing: A problem-oriented approach. *Crime and Delinquency, 25*, 236–258.

Greene, J. (1999). Zero tolerance: A case study of police policies and practices in New York City. *Crime and Delinquency, 45*(2), 171–187.

Habermas, J. (1989). *The structural transformation of the public sphere: An inquiry into a category of bourgeois society.* Cambridge, MA: MIT Press.

Haggett, P. (1977). Human ecology. In A. Bullock & O. Stallybrass (Eds.), *The Fontana dictionary of modern social thought* (p. 187). London: Fontana.

Harvey, D. (1996). *Justice, nature and the geography of difference.* Cambridge, MA: Blackwell.

Herbert, S. (1997). *Policing space: Territoriality and the Los Angeles police department.* Minneapolis: University of Minnesota Press.

Hillier, B., & Hanson J. (1984). *The social logic of space.* Cambridge: Cambridge University Press.

Holston, J. (1995). Spaces of insurgent citizenship. *Planning Theory, 13*, 30–50.

Housing and Urban Development. (2005). *The 2015 annual homeless assessment report (AHAR) to Congress.* Retrieved from https://www.hudexchange.info/resources/documents/2015-AHAR-Part-1.pdf.

Kelling, G., & Coles. K. (1998). *Fixing broken windows: Restoring order and reducing crime in our communities.* New York: Free Press.

Klinger, D. A. (1997). Negotiating order in patrol work: An ecological theory of police response to deviance. *Criminology, 35*(2), 277–306.

Koper, C. S. (2014). Assessing the practice of hot spots policing: Survey results from a national convenience sample of local police agencies. *Journal of Contemporary Criminal Justice, 30*(2), 123–146.

Koper, C. S., Egge, S. J., & Lum, C. (2015). Institutionalizing place-based approaches: Opening 'cases' on gun crime hot spots. *Policing, 9*(3), 242–254.

Lily, J., Cullen, F., & Ball, R. (2002). *Criminological theory: Context and consequences* (3rd ed.). Thousand Oaks: Sage.

Los Angeles County Sheriff's Department West Hollywood Station. (1996). *Operation outreach: Project summary.* Retrieved from http://www.popcenter.org/library/awards/goldstein/1996/96-26.pdf.

Lum, C., & Koper, C. S. (2012). Incorporating research into daily police practices: The matrix demonstration project. *Translational Criminology: The Magazine of the Center for Evidence-Based Crime Policy (George Mason University), Fall 2012*, 16–17.

Newman, O. (1972). *Defensible space: Crime prevention through urban design.* New York: Macmillan.

Newman, O. (1976). *Design guidelines for creating defensible space.* Washington, DC: Government Printing Office.

Newman, O. (1981). *Community of interest.* Garden City: Anchor Press/Doubleday.

Newman, O. (1996). *Creating defensible space.* U.S. Department of Housing and Urban Development, Office of Policy Development and Research.

Niederhoffer, A. (1967). *Behind the shield: The police in urban society* (pp. 207–28). Garden City, NY: Doubleday.

Sherman, L., Gartin, P., & Buerger, M. (1989). Hot spots of predatory crime: Routine activities and the criminology of place. *Criminology, 27*(1), 27–56.

Skogan, W. (1992). *Disorder and decline: Crime and the spiral of decay in American neighborhoods.* Berkeley: University of California Press.

Smith, M., & Clarke, R. (2000). Crime and public transport. *Crime and Justice, 27*, 169–233.

Stark, R. (1987). Deviant places: A theory of the ecology of crime. *Criminology, 25*(4), 893–909.

Steventon, J. (1996). Defensible space: A critique of the theory and practice of a crime prevention strategy. *Urban Design International, 1*(3), 235–245.

Taylor, R. B., Gottfredson, S. D., & Brower, S. (1980). The defensibility of defensible space. In T. Hirschi & M. Gottfredson (Eds.), *Understanding crime* (pp. 17–36). Beverly Hills: Sage.

Walker, S. (1984). "Broken windows" and fractured history: The use and misuse of police history in recent police patrol analysis. *Justice Quarterly, 1*(1), 57–90.

Weisburd, D., & McEwen, T. (1998). Crime mapping and crime prevention. In D. Weisburd & T. McEwen (Eds.), *Crime mapping and crime prevention* (pp. 1–23). Massey: Willow Tree Press.

Wilson, J., & Kelling, G. (1982, March). Broken windows: The police and neighborhood safety. *The Atlantic*. Retrieved from http://www.theatlantic.com/doc/198203/broken-windows.

Winton, R., & DiMassa, M. (2007, March 3). ACLU seeks court injunction in skid row cleanup. *Los Angeles Times*. Retrieved from http://articles.latimes.com/2007/mar/03/local/me-skidrow3.

Zapotosky, M. (2008, November 15). Crime drop linked to data monitoring: St. Mary's system streamlines policing. *Washington Post*. Retrieved from http://www.washingtonpost.com/wp-dyn/content/article/2008/11/15/AR2008111500133.html.

2

Remapping the City: Public Identity, Cultural Space, and Social Justice*

Jeff Ferrell

Contemporary public controversies and conflicts often seem oddly out of balance. Neighborhood groups, criminal justice agencies, politicians and political activists, ethnic minorities and majorities, the old and the young all fight high-profile, often heated battles over what might appear the most unimportant, even peripheral of public issues and public spaces: parking lots and street corners, sidewalks and shopping districts. As they battle, the participants seem also to signal a shift in the very nature of public policy and political debate, such that notions of social order and social justice now rest on these new spatial foundations. At the same time, media coverage of these issues, and political campaigning around them, regularly highlight the dangers inherent in this contested remapping of the city's spaces. At the extreme, media and political campaigns suggest that, if not addressed, these new dangers portend a panicky decline into social decay.

* Source: Ferrell, J. (2001). Remapping the city: Public identity, cultural space, and social justice. *Contemporary Justice Review, 4*(2): 161–180. Reprinted with permission from Editor-in-Chief Dennis Sullivan with the support of Professor Ferrell. Thanks to you both.

Consumption, Control, Cultural Space

Cities around the United States increasingly stake their economic vitality, and certainly their public images, on urban redevelopment and design schemes built around new downtown sports arenas, parking garages, microbreweries, pedestrian shopping malls, and gentrified inner-city neighborhoods. If, as Marx (1972) noted, history arrives the first time as tragedy and the second as farce, contemporary city planning suggests that urban development, urban identity, and urban history are forged first out of industry, commerce, and labor, but next from the marketing of consumption, symbol, and amusement. In this sense, contemporary cities take on more and more the character of corporate theme parks, selling idealized images of themselves, and cartoonish echoes of their former identities, to residents and visitors in the form of converted loft living spaces, almost-hip storefronts, and rebuilt historic districts. These "cultural strategies of economic development" undergird urban revitalization schemes in cities across the United States, from Denver's reinvented LoDo District to Monterey's repackaged Cannery Row and Akron's retreaded downtown, and in so doing organize new "consumption spaces" (Zukin, 1997, pp. 227, 240) inside old urban structures.

Significantly, this trendy transmogrification of urban life is presented to the public not only as a form of economic salvation, essential to reviving the fortunes of the urban core, but as a form of social and cultural salvation as well, as a strategy for restoring urban civility and a sense of shared community. Foci of civic pride, staging areas for "public" events, facilitators of daily interaction, these sports arenas, reborn shopping districts, and revitalized neighborhoods are marketed as a Durkheimian social adhesive through which ethnically and economically fractured cities can be reassembled. In this way, debates over urban economic and cultural redevelopment regularly evolve into debates over social well-being, social order, and social justice; and those who would impede or intrude on this redevelopment of image and economy regularly find themselves characterized as social misfits, or even policed as criminal threats to the common good.

When successful, these urban redevelopment schemes attract remarkable numbers of middle class, mostly Anglo consumers, and a growing segment of middle-class residents. As these new city center residents flood into retrofitted processing plants and converted lofts, housing prices soar, and low-income and minority residents—that is, those not already driven out of the revitalized central city by the pre-developmental destruction of low-cost housing and evacuation of industrial jobs—now face even greater economic pressures toward dislocation. But unlike the poor, yet another growing segment of the middle and upper classes relocates outside the central city by choice, removing itself to planned and gated communities at the outskirts of the city, and commuting back into the city center along ever more congested freeways in search of good restaurants and other touches of urban flavor. Given the carefully marketed seductions of the redeveloped central city, though, why do many middle- and upper-class citizens choose to live so far from it, locked behind guard houses and gates, wrapped in the enforced security of housing codes, homeowners' associations, and legal covenants? What about the contemporary city do they fear?

Perhaps they fear the reality, or at least the mediated image, of growing numbers of homeless children and adults, pushed into the streets in part by the very urban redevelopment schemes that open loft space and coffee houses to others. Perhaps they find distasteful the ways in which these homeless populations intrude upon moments of urban leisure and entertainment, begging outside a restaurant or sleeping along an otherwise lovely riverwalk, and thereby offering an uncomfortable visual reminder of social inequality. Or perhaps they fear the growing array of people and groups who seem to value their own dangerous public identities, their own edgy markers of subcultural status and excitement, more than they value their own safety or the safety of others—and worse, seem actually to take some perverse pleasure in spoiling that which urban planners, political leaders, corporate developers, and middle-class consumers most value about the redesigned city.

Within the large and varied homeless population, for example, countless young "gutter punks" occupy street corners and park benches, hang outside coffee houses and cafes, less embarrassed by their degraded identities than embracing and flaunting them. Street corners are also a surrogate home to more and more young people identifiable as gang members—identifiable, that is, either because they themselves publicly proclaim this status through risky matters of turf and color, or because they are so identified for public perusal by policing agencies and the mass media. Between the corners, Hispanic and Mexican-American street "cruisers" and "low riders" glide back and forth in wildly modified automobiles, and down stair rails and across retaining walls skateboarders and "skate punks" grind out outrageous, highflying tricks. On these same walls—and on elevated freeway signs, freight trains, and most any other mobile or immobile surface—hip-hop graffiti writers and other outlaw public artists risk injury and arrest while inscribing swarms of stylized names and images.

Riskier still are the activities of BASE jumpers, who illicitly assault skyscrapers, buildings under construction, and bridges and then parachute off them. Adding to these physical interruptions and intrusions into the cityscape are various auditory ones as well: street musicians laying down cacophonous soundtracks along subway platforms and restored pedestrian malls; "ravers" taking over warehouses for unanticipated, all-night, high-decibel parties; punks and progressives setting up and blasting out pirate radio stations from secret locations around town. And, beyond and around all this, countless kids—tattooed, pierced, draped in oversized clothes, "distorted in the interest of design" (Ellison in Cosgrove, 1984, p. 39; see Ferrell, 1995)—slouch down city streets and trendy shopping corridors, seemingly toward nowhere in particular.

Witnessed through the oversized windows of a $2,000-a-month retrofitted loft or the windshield of an oversized SUV, this cavalcade of difference and defiance may appear not just mildly distasteful or disturbing, but downright threatening, even criminal. It increasingly appears that way from inside city council chambers and the statehouse, from inside the police station and the police cruiser, as well. As part of broader shifts over the past decade or so toward punitive criminal justice policies and "community" policing, policy and policing directed at reconstructed urban spaces and those outsiders who occupy or intrude upon them has also evolved harshly and dramatically.

Those identified as gang members face neighborhood roundups, civil injunctions prohibiting public gatherings, even deportation. Street cruisers, skateboarders, and others encounter new statutes and regulations regarding vehicle modification and movement, noise levels, trespass, and loitering. Aggressive local, state, and national campaigns are instituted to remove graffiti writers and graffiti images from city centers, and to closely regulate or even eliminate street musicians and all-night rave gatherings. Pirate radio operators confront the legal clout of the Federal Communications Commission, and thus confiscation of their equipment and thousands of dollars in fines. Those stylishly slouching kids now face new impediments also: more numerous and more restrictive dress codes at school and work, widespread curfews when away.

The contemporary criminalization of the homeless is perhaps the most thoroughgoing. Their daily activities are disrupted by park benches redesigned to prevent sleeping, and padlocked public bathrooms; their daily lives are all but outlawed through a plethora of new statutes and enforcement strategies regarding sitting, sleeping, begging, loitering, and "urban camping;" and those street-level organizations like Food Not Bombs that would feed or otherwise assist them likewise encounter aggressive, pre-emptive enforcement of zoning and public health statutes. Thus, in New York City, Mayor Giuliani targets "quality of life" crimes like panhandling and obstructing public sidewalks. In San Francisco, authorities set up sting operations against beggars, arrest Food Not Bombs members for publicly distributing food, and propose to ban standing on street corners for longer than five minutes (Nieves, 1999a). In Tempe,

Arizona, officials strategize prior to Super Bowl XXX on ways to "force homeless people out of sight" (Petrie, 1995, p. A1). And in neighboring Phoenix, the executive director of the Downtown Phoenix Partnership leads a "cleanup campaign" against the homeless, arguing that "it's part of an image issue for the city" (Wagner, 1996, p. B1).

In all these policy and policing initiatives, and in the often high-profile political and media campaigns that surround and support them, we hear the echoes of the urban redevelopment debates. Public officials, criminal justice agents, and corporate developers time and again argue that those who occupy the streets in defense of their gang, their barrio, or their way of life, who by taking to the streets intrude on urban development and gentrification, are best understood as urban undesirables responsible for the destruction of city life itself. Likewise, those who beg, sit and sleep on sidewalks, skateboard, write graffiti, play street music, or broadcast pirate radio are not simply choosing alternative lifestyles. They are committing crimes, "quality of life" crimes, that if left unattended threaten to unravel economic revitalization, undermine the possibility of harmonious public life, and ultimately undo the emerging social order.

Joined in this collective conflict over city streets, city development, and city design, the participants—urban planners, yuppies, police officers, gang members, gutter punks, street cruisers—are linked by something else as well. Together, they participate in patterns of confrontation and everyday interaction grounded in the particular places and particular situations they occupy. That is, they find themselves caught up in conflicts over cultural space. This notion of "cultural space" (Ferrell, 1997; 1998) suggests that public spaces and city sectors—parks, streets and street corners, shopping districts, residential enclaves—function not only as utilitarian arrangements, but as deep repositories of meaning for those who own them, occupy them, or move though them.

This meaning is in turn encoded and contested in the realms of image and perception, such that the occupation of these areas is always as much symbolic as physical, the presence of particular populations confirmed as much through stylized public identities as though simple census counts. Thus, the various constellations of cultural space already glimpsed in the restored storefronts and gated communities of the affluent, the street corners of gang members and gutter punks, the back alleys of graffiti writers and the homeless-incorporate, along with issues of urban development and migration, are other issues essential to defining self and society. These cultural spaces mark the changing boundaries of private property and public propriety, shape the emerging image of the city and its residents, and drive the contested remapping of cultural identity, class affiliation, and public meaning.

Because these cultural spaces are meaningful, because they matter so profoundly in the construction of identity and perception, because they are worth fighting for, they emerge as essential contemporary zones of conflict, control, and resistance. As already seen, conflicts over cultural space incorporate not only the emerging political economy of the city, but new forms of politics, criminalization, and legal control. It is not by accident that these cultural space controversies are so often publicly presented in the language of social problems and social breakdown, so often publicly encased in the vocabulary of crime and criminal threat; and it is not surprising that many of the most controversial new forms of social and legal control, and most spectacular forms of public resistance, have developed within and around these conflicts. As Foucault (1977), Platt (1974), Schlossman and Wallach (1978), Ferrell (1990), and other historians of crime and justice have demonstrated, emerging institutions, and evolving patterns of production and consumption, become at the same time domains for new forms of crime and criminalization, control and resistance. In the present case, then, an inquiry into contemporary constellations of public conflict becomes, inevitably, an inquiry into the interconnections between crime and crime control, political economy, cultural space, and the construction of public identity.

Focused as it is on the contested meaning of public spaces and the symbolic imagery of public controversies, this inquiry requires forms of criminological analysis attentive to broad issues of representation, meaning, and power. That is, it requires a form of *cultural criminology* (Ferrell & Sanders, 1995; Ferrell, 1999; Ferrell & Websdale, 1999) that can explore the convergence of crime, crime control, and cultural processes within contemporary public conflicts. This convergence shapes the political and economic frameworks of these conflicts, as city officials and corporate developers work to reinvent and market the image of the city, to create urban "consumption spaces" that symbolize safety and status, and to legally exclude from these spaces those who would intrude on their symbolic value. It drives the new techniques of regulation and control that emerge in and around these spaces—techniques that involve the policing of public perception as much as the policing of populations. And it animates the subcultural dynamics of those labeled as criminal threats to these new arrangements; through such subcultural dynamics, they transform their criminalized identities into symbolic displays of defiance and resistance and construct alternative public meanings.

At the same time, of course, any inquiry into contemporary cultural space controversies must be attentive to spatial dynamics, and to the encoding of cultural processes and power relations in public space. Certainly, the insights offered by emerging perspectives in cultural and postmodern geography (Merrifield & Swyngedouw, 1997; Rotenberg & McDonogh, 1993; Soja, 1989) are essential for uncovering the symbolic meaning of spatial arrangements and for analyzing the ways in which these arrangements function to enforce existing configurations of power. Similarly, Georges-Abeyie's (1990a; see 1990b) notion of "petit apartheid" suggests that patterns of ethnic hostility, intra-ethnic and inter-ethnic criminality, and discriminatory policing emerge not as free-floating phenomena, but in the context of expanding "residential spatial segregation," within "specific ecological zones of the alleged ghetto, slum-ghetto, or non-ghetto," and thus out of complex and changing "spatial dynamics" (pp. 12–13). In his analysis of street politics and street sensibilities, Keith (1997) thus argues that, through "the return to spatiality" in social theory, we can "reconnect economy and culture" (p. 139); to this we might add crime and crime control, and contested constructions of public identity, as well.

And it is here, in this tangle of cultural, spatial, and interactional dynamics, that we begin to see a key linkage between contemporary cultural space battles, the public negotiation of identity, and the everyday practice of justice and injustice. As new cultural spaces are carved out by city planners and corporate developers, they serve to redesign city life along new lines of spatial exclusion, and to organize new forms of control against those deemed foreign to these spaces. It is in this context, and in the interest of enforcing and maintaining these new spatial arrangements, that new indignities and new illegalities emerge. Yet it is also in this spatial context that new forms of resistance and identity are invented in counterpoint, and that new configurations of social justice are imagined.

Gutter Punks, Street Kids, and the Spatial Politics of Mill Avenue

> What is punk?... Punk is doing something totally insane, or saying "Fuck off" to the authorities.... Punk is living on the streets, "squatting" in a run-down house, stealing money for food, eating out of a garbage can, wearing the only clothes you have day after day. Punk isn't a hairstyle or even a hair color ... it's the way you live out on the streets.... "You can take the punk off the street, but you can't take the street out of the punk."(Anonymous in Arizona, 1997, p. 12)

Tempe, Arizona, officials and their version of neighboring Phoenix's Downtown Phoenix Partnership—the Downtown Tempe Community (DTC) have their own image issue, and one that didn't go away with the final play of Super Bowl XXX. Tempe city officials and their developer allies are determined to build the city's main downtown commercial thoroughfare, Mill Avenue, into an upscale consumer destination, and standing in their way—or as we shall see, sitting in their way—is a group DTC officials regularly deride as street kids, slackers, and gutter punks.

"Gutter punk" does in fact accurately describe many of those on Mill. A subterranean stratum emerging out of—or more accurately, underneath the larger punk scene in the 1990s, the world of gutter punks is occupied by kids for the most part cut loose from traditional networks of support. While many of them embrace the particular stylistic or musical codes of the larger punk movement, they define themselves more by their willingness and ability to live on their own terms, and to find among themselves the ability to survive on the margins. Traveling around the country by freight train or Greyhound bus, squatting together in abandoned buildings, and hanging out on the streets, gutter punks practice the anarchic, do-it-yourself, anti-authoritarian politics of punk with a remarkable seriousness of purpose, and defiantly take these politics to extremes not always embraced by others. In doing so, of course, they present themselves to legal authorities and store owners, to shop patrons and passers-by, as outsiders with the audacity to be young, homeless, and publicly adventuresome at the same time.

Tempe officials are not the first to encounter gutter punks, and to confront their occupation of public space; as punk and gutter punk subcultures have emerged around the United States, Canada, and elsewhere, so have conflicts over their public presence. In Montreal, for example, police arrest and fine gutter punks for a crime that Giuliani would appreciate—unauthorized car windshield-washing—and city officials move to rezone a public punk meeting place, Berri Square, so as to institute a curfew. When local punks, Food Not Bombs, and members of the anarchist group Demanarchie demonstrate against the rezoning, more arrests are made. And when authorities move to drive panhandling gutter punks out of the Berri subway station, the situation spills over into a conflict of sonic, even operatic, proportions. Drawing on a similar strategy utilized in Toronto, the public transit authority decides to broadcast opera music in the station, believing it to somehow serve as a form of sonic punk-repellent. But of course the punks stay to enjoy the arias, and to participate in the failed opera buffa created by the authorities (Leblanc, 1999).

In another French-flavored city a couple of thousand miles south, a similar conflict unfolds. In response to the public presence of French Quarter gutter punks, New Orleans business and tourist associations call for more aggressive policing, and for new laws prohibiting public sleeping. With their "spiked leather bracelets, nose rings, close-cropped hair and tattoos," and their "lack of respect for themselves or anybody else," the gutter punks are accused of polluting the carefully maintained tourist appeal of the Quarter. The president of the convention and visitors bureau publicly complains that it's all "just a disgrace. This is what we're inviting our tourists to see?" But Coral Cronin, a 16-year-old gutter punk, offers a rebuttal: "They've got to realize this is a city. It's not a Disneyland" (Associated Press, 1995).

Back in Tempe, it is a Disneyland and increasingly so, as officials and developers invite tourists and local consumers to see Mill Avenue gradually be remade into a commercial wonderworld. Drawing, ironically, on the youthful appeal generated by nearby Arizona State University, Tempe officials have worked to bring in major retailers as a way of transforming Tempe's "decrepit central core" into a uniformly appealing location for shopping and nightlife; as the local newspaper glowingly reports, "Tempe planners spent the last 10 years attracting businesses and investors to help them create a sort of theme-park downtown" (Balazs, 1999, p. A1; Hermann, 1998, p. A10). As a result, the traditional mom-and-pop shops of Mill Avenue are closing, replaced by what local activist Randall Amster (2000) describes to me as "a sort of Manhattanization of our little spot here in the desert ... a kind of chain-store process ... The Gap and Abercrombie & Fitch and Starbucks...." Indeed, one local shop manager—her own shop soon enough driven out of business—reports that "we've watched one small store after another close ... The big national chains are taking over and Mill Avenue is becoming an open-air mall" (Fiscus & Hermann, 1999, p. A18).

And the process continues. A new $70 million, high-end retail and condominium project has Tempe's mayor salivating over "having people with that kind of disposable income walking around your downtown" (Fiscus, 2000, p. B7). A damming and refilling project that has made "Town Lake" out of the bone-dry bed of the nearby Rio Salado—drained dry over the years by too much development and population growth and too many artificially green desert lawns—has already driven up neighboring home prices, just as the police have of late begun to drive the homeless from neighboring parks. And when a proposed 900,000 square foot shopping, entertainment, and office complex is completed next to the lake, longtime residents fear, it will once and for all "break the backs of the mom-and-pop businesses along Mill Avenue" (Diaz, 2000b; Diaz & Stanley, 1999, p. A4).

Of course, this sanitization and homogenization of the local business climate requires a certain cultural sanitization as well. Local authorities, therefore, increasingly target the homeless folks, slackers, and gutter punks who have traditionally hung out in and around the avenue's shops and coffee bars, arresting them repeatedly for urban camping, trespassing, and loitering. A city council member proclaims that "we're very concerned and we need to do something" about Mill Avenue's youth population. Tempe police actively enforce the local anti-cruising and car stereo volume ordinances, and orchestrate regular curfew sweeps. And the executive director of the Mill Avenue Merchants

Association adds, "We don't want to run the kids out. But there's not a whole lot to do but hang out. Twenty-one and older is definitely the target market down here" (Cannella, 1996, pp. A1, A10).

To further ensure the comfort of its emerging target market, the Downtown Tempe Community supplements curfew sweeps and anti-cruising ordinances with a touch of one-on-one soft control. Euphemistically described in the local media as an "ambassador to the homeless" (Jones, 1999, p. B1), Rhonda Bass is employed by the DTC as the point person in what she more realistically describes to me as "a security program, an outreach program." Formerly working in the DTC office on issues of tourism promotion, she now patrols Mill Avenue with a cell phone and radio, on the lookout for those she characterizes as:

> homeless kids, slackers ... old Deadheads that are lost or something ... hardcore homeless people ... younger kids [that] travel more in little gangs.... They're all on some kind of substance ... or not mentally capable of understanding or taking care of themselves. They're all kind of extreme. (Bass, 1999)

Upon encountering such human extremities, she works to get them off the avenue, either through the temporary provision of social services or by calling in the local police since, as she says, the presence of the homeless affects business owners and "it does hinder their businesses when you have a group of 10, 20 smelly human beings sitting outside of their shops just aggravating people when they walk by." She reports that business owners are pleased with the program, and that her boss at the DTC is pleased with her efforts—"the only thing he asks is that our streets are safe and clean" but adds that the younger street kids, the gutter punks especially, seem to resent her offers of assistance. Strange—perhaps their pervasive mental incapacitation leaves them unable to recognize the real meaning of that which they are offered.

For the DTC and Tempe authorities, though, even curfew sweeps, anti-cruising ordinances, and the street cleaning work of Rhonda Bass haven't been enough to rid the avenue of the smelly human beings sitting outside the shops. So, in December 1998, the Tempe City Council and the DTC pushed through a new ordinance that criminalized "sitting or lying down on public sidewalks in the Downtown Commercial District," with a maximum $500 fine and 30-day jail sentence (Article V, Sec. 29-70, Ord. No. 98.57). Modeled on "sitting bans" in other cities around the United States, the ordinance was defended by Tempe's mayor and others as not targeting the homeless, but rather issues of safety and accessibility; as Rhonda Bass argues, "it's not a strike against the homeless people or anything. It was just to kind of free-flow our streets more so the pedestrians have more room."

Whatever its alleged intent, the positive effects of the ordinance were soon celebrated. The local media reported a few months after its January 1999 implementation that "Mill Avenue is clearly safer at night than it has been in recent months.... As recently as December, potential visitors were turned off by an environment populated by unruly youths." Business owners noted that "we used to have panhandlers out in front every night. Now we don't have any," and approvingly likened the local clampdown to the one in San Francisco, where "street people really got out of hand." Rod Keeling, executive director of the DTC, added, "everybody that I've talked to over the past six months has noticed a marked improvement" (Barajas, 1999, pp. 4–5).

Apparently Rod Keeling hasn't talked to Leif, Kat, and their friends. Wandering down Mill a couple of months after the sitting ban goes into effect, I hook up with them in front of a local bookstore. Even among the ragged company of Mill's gutter punk community, Leif stands out his face tattooed with a variety of new tribal designs. His friend, Kat exhibits a rather more graceful dishevelment. Passing around Ice House beers poured surreptitiously into plastic soda cups, rolling cigarettes or cadging them from passersby, they invite me to sit down with them—on the flat edge of a low flowerbed, that is. They know the details of the new ordinance—know that sitting on the sidewalk is prohibited, but that sitting on "permanently affixed" structures isn't—and so we sit 18 inches above illegal, and talk.

Describing their lives on the streets, Leif talks about the ways the kids consistently help each other out by sharing squats; as he says, his problems are "more about food than about a place to sleep" (Leif, 1999). He notes that this lack of food results directly from the difficulty in finding a decent job, but figures it matters less to him and his friends than to others anyway, since "we're not so materialistic." Kat (1999) agrees, noting that her friends on the streets "are nicer than all the Babylon people, more about brotherly love than in their material world." She and Leif go on to emphasize the sense of community and support that exists on the street. "It's all about friendship—that's what counts," says Kat. "If you're a good person, you'll run into somebody who will help. It's totally karma."

By this time another dharma bum has arrived—Scum, carrying a "fresh" six-pack of Ice House under his shirt—and talk turns to the emerging economics and control of Mill Avenue. Kat (1999) argues that "they're upset because they envy our way of life and can't handle it, so they like to make dumb laws to fuck with us," and compares Tempe's sitting ordinance to laws regulating hitchhiking, and to her prior arrest in another city for standing too long in the same spot. "Of course I threw the ticket away." Leif (1999) notes that, despite the new ordinance, "we sit wherever we want. We don't sit on the ground when they're looking. We find ways around it, to invade them." And indeed, Leif does know when they're looking; as we're talking, he points out the private security personnel—"weekend badges"—watching us from the balcony of a Hooter's restaurant across the street. As I get up to leave, Leif invites me to an informal drum circle that he and friends will be holding later on the street, if the police don't break it up. Due in Tucson by evening, I can't make it. But walking back down Mill, I do run into a different sort of circle, this one apparently quite legal. A group of Girl Scouts rings a cookie sale table they've set up right in the middle of the sidewalk.

If Rod Keeling is under the impression that everyone sees the new sitting ordinance as an improvement, that Mill Avenue is now safely in the hands of Gap stores and Girl Scouts, he probably hasn't talked with Randall Amster, either. Amster's critique of the emerging Mill Avenue goes beyond the "chain-store process" and "Disneyfication mode" that he argues underpin its economic development. He (Amster, 2000) also points out to me the close economic and political ties between the city of Tempe and the DTC—the way in which the DTC functions as the city government's "alter ego"—and describes this "concerted effort of corporate and governmental entities" as "a kind of neo-fascism." Out of this arrangement, he argues, has come a "rise in persecution of people and things that don't fit into the larger plan," a "sanitization process" whereby gutter punks and other street folks have "basically become the equivalent of street trash." As an alternative to such arrangements, and as a foundation for opposing them, Amster cites a remarkable mix of political traditions, including "anarchist direct action, the Wobblies, the IWW ... the civil rights movement ... the philosophies of Gandhi and King ... passive resistance, civil disobedience ... the burgeoning WTO, World Bank anti-globalization movement." And, describing an alternative vision to that of city planners and business groups, Amster notes that:

> for me, it's all about maintaining public spaces. The conceptual link that I operate from is trying to preserve spaces that are historically dedicated to the public, because it's my belief that without public spaces, any kind of talk about democracy basically goes out the window ... I'd like to see the public spaces in Tempe become revitalized again; that would be my ultimate goal ... keeping the spaces that historically were for the public ... vigorous meetings spots and places that everyone can enjoy. (2000)

Toward this end, Amster and his friends did indeed decide on a bit of anarchist direct action—and they aimed it directly at the new sitting ordinance. Putting together Project S.I.T. (Sidewalk Initiative Team)—a group whose website features an anarchist/sitter logo, and a commemoration of the Wobbly's first U.S. sit-down strike in 1906—Amster and others set in motion a series of Mill Avenue street sit-ins in protest of the new ordinance. Beginning with a January 1999, Martin Luther King Jr. Day protest, groups of activists, homeless folks, Arizona State University students and faculty, and local children sat in circles on the sidewalks of Mill Avenue, in intentional violation of the ordinance. Some of the sit-ins drew intense media coverage, others less; one included a pounding drum circle of the sort Leif described, and drew the praise of an onlooker the media described as "a homeless man ... whose right arm bears the tattoo 'Food Not Bombs'" (Trujillo, 1999, p. B5). But in every case, as Randall Amster recalls, the sit-ins reclaimed and reinvented the very sorts of cultural space that he and others cherished and the very sorts that the new ordinance was designed to erase:

> They were like little mini-moments of autonomous zones. There was this aspect of liberating a street corner just for a day or so, and really creating a kind of space for spontaneity. We had people playing drums. We had a bunch of street people join us.
>
> One sort of crazy couple ... had a van, on the side was painted "Fuck the Police" ... it was definitely a day of spontaneity and open-endedness that you can't really find down there anymore. (Amster, 2000)

For Amster and Project S.I.T., these disorderly street politics generated an added benefit as well. Trained as a lawyer—though having earlier "left the legal profession because my anarchistic feelings made it impossible for me to practice law"—Amster intended to mount a legal challenge to the sitting ordinance, but knew that such challenges often fail when those bringing them cannot demonstrate direct involvement in the issue at hand. In this case, though, direct action in the street evolved into the basis for legal action in the courts:

> The idea was that by sitting my own butt on the sidewalk, and along with all the other folks that joined us, conceptually we were able to link our rights with the rights of the street people, really the target of the ordinance.... Now I have to say that I can't take credit for that in terms of seeing it ahead of time and really pushing that—that's just the way it naturally evolved.... We were able to show that there was clearly a time when sitting was used specifically to convey something. In other words, the act of fifty people sitting down in defiance of the law that makes sitting down a crime, on Martin Luther King Jr. Day, was in itself an expressive act. (Amster, 2000)

Establishing this linkage between expressive street protest and the rights of gutter punks and other street people, Amster was able to challenge the legality of the ordinance, and in early 2000 a U.S. district court judge overturned Tempe's sitting ban, ruling it unconstitutional (Diaz, 2000a).

So it seems that for Rod Keeling, the DTC, and Tempe city officials, even with all their cash and political clout, you can't always get what you want. But of course, if you keep trying, you might get what you need. Randall Amster (2000) points out that the city has been "slowly selling off the sidewalks downtown," deeding them to developers in such a way as to "convert public space to private." In this way, as he says, "you could win the legal battle, the immediate battle, the public opinion battle, and in the end the city could still just sell it right from under you and say, sorry, now it's private property and yon no longer have any First Amendment rights." Moreover, victory in the immediate battle hardly halts the ongoing and ever inventive spatial sanitization work of economic and political authorities, an excremental whiff of which filtered out of the DTC back in 1997.

Early in that year, Keeling and the DTC proposed to ban cats and dogs from downtown sidewalks, arguing that their presence had become a public health matter, since "we have had people step in dog waste and track it into stores. We've had a woman slip and fall." In a letter to Tempe's mayor and city council, Keeling elaborated, alleging that Mill Avenue's street kids create "public disorder" with their "public sexual activity ... defecation and urination in public areas, and possession of dogs, cats, and other animals that can intimidate the public" (*The Arizona Republic*, 1997, p. B1; Cannella, 1997, p. B3). After all, Keeling later argued, "the lifestyle we're talking about is horrific.... The human carnage is unbelievable. Our community shouldn't let this behavior go on.... It includes kids from 12 up to their 20s." A Mill Avenue business owner added that such kids are typically covered in "body piercings, tattoos, and reeking of body odor" (Petrie, 1998, p. B2).

Though the proposed ban ultimately wasn't passed by the city council due, apparently, to opposition from middle-class pet owners, and concerns about pet-owning shop patrons—the campaign for its passage did reveal a particularly inventive, and odious, ideology. This ideology surfaces time and again in conflicts over cultural space, as likely to be directed at graffiti writers (Ferrell, 1996) or gay men (Delany, 1999) as it is at gutter punks. In every case, its essentials are the same: drawing on evocative images of filth, disease, and decay, economic and political authorities engage in an ideological alchemy through which unwanted individuals do indeed become the sort of "street trash" Amster describes. And when successful, this alchemy quite effectively demonizes economic outsiders, stigmatizes cultural trespassers, and thereby justifies the symbolic cleansing of the cultural spaces they occupy.

Even now, after years of such cultural and spatial cleansing—after years of economic homogenization and privatization, of curfew sweeps and anti-cruising enforcement, of anti-sitting ordinances and homeless "ambassadors"—the promotional literature of the DTC ironically invites visitors to a Mill Avenue marketed as "urban and eclectic by day, with a pulsating street scene at night," a place where "culture is abundantly on display" (Downtown Tempe Community, n.d.). But the work of city officials and the DTC sends a darker cultural message, writes an ironic subtext to be read by the homeless and the marginalized, by Kat and Leif, by street dogs and alley cats, by gutter punks and by the anarchist activists that defend them: Don't sit. Don't stay. Don't beg.

Toward Spatial and Social Justice

Wide-ranging contemporary conflicts over cultural space, and particular public controversies like that on Mill Avenue, all reveal complex configurations of inequality and injustice. Clearly, these conflicts reinforce patterns of power and privilege, as they spawn new aggressions and indignities against the disadvantaged, enforce new forms of spatial exclusion within urban areas, and promote a type of spatial cleansing whereby unwanted populations are removed, by the force of law and money, from particular locations and situations. But this spatial cleansing is at the same time a cultural cleansing; as economic, political, and legal authorities work to recapture and redesign the public spaces of the city, they work to control public identity and public perception as well, to remove from new spaces of consumption and development images of alternative identity. Forces of economic development and corporate control, of legal and political domination, of symbolic erasure and perceptual policing all intersect and intertwine in the cultural spaces of the city—and do so not as discrete entities, but as entangled lines of power each constituting (Henry & Milovanovic, 1996) and contributing to the other. In so doing, these combined forces produce new forms of social control and surveillance, and with them sanitized remappings of segregation and separation, aimed not only at marginalized populations but at the public identities they inscribe in the spaces of the city.

The potent complexity of these forces suggests that any attempt to resist and overcome them must engage a variety of issues, from the reconfiguration of discriminatory criminal justice practices and the political system that supports them, to the remaking of an economic system that generates both growing class divides and the spatial patterns by which these divides are encoded in everyday life. But the experiences of Leif and Kat, of Randall Amster and Project S.I.T., suggest something else as well: that resistance to injustice must emerge, not just in courtrooms and political campaigns, but in the streets and spaces, in the everyday cultural politics, of the city. At a minimum, gutter punks and street activists throw alternative identities up against enforced uniformity, offer moments of autonomous pleasure in the face of orchestrated entertainment, celebrate a sort of shambling marginality in counterpoint to an emerging economy and aesthetics of middle-class consumer life. Beyond this, as the actions of Randall Amster and the Project S.I.T. participants show, they also succeed in organizing eclectic communities of difference, and effective political resistance, inside the spaces they share.

This sort of activism for spatial and social justice is of course not confined to Tempe. Urban kids in the U.S. and other countries are working to build a Youth Peace Movement, and within it linking "union [politics], street culture, and indigenous activism, along with racial/ethnic participation" (Childs, 1997, p. 255). Activists who have orchestrated a growing street gang truce in the U.S. are not only developing resources to combat police violence, but supporting "a project to hire jobless youth to recycle waste plastic into sturdy dome-homes for the homeless, [and] neighborhood 'cooperative zones' as an alternative to the cruel hoax of 'enterprise zones'" (Zinzun, 1997, p. 265).

Artists like Judy Baca are bringing together hip-hop graffiti writers and other young people from diverse cultural backgrounds to create public murals celebrating community heritage and cultural history (Lippard, 1990; see Sanchez-Tranquilino, 1995). Urban environmental movements like Critical Mass and Reclaim the Streets are attempting to "demolish the divisions between art and life" (Jordan, 1998, p. 129) by situating moments of cultural transformation and symbolic resistance in the spaces of daily existence. Critical Mass—a fluid, decentralized, "organized coincidence" of bicyclists and bicycle militants—stages collective rides and other events designed to celebrate alternative transportation and to disrupt the dominance of automotive traffic in urban areas. Members of the Reclaim the Streets movement illicitly barricade avenues and intersections; defy attempts to reopen them to the usual flow of traffic, commerce, and gentrification; and convert them instead into informal, inclusive street parties and parks.

This activism around issues of cultural space suggests that essential issues of human dignity and identity, of social welfare and social justice, are at issue in the everyday conflicts between marginalized populations and those who would erase them from public view. In fact, a variety of contemporary cases confirm just what the stakes are, day to day, in this street fight over cultural space. Reporting on the proliferation of anti-homeless ordinances, *The New*

York Times notes that such ordinances seem aimed at "soothing shoppers' eyes" and at redeveloping urban neighborhoods in such a way that they're "scrubbed clean" (Ybarra, 1996, p. 5; Nieves, 1999a, p. 4). Explaining the rise in homelessness itself, an Urban Institute researcher adds that the well-to-do in such neighborhoods "are pushing the price of housing up and taking over more space" (*New York Times*, 2000, p. A6), thereby contributing to the very homelessness problem they seek to ignore. And accounting for the growing number of fatal assaults on the homeless, the executive director of the Chicago Coalition for the Homeless cites urban gentrification and the heavy-handed enforcement of anti-homeless laws, which provide "the underpinning of these hate crimes" by promoting the image that "these people don't count. These people are criminals for being poor" (Nieves, 1999b, p. A36).

Along Mill Avenue, across the United States, and around the world, the lessons are the same. Identity is forged in the cultural spaces of everyday life, inside the emerging map of the city. Social justice demands spatial justice.

References

Amster, R. (2000, March 14). Interview. Tempe, Arizona.

Anonymous in Arizona. (1997). More core. *Thrasher, 198*, 12.

The Arizona Republic. (1997, January 9). Animal ban urged in downtown Tempe. *The Arizona Republic*, Bl.

Associated Press. (1995, November 3). "Gutter Punks" degrade French Quarter. *Arizona Daily Sun*, 9.

Balazs, D. (1999, November 17). Valley downtowns taking off. *The Arizona Republic*, A1, A12.

Barajas. V. (1999. August 19). Tempe's got the hookup. *The Arizona Republic*, 4–5.

Bass, R. (1999, July 9). Interview. Tempe, Arizona.

Cannella, D. (1996, May 31). Slackers congregate for run of the mill. *The Arizona Republic*, A1, A10.

Cannella, D. (1997, January 11). Proposed dog ban aims at "slackers." Tempe critics say. *The Arizona Republic*, B1, B3.

Childs, J. B. (1997). The new youth peace movement: Creating broad strategies for community renaissance in the United States. *Social Justice, 24*, 247–257.

Cosgrove, S. (1984). The zoot-suit and style warfare. *Radical America, 18*, 39–51.

Delany, S. R. (1999). *Times Square red. Times Square blue.* New York: New York University Press.

Diaz, E. (2000a. February 1). Federal judge strikes down Tempe law against sitting on sidewalks. *The Arizona Republic*, 82.

Diaz, E. (2000b. February 7). Lake brings new life to neighborhood. *The Arizona Republic*, A1, A11.

Diaz, E., & Stanley, J. (1999, September 18). Tempe center size debated. *The Arizona Republic*, Al, A4.

Downtown Tempe Community, Inc. (n.d.). Downtown Tempe People and Parking Guide.

Ferrell, J. (1990). East Texas/Western Louisiana sawmill towns and the control of everyday life. *Locus, 3*, 1–19.

Ferrell, J. (1995). Style matters; Criminal identity and social control. In J. Ferrell & C. R. Sanders (Eds.), *Cultural criminology* (pp. 169–189). Boston: Northeastern University Press.

Ferrell, J. (1996). *Crimes of style: Urban graffiti and the politics of criminality.* Boston: Northeastern University Press.

Ferrell, J. (1997). Youth, crime and cultural space. *Social Justice, 24*, 21–38.

Ferrell, J. (1998). Freight train graffiti: Subculture, crime, dislocation. *Justice Quarterly, 15*, 587–608.

Ferrell, J. (1999). Cultural criminology. *Annual Review of Sociology, 25*, 395–418.

Ferrell, J., & Sanders, C. R. (Eds.). (1995). *Cultural criminology.* Boston: Northeastern University Press.

Ferrell, J., & Websdale, N. (Eds.). (1999). *Making trouble: Cultural constructions of crime, deviance, and control.* New York: Aldine de Gruyter.

Fiscus, C. (2000, March 2). Brickyard on mill. *The Arizona Republic*, B1, B7.

Fiscus, C., & Hennann, W. (1999, September 12). Mom-pop shops losing ground to chain stores. *The Arizona Republic*, A18.

Foucault, M. (1977). *Discipline and punish: The birth of the prison.* London: Tavistock.

Georges-Abeyie, D. (1990a). The myth of a racist criminal justice system? In B. D. MacLean & D. Milovanovic (Eds.), *Racism, empiricism, and criminal justice* (pp. 11–14). Vancouver: The Collective Press.

Georges-Abeyie, D. (1990b). Criminal justice processing of non-white minorities. In B. D. Maclean & D. Milovanovic (Eds.), *Racism, empiricism, and criminal justice* (pp. 25–34). Vancouver: The Collective Press.

Hennann, W. (1998, March 4). Downtown Tempe fills need for "someplace." *The Arizona Republic*, A1, A10.

Henry, S., & Milovanovic, D. (1996). *Constitutive criminology.* London: Sage.

Jones, M. L. (1999, April 5). "Ambassador" to homeless. *The Arizona Republic*, B1, B2.

Jordan, J. (1998). The art of necessity: The subversive imagination of anti-road protest and reclaim the streets. In G. McKay (Ed.), *DIY culture: Party and protest in nineties Britain* (pp. 129–151). London: Verso.

Kat. (1999, March 6). Interview. Tempe, Arizona.

Keith, M. (1997). Street sensibility? Negotiating the political by articulating the spatial. In A. Menifield & E. Swyngedouw (Eds.), *The urbanization of injustice* (pp. 137–160). New York: New York University Press.

Leblanc, L. (1999). Punky in the middle. In J. Ferrell & N. Websdale (Eds.), *Making trouble: Cultural constructions of crime, deviance, and control* (pp. 203–229). New York: Aldine de Gruyter.

Leif. (1999, March 6). Interview. Tempe, Arizona.

Lippard, L. R. (1990). *Mixed blessings: New art in multicultural America.* New York: Pantheon.

Marx, K. (1972). The eighteenth Brumaire of Louis Bonaparte. In R. Tucker (Ed.), *The Marx-Engels reader* (pp. 436–525). New York: W.W. Norton.

Merrifield, A., & Swyngedouw, E. (Eds.) (1997). *The urbanization of injustice.* New York: New York University Press.

The New York Times. (2000, February 1). 1.35 million kids likely homeless in year, study says. *The Arizona Republic*, A6.

Nieves, E. (1999a, December 7). Cities try to sweep homeless out of sight. *The New York Times*, 4–5.

Nieves, E. (1999b, December 26). Fatal beatings of U.S. homeless are increasing. *The Arizona Republic*, A36.

Petrie, B. (1995, September 27). Tempe may squeeze out homeless. *The Arizona Republic*, A1, A12.

Petrie, B. (1998, December 17). Tempe set to ban sidewalk sitting. *The Arizona Republic*,81, 82.

Platt, A. (1974). The child-saving movement and the origins of the juvenile justice system. In R. Quinney (Ed.), *Criminal justice in America* (pp. 362–383). Boston: Little Brown.

Rotenberg, R., & McDonogh, G. (Eds.) (1993). *The cultural meaning of urban space.* Westport, CT: Bergin and Garvey.

Sanchez-Tranquilino, M. (1995). Space, power, and youth culture: Mexican American graffiti and Chicano murals in East Los Angeles, 1972–1978. In B. J. Bright & L. Bakewell (Eds.), *Looking high and low: Art and cultural identity* (pp. 55–88). Tucson: University of Arizona Press.

Schlossman, S., & Wallach, W. (1978). The crime of precocious sexuality: Female juvenile delinquency in the progressive era. *Harvard Educational Review, 48*, 65–94.

Soja, E. (1989). *Postmodern geographies.* London: Verso.

Trujillo, L. (1999, January 31). Sit-in targets Tempe law. *The Arizona Republic*, B5.

Wagner, D. (1996, April 16). Cracking down on beggars. *The Arizona Republic*, 81, 83.

Ybarra, M. (1996, May 19). Don't ask, don't beg, don't sit. *The New York Times*, Sect. 4, 5.

Zinzun, M. (1997). The gang truce: A movement for social justice: An interview with Michael Zinzun. *Social Justice, 24*, 258–266.

Zukin, S. (1997). Cultural strategies of economic development and hegemony of vision. In A. Merrifield & E. Swyngedouw (Eds.), *The urbanization of injustice* (pp. 223–243). New York: New York University Press.

3

Policing Cyberspace: Mass Surveillance and the Expansion of the State

Frank Tridico

Matters of public interest such as privacy and civil liberties are often in conflict with State power, particularly with proactive policing. After 9/11, the State has moved toward a more *proactive*, rather than *reactive* form of policing, engaging in four areas of change: (1) increased surveillance, (2) aggressive entrapment, (3) more of a centralized system, and (4) increased technology to combat crime and threats to national security. The move to proactive policing involves imposition on privacy and civil liberties, because it necessitates the State to assess whether crime is in the early stages or is in the process of being committed. It brings law enforcement closer to impending threats in an effort to secure warrants and arrests prior to the commission of crimes, contain the threat while it is occurring, and secure vital evidence that can be used against suspects in legal proceedings. The move to proactive policing differs greatly from the traditional reactive model that addresses crime as it is occurring or after it has occurred.

To understand State power and criminal justice policy, it must be examined in three contexts. The State (which includes government, federal agencies, courts, and varying levels of law enforcement) is both conservative in structure and design, running as a centralized body, and resisting change while affording itself greater immunity. With respect to criminal justice policy, conservatives have advanced a law-and-order approach, and liberal legislators have either generally supported the approach or have not opposed it. Second, the United States Supreme Court has had majority representation by conservative Justices for most of its history. In only brief periods in history such as the Warren Court of the 1960s have there been more than four liberal Justices. Conservative Justices have interpreted the Constitution in a manner that has largely benefited the State by affording it constitutional legitimacy in many of its rulings. For example, almost every major ruling regarding the Fourth Amendment after *Mapp v. Ohio* (1961) has increased State power vis-à-vis law enforcement policy. Landmark rulings such as the exclusionary rule in *Mapp* have been offset by incremental provisions in cases that have placed greater emphasis on proactive policing. Third, the aforementioned allows for both legal authority and constitutional legitimacy to expand the power of the State to address national security concerns.

From a spatial policing paradigm, there are three areas of coverage in law enforcement: (1) the global, which utilizes a centralized system (Interpol) and international collaboration and information sharing to combat crimes such as child pornography, human trafficking, and terrorism; (2) the federal, which has moved toward a more centralized system (Homeland Security) to primarily address national security concerns; and (3) the regional, or local, which operates at a more limited scope to primarily address child pornography and sexual exploitation of minors through the Internet.

The chapter focuses first on cyber policing at the macro levels (global and federal), and then on the micro or regional areas.

International Cooperation: Five Eyes Intelligence-Sharing Network

Given the secrecy of intelligence gathering surveillance programs, information about them is more likely to be identified through breaches, errors, leaks to media sources, or court challenges. In late January 2016, Canada placed put a hold on sharing top-secret spy data with the Five Eyes countries, including the United States, after it was discovered that its National Security Agency (NSA) counterpart had shared information containing the personal details of Canadians. Authorities stated that this decision was made once it was learned that the Communications Security Establishment (CSE) agency had not properly hidden the metadata of Canadian citizens before sharing it with its international allies. Metadata includes the numbers and time stamps of phone calls, but excludes content. The CSE is equivalent to the NSA in the United States, which monitors electronic communication (RT, 2016).

Canada is a member of the Five Eyes intelligence-sharing network. Other members include the United States, the United Kingdom, Australia, and New Zealand. Although spying on Canadians specifically is against the law, individuals may inadvertently become entangled in the process when the CSE investigates other targets. While metadata can be obtained through telephony content, much of this is also attained through cyberspace, where personal data and communication between parties of interest can be assessed.

Interpol

Mass surveillance has coincided with the expansion and scope of the State not only in the United States, but throughout the aforementioned common law countries. While the intelligence-sharing network Five Eyes is relatively new, other more established international networks such as the International Criminal Police Organization (Interpol) have been used to share intelligence and engage in aggressive surveillance programs. Interpol was formed in September 1923, has an operating budget of 78 million euros (2013 figures) and has a jurisdictional structure that expands to 190 participating countries.

The role of Interpol is defined in Article 2 of its constitution, which states it (1) ensures and promotes the widest possible mutual assistance between all criminal police authorities within the limits of the laws existing in the different countries and in the spirit of the Universal Declaration of Human Rights, and (2) establishers and develops all institutions likely to contribute effectively to the prevention and suppression of ordinary law crimes. Interpol provides administrative liaison among law enforcement agencies of member countries, providing communications and database information sharing. Such information sharing is crucial when combating international crime as they help to overcome language, cultural, and organizational structural differences of member states. While national agencies have their own crime databases, the information is likely to be limited within their respective jurisdictions. Interpol's databases can track criminals and crime trends globally through collections of fingerprints, photographs, lists of wanted persons, DNA samples, and travel documents. Interpol has a lost and stolen travel document database in excess of 12 million units. This alone affords international community an integral resource with respect to regional and international security threats (Interpol, 2013).

Interpol officials can provide information sharing and analysis to member states. Interpol agents and member states communicate through an encrypted Internet-based network known as I-24/7. Some member states have expanded access to airports and border access points for more immediate access to information sharing (Anheier & Juergensmeyer, 2012). Interpol issued 13,637 notices in 2013, of which 8,857 were Red Notices, compared to 4,596 in 2008 and 2,037 in 2003. With respect to terrorism, Interpol initiated *Operation Hawk*, which combines comprehensive counter-terrorism training with border security operations. Specifically, the program aims at detecting the trafficking of radiological or nuclear material and chemical precursors. During parallel operations in Thailand and Malaysia, Thai customs officials discovered more than 154.3 pounds of sodium chlorate, a chemical precursor used to make improvised explosive devices (IEDs) (Interpol, 2013).

With respect to border security, Interpol's Integrated Border Management Task Force coordinates operations designed to assist member states with border protection vis-à-vis increased screening of passengers and vehicles against Interpol's databases. In 2013, 12 operations focusing on border security took place with some counter-terrorism aspects. More than 22,200 passengers were screened against Interpol's databases during Smuggling Training Operation Programme (STOP) operations in Kazakhstan and Tajikistan, resulting in four positive hits. Approximately 1,400 individuals, vehicles, and cargo were screened in relation to radiological or nuclear materials. Access to Interpol's I-24/7 system was made available to remote locations in Tajikistan, areas that could serve as soft or vulnerable security concerns (Interpol, 2013). With regard to databases, Interpol member countries conducted more than 1.2 billion searches of its criminal databases in 2013. This accounted for an average rate of 3.3 million searches per day or 38 searches per second, making it an invaluable international resource for proactive policing.

Three types of databases exist: (1) nominal, (2) fingerprints, and (3) DNA profiles. The nominal database contains records on wanted persons, known criminals, and missing persons. The number of searches of the database has more than doubled from 2011–2013. The fingerprint database contains fingerprints used to identify fugitives and missing persons which have been submitted by 180 member states. The DNA profiles database was created in 2002 with a single DNA profile and has increased exponentially. Users made an average of 31 searches per day in 2013. DNA profiles provide more advanced screening for member states to assist in identifying suspects abroad (Interpol, 2013).

The following accounts for a comparative statistical breakdown of records, searches, and hits by member states in three five-year intervals: 2003, 2008, and 2013.

The most identifiable exponential growth is seen in the fingerprints database, where there are 163,676 more units added, or an increase of 571% to its database over 10 years. Further exponential growth can be identified in the DNA profiles database, which has 85,859 more units added, or an increase of 256% over 10 years. The nominal database showed slight increases in 2008,

Table 3.1: Interpol Records for Nominal, Fingerprints, and DNA Profiles Databases

Database	2003	2008	2013
Nominal Database	154,094	174,256	155,691
Fingerprints Database	34,741	83,876	198,417
DNA Profiles Database	54,876	81,600	140,735

and it retracted to figures from a decade prior in 2013. Although this creates a perception of decreased value, accentuated emphasis should be given to the fingerprints and DNA profiles databases, which offer more specific intelligence to the international community to track individuals abroad.

The most identifiable exponential growth over two five-year cycles is for Interpol searches for the nominal database. An increase of 296,745,857 inquiries was made from 2013 figures as compared to 2003, demonstrating greater accessibility and valued resources for participating states. Although the number of searches for fingerprints was comparatively smaller, there was also exponential growth here, with 12,529 more searches in 2008 than in 2003, and 21,843 more searches in 2013 than in 2003. With regard to DNA Profiles database searches, there has been a sharp decline, from 41,903 in 2003 to 9,756 in 2008, and a slight rise to 11,328 in 2013. This suggests that most member states are still not participating or offering DNA profile specimens for varying reasons (e.g., some states have insufficient technology to collect and/or compare DNA and still rely on other areas).

With regard to successful hits, Interpol has been a valuable international resource for member states with regard to the nominal database. There has been an increase of hits over two five-year cycles: an increase of 75,963 in 2008 when compared to 2003, and an increase of 199,041 hits in 2013 when compared to 2008, and 275,004 more hits in 2013 than 10 years prior. A signifi-

Table 3.2: Interpol Searches for Nominal, Fingerprints, and DNA Profiles Databases

Database	2003	2008	2013
Nominal Database	215,401	7,302,822	296,961,258
Fingerprints Database	4,927	17,456	26,770
DNA Profiles Database	41,903	9,756	11,328

Table 3.3: Interpol Hits for Nominal, Fingerprints, and DNA Profiles Databases

Database	2003	2008	2013
Nominal Database	21,307	97,270	296,311
Fingerprints Database	72	1,032	1,283
DNA Profiles Database	49	25	86

cant number of hits for the fingerprints database can be evidenced both in 2008 and 2013 when compared to 2003. These account for individuals that would potentially not have been identifiable by other means once they cross over jurisdictions and into other regions. Limited growth is evidenced in DNA profiles database over two five-year cycles, perhaps suggesting an area Interpol can focus on with member states to utilize for future investigations.

Interpol is particularly effective at combating child pornography. At the end of 2013, approximately 3,809 victims from 50 member states had been identified by investigators and victim identification specialists using the Interpol International Child Sexual Exploitation (ICSE) database. To further enhance identifying abuse victims, the Interpol Victim Identification Laboratory (ViLab) was created. Based on a system shared with Interpol by the Royal Canadian Mounted Police, the ViLab is a mobile investigative resource that allows trained users to view child sexual abuse images from ongoing and unsolved investigations to help identify locations. Interpol has been effective at helping law enforcement in identification of victims and apprehending individuals exploiting minors. Investigations of online predatory rings and the creation, possession, and/or dissemination of child pornography are aided.

Other Statistics

The Interpol Annual Report (2013) accounted that more than 13,000 notices that were issued in that year, of which 8,857 were Red Notices for wanted persons. A total of 1,749 persons were arrested based on an Interpol notice during 2013. One of the notices issued led to the arrest of a suspect in the Srebrenica massacre. Aleksandar Cvetkovic, a suspect in the mass killings at Srebrenica during the 1992–1995 Bosnian War was extradited from Israel to Bosnia and Herzegovina following close collaboration between the NCBs in those countries and Interpol's Fugitive Investigative Support (FIS) unit. FIS coordinated actions between Israeli Ministry of Justice, the Bosnia and Herzegovina

War Crimes Prosecution Service, and the International Criminal Tribunal for the former Yugoslavia to help secure Cvetkovic's arrest.

Orange notices were circulated for the Boston Marathon Bombing suspects. At the request of U.S. authorities, Interpol issued a global Orange Notice detailing the features of the bombs used in the attack and identifying information of the suspects, Dzhokar Tsarnaev and Tamerlan Tsarnaev.

Interpol's criminal intelligence analysis provides operational and strategic analysis for crime-related projects, investigations, and operations. In 2013, Interpol provided 14 analytical reports regarding terrorism, 21 reports on organized crime and specialized crime areas, and three reports on drug trafficking. Interpol also provided training for 218 law enforcement officers from 68 countries in criminal intelligence analysis in 2013, a valuable contribution to regions with limited technology, resources, expertise, and strong centralized organizational frameworks. Interpol is working with member states to identify and interdict foreign nationals traveling to conflict zones in order to engage in terrorism-related activities. Data is collected and shared to track the movement of transnational fighters. In 2013, Interpol provided two analytical reports accounting for demographic data, recruitment networks inciting and facilitating travel, travel routes and modi operandi used by transnational fighters (Interpol, 2013).

Toward a More Centralized International Intelligence System

Interpol is a crucial asset in working with member states to identify emerging strategies of terror suspects as they travel globally, particularly with relative ease due to the Schengen Area consisting of 26 European countries that have abolished passport and other types of border controls. There, the agreement allows for both freedom of movement for European citizens, Schengen visa holders, and these who can travel in the area visa-free. The current Syrian refugee crisis has contributed to a massive exodus of persons out of the region and to other parts of the Middle East and Europe. ISIS is now in control of a large area of land including parts of Syria and Iraq, with expanding territory in the region. Transnational fighters have traveled to the region to fight for ISIS. Proxies have been used for terrorist activities in other countries. The ongoing movement of transnational fighters, refugee crises, political instability throughout the Middle East, and the emergent threat of terrorism has created more challenges for member states, and a greater onus for Interpol to expand its intelligence globally.

Mass surveillance and the expansion of the State coincide in large part due to emergent threats to national security. The timeline of the National Security Agency shows incremental increases in powers over time, but particularly when catastrophic events such as terrorist acts occur. When that occurs, the State seeks greater powers, particularly in areas of surveillance and is sometimes in conflict with the interpretation of existing laws and the United States Constitution. However, it should be noted that it is the Chief Justice of the U.S. Supreme Court that appoints U.S. district judges to the Foreign Intelligence Surveillance Court (FISC). It should also be noted that FISC has approved 99.97% of the 34,626 electronic surveillance requests from 1979–2013 with 60.4% of those from 2001–2013. This demonstrates that the FISC has served to reinforce the powers of the State with regard to electronic surveillance, including that which has been applied domestically and to U.S. citizens. FISC, as an extension of the State, has helped to preserve the power, legitimacy, and expanded reach of the State.

Public scrutiny, particularly after the Edward Snowden leaks, which brought surveillance programs into public purview, has had some limited political influence. This has led to the State coming forward to control the parameters of such discourse by defining the scope and justification of surveillance in relation to national security. It has provided some overtures to the public in terms of acknowledgment of preserving privacy interests, and implementing some amendments to address such concerns without compromising the scope and reach of the programs.

There is a concerted move toward centralized systems of surveillance and metadata collection within nation-states. There is a growing cooperation of centralized systems of information sharing of metadata between countries as has been noted by the Five Eyes intelligence-sharing network. There is growing cooperation on information sharing across states on a case-by-case basis, but more likely this will eventually be integrated with Interpol. The future of surveillance is centralization at the nation-state level, some level of international centralization in matters metadata collection, and information sharing pertaining to terrorism. Ironically, terrorism, which seeks to dismantle the organizational structure of the State and bring about political instability, will facilitate the broadened powers of the State to preserve political stability.

Federal Level: The Move toward a Centralized, More Powerful System

Under the Foreign Intelligence Surveillance Act of 1978, the government is required to obtain a judicial warrant before federal intelligence agencies are able to conduct electronic surveillance within the United States with respect to national security. The Foreign Intelligence Surveillance Court (FISC) was established by Congress to approve or deny warrant applications related to national security investigations. There are 11 U.S. district court judges from at least seven judicial circuits who serve terms for up to seven years. These judges are appointed by the Chief Justice of the U.S. Supreme Court. There must be at least three judges that reside within 20 miles of the District of Columbia to ensure the court can be convened on immediate notice.

Under the Fourth Amendment, a search warrant must be based on probable cause to believe that a crime has been or is being committed. This is not the general rule under FISA. Surveillance under FISA is permitted based on a finding of probable cause that the surveillance target is a foreign power or an agent of a foreign power, irrespective of whether the target is suspected of engaging in criminal activity. However, if the target is a "U.S. person," there must be *probable cause* to believe that the U.S. person's activities may involve espionage or other similar conduct in violation of the criminal statutes of the United States. Although FISA surveillances must have an intelligence purpose, courts allow FISA-obtained information to be used in criminal trials.

The Electronic Privacy Information Center (2016) describes the protocol for surveillance applications to the Court. The Attorney General must personally approve each final FISA application. The application must contain the following criteria:

(1) a statement of reasons to believe that the target of the surveillance is a foreign power or agent of a foreign power, (subject to the relevant amendments made by the USA PATRIOT Act)
(2) a certification from a high-ranking executive branch official stating that the information sought is deemed to be foreign intelligence information, and that the information sought cannot reasonably be obtained by normal investigative techniques;
(3) statements regarding all previous applications involving the target;
(4) detailed description of the nature of the information sought and of the type of communication or activities to be subject to the surveillance;
(5) the length of time surveillance is required;
(6) whether physical entry into a premise is necessary, and
(7) identify specific procedures to minimize the acquisition, use, and retention of information concerning non-consenting U.S. persons.

With regard to U.S. persons, the FISC judge must find probable cause that *one* of four conditions has been met:

(1) the target knowingly engages in clandestine intelligence activities on behalf of a foreign power which may involve a criminal law violation;
(2) the target knowingly engages in other secret intelligence activities on behalf of a foreign power under the direction of an intelligence network and his activities involve or are about to involve criminal violations;
(3) the target knowingly engages in sabotage or international terrorism or is preparing for such activities; or
(4) the target knowingly aids or abets another who acts in one of the above ways.

If the request is denied, the government can appeal the decision to a court of review. However, surveillance requests are granted in 99.97% of all cases. Since 1979, over 34,000 warrant applications requesting the authority to conduct domestic electronic surveillance, physical searches of premises, or a combination of both have been submitted to the court by federal intelligence agencies. Of these, approximately 20,909 requests have been made since September 11, 2001 (*Washington Post*, 2013). The period from 2001–2013 (13 years) accounts for 60.4% of the total number of surveillance requests, as compared to 39.6% of the total number of surveillance requests over a 21-year span from 1979–2000. Only 11 requests were denied by the court between 2001 and 2013. This demonstrates a consistent application of broad powers afforded to the State by the court. The U.S. Attorney General must provide Congress with the total number of granted, modified, or denied applications. The Attorney General meets with select intelligence committees in the House of Representatives and Senate on electronic surveillance at least twice a year. The following accounts for a breakdown of the 34,626 electronic surveillance requests over six presidencies.

It should be noted that the aforementioned figures do not account for the totality of the Obama presidency and only include electronic surveillance requests submitted up until 2013. The George W. Bush and Obama presidencies have accounted for almost two-thirds of the total number of electronic surveillance requests since 1979, suggesting a bi-partisan acceptance of affording more powers to the State in terms of expansive surveillance.

While there is some transparency vis-à-vis select intelligence committees, limited information is provided to the media, the broader public, or accessible in terms of comprehensive data. For example, limited transparency makes it difficult to discern the following:

Table 3.4: Total Number of Electronic Surveillance Requests Submitted to FISA, 1979–2013

President	No. of Requests	% of Total Requests	Requests Denied
Jimmy Carter	518	1.5%	0
Ronald Reagan	4,924	14.2%	0
George H. W. Bush	2,218	6.4%	0
Bill Clinton	6,057	17.5%	1
George W. Bush	14,353	41.5%	9
Barack Obama	6,556	18.9%	1

Rounded to nearest tenth percentage. Source: *Washington Post*, July 10, 2013.

(1) The standard and specific differences between the 99.97% of electronic surveillance requests approved and the 0.03% that were denied from 1979–2013. Without access to content within the application requests, it is virtually impossible to provide detailed scrutiny to assess whether any number of approved ones could have potentially been denied.
(2) Whether electronic surveillance requests were applied to unique targets, or whether they involved numerous applications for similar parties. These figures can show whether heightened concerns to national security are broader or narrowed in scope.
(3) Whether the bulk of electronic surveillance applications granted over specific periods of time have been applied for information gathering only, or if that surveillance has led to information that specifically led to prosecution of threats to the homeland. These figures can show whether, and to what extent, proactive measures have tangibly led to the elimination of threats.

The National Security Agency History

The National Security Agency (NSA) is a United States intelligence organization. This agency is tasked with collecting and analyzing data and information for foreign intelligence and counter-intelligence purposes. The NSA's mission statement reads as follows: "The NSA core mission is to protect U.S. national security systems and to produce foreign signals intelligence information." The scope, capacity, and operational procedure of this mission statement has changed significantly since the enactment of this agency. After the terrorist attacks of September 11, 2001, surveillance abroad as well as in the homeland may be used to protect the national security systems as well as produce intelligence in compliance with the agency's mission statement. The history of the NSA shows the change in their procedures of collection as well as the capacity and scope the agency uses to acquire information pertaining to national security.

Early Twentieth Century

The NSA was established in 1952 by President Truman. The agency's duty was to protect U.S. national security by collecting and analyzing intelligence. By 1973, the Supreme Court ruled that warrants need to be acquired to collect domestic data and intelligence. After this ruling, the Senate created a central committee to investigate alleged illegal domestic spying. The committee uncovered widespread abuse of government wire-tapping and eavesdropping practices. The committee recommended reforms to these domestic intelligence gathering practices, and in 1978 the Foreign Intelligence Surveillance Act (FISA) was enacted into law.

The Foreign Intelligence Surveillance Act (FISA) was enacted to protect United States citizens from illegal spying by government agencies. The new law was used to govern the surveillance activities by law enforcement when conducting domestic intelligence gathering on foreign states. This law required intelligence agencies to obtain warrants from the Foreign Intelligence Surveillance Court (FISC) that held safeguards to protect individuals from illegal surveillance by government agencies. These safeguards included that the court could not grant a warrant for domestic surveillance that an ordinary judge would find overreaching. This ensured that the government agencies including the NSA were governed by a court that held the same standards of probable cause for search and seizure used in all criminal procedures.

In December 2000, the NSA released a report detailing their mission for the new century. This report declares that in order to perform their mission of protecting national security from foreign states the agency must be allowed to have a constant presence on telecommunication networks to analyze the large amounts of data in order to gather intelligence. This plan would include phone records and Internet communications. The popularity of Internet communications and the ability to tap into servers would benefit the NSA by allowing them to monitor communications throughout the world. This would greatly enhance their surveillance ability to collect data in the interest of national security.

History of Surveillance in the United States

After the terrorist attacks on the World Trade Center and the Pentagon on September 11, 2001, the NSA was asked by the White House what more they could legally do to prevent any further terrorist attacks by gathering domestic intelligence. The NSA responded that by connecting their surveillance to terrorist activities the NSA could circumvent the FISA courts to collect domestic data from U.S. citizens within the context of national security interests. The first surveillance program used in this plan was the collection and sharing of all U.S. phone numbers that called to Afghanistan. This program was done without warrants or authorization from the FISC enacted to govern the intelligence agency.

On September 14, 2001, the first phases of expanded surveillance initiated. The Electronic Frontier Foundation (2016) cites that the State began targeting of terrorist-associated foreign telephone numbers on communication links between the U.S. and foreign countries where terrorists were known to be operating. Only specified, pre-approved numbers were allowed to be tasked for collection against links that originated in the United States.

When the State asked what could be done to secure the homeland, they were informed that analysts could chain through masked U.S. telephone numbers to identify foreign connections to those numbers. This could be done without identifying the U.S. telephone number or the party it belonged to. However, in December 1999, the Department of Justice had declared this type of search contravened the Foreign Intelligence Surveillance Act (FISA) when applied to *metadata* belonging to *U.S. persons* because it was considered "electronic surveillance" under its provisions (Electronic Frontier Foundation, 2016).

By September 26, 2001, any Afghan telephone number in contact with a U.S. telephone number was presumed to be of foreign intelligence value and was subject to dissemination by the FBI (Electronic Frontier Foundation, 2016). On October 4, 2001, President George W. Bush authorized a secretive order that allowed for the NSA's Domestic Surveillance Program (Lichtblau, 2009). This program was then declared legal by the NSA's General Counsel. The NSA held that this authorization allowed them to spy on four types of data: (i) telephony content; (ii) Internet content; (iii) telephony metadata; and (iv) Internet metadata (Electronic Frontier Foundation, 2016).

While there have been greater challenges to telephony content and metadata, there has been less on the State's imposition on Internet content and metadata. Both the public and the courts have demonstrated a greater reverence to personal privacy provisions to telephony communication, whereas cyberspace is regarded as less private, or more communal, requiring less protection. The latter has afforded the State greater leverage in expanding its surveillance beyond telephony content and metadata.

Attorney General John Ashcroft certified the program and the NSA began to send letters to private telecommunication companies asking for data. The NSA was able to gain access to Internet and phone content records of citizens. In 2002, all telecommunications companies previously asked to provide bulk data were signed into a formal voluntary agreement to give their data on specific targets to the U.S. government and the NSA. By 2003, this agreement included surveillance rooms in companies to collect mass data, which was directed and led by the NSA (Electronic Frontier Foundation, 2016).

The Electronic Frontier Foundation (2016) recounts that the NSA created a special division for advanced analysis in 2004 for the analysis and production of metadata gathered from their surveillance program. During this time, Attorney General Ashcroft was hospitalized and Deputy Attorney General James Comey became the acting Attorney General. The White House was told that he would not extend the NSA's spying program (Gellman, 2008). This is influenced by the Justice Department's interpretation of its legality. The White House decided to extend the program without the support of the Justice Department. Due to the Justice Department not providing approval, the collection of Internet metadata was halted for three months. However, President George W. Bush amended this order and the bulk collection of Internet metadata continued within the division for advanced analysis and production. In 2004, analysis and production of metadata and content was consolidated into advanced analysis. Specifically, they separated assessment into three areas: Internet metadata, telephony metadata, and content (Electronic Frontier Foundation, 2016).

In December 2005, *The New York Times* reported that the NSA was spying on U.S. citizens. This prompted President Bush to confirm the NSA's secretive domestic spying program. *The New York Times* also revealed that large companies were giving government access to their communication streams. After this exposure, telephone companies began to demand that voluntary letters of participation with the program be changed to court orders (Electronic Frontier Foundation, 2016).

On January 9, 2006, all FISC judges were briefed on the NSA's domestic spying program. This is the first time the FISC was fully involved with the NSA's surveillance program. With their support, the NSA was then allowed to begin their dragnet collection of telephony metadata. This allowed the NSA to collect metadata without a filter to be stored and analyzed by the agency and to not have to identify a single target. The FISC also authorized the first court order to collect mass phone records. The FISC declared that this order was supported by Section 215 of the USA PATRIOT Act, which amended the original FISA, placing greater emphasis on the government's surveillance abilities on suspected terrorists or individuals linked to terrorism. This order was renewed 11 times from its enactment to the end of 2008 during the presidency of George W. Bush (Electronic Frontier Foundation, 2016).

In 2007, the FISC stated that they would begin issuing the orders that authorize government agencies to target for the collection of communications when there is probable cause that the communications involved agents of recognized terrorist groups. This now made the FISC responsible to approve any electronic surveillance that was executed to further the surveillance of any terrorist or terrorist activities. This allowed for the program to run indefinitely under the authorization of the FISC and to no longer need reauthorization from a sitting U.S. president. Under this new structure, the FISC only needed to approve the reauthorization of court orders that renewed the mass collection of calling records from private companies. These court orders are supported by the interpretation of Section 215 of the USA PATRIOT Act that is continually reauthorized (Electronic Frontier Foundation, 2016).

Congress passed the FISA Amendments Act on July 9, 2008. This new act allowed for telecommunication companies to have immunity from federal or civil cases against them for their participation with government agencies in surveillance operations. This immunity is applicable as long as it is deemed that the actions of the government are constitutional (Electronic Frontier Foundation, 2016).

On March 2, 2009, the FISC ordered that the NSA must obtain their court approval to search the metadata acquired by their mass surveillance collection authorized by Section 215. This order compelled the NSA get court approval to analyze the metadata collected on a case-by-case basis unless there is a threat of imminent danger or loss of life. During the presidency of Barack Obama, the NSA's power to collect bulk data from domestic telecommunications changed and limited their domestic surveillance program. In 2011, the Obama administration ordered the NSA to no longer collect Internet metadata, but *increased* its ability to collect and track Internet traffic from Internet providers and search engine servers. This allowed them to store this information by having it funneled to their servers for collection and analysis (Electronic Frontier Foundation, 2016).

In 2015, Section 215 of the USA PATRIOT Act expired. This was then replaced by the USA Freedom Act. The USA Freedom Act limited the collection of bulk calling records. It required that the NSA provide a reasonable, articulatable suspicion and a specific term of time and details that prove that the data is connected to terrorism to attain phone records (Electronic Frontier Foundation, 2016).

FISA Warrantless Surveillance Reauthorization

The Electronic Privacy Information Center (2016) contends that the Protect America Act of 2007 altered the structure of FISA surveillance. The act altered the definition of electronic surveillance, created additional procedures for authorization of intelligence gathering on a program-wide basis, and set up a procedure for the courts to review those programs. FISA's new Section 105A declares that "nothing in the definition of electronic surveillance ... shall be construed to encompass surveillance directed at a person reasonably believed to be located outside of the United States." Since the FISA court procedures govern the use of electronic surveillance, this change in definition removes such surveillance from the review of the FISA court. There may be surveillance that is electronic, but if it does not fit into the FISA law's definition of electronic surveillance then the FISA court does not control it. This provision permits the warrantless surveillance of Americans when the surveillance is "directed at" someone believed to be outside the United States, regardless of whether that person outside the United States is an American or not.

Section 105B creates a set of procedures for the administration to use when acquiring information that is not electronic surveillance. The government must certify that the acquisition is not electronic surveillance. Certifications are also required that minimization procedures are followed and that "a significant purpose" of the acquisition is to obtain foreign intelligence information. The benefit the State gains from following this procedure is that holders of information, such as telecommunications companies, are forced to comply. The holders of information are also immunized from lawsuits for having provided this information, notwithstanding any privacy laws that would otherwise hold the companies liable for releasing the information. These certifications are valid for up to a year (Electronic Privacy Information Center, 2016).

Review of the procedures in 105B is provided by Section 105C. If the FISA court overturns the program, then the government can appeal to the FISA Court of Review and on to the Supreme Court. Even if overturned, the program can continue while these reviews and appeals are pending. The changes to the law are set to expire six months after enactment. However, any programs in place at the time of the expiration can continue their full course of up to a year (Electronic Privacy Information Center, 2016).

The National Security Agency and the FBI are tapping directly into the central servers of nine leading U.S. Internet companies, extracting documents, photographs, e-mails, audio and video chats, and connection logs that enable government analysts to track foreign targets, according to a top-secret document obtained by *The Washington Post* (Gellman & Poitras, 2013).

PRISM

The program code-named PRISM was initiated after Congress passed the Protect America Act in 2007 and the FISA Amendments Act of 2008, which immunized private companies that cooperated voluntarily with U.S. intelligence collection. PRISM recruited its first partner, Microsoft, and began six years of rapidly growing data collection for surveillance. The court-approved program is focused on foreign communications traffic, which often flows through U.S. servers even when sent from one overseas location to another (Gellman & Poitras, 2013).

Gellman and Poitras (2013) account that an internal presentation of 41 briefing slides on PRISM, dated April 2013 and intended for senior analysts in the NSA's Signals Intelligence Directorate, described the new tool as the most prolific contributor to the president's daily briefing. According to the slides and other supporting materials obtained by *The Washington Post*, NSA reporting increasingly relies on PRISM as a crucial source of material, accounting for nearly one in seven intelligence reports. Gellman and Poitras (2013) cite that Internet companies such as Yahoo and AOL have been offered immunity from lawsuits to allow for State intervention to facilitate surveillance. The companies accept a directive from the Attorney General and the Director of National Intelligence to open servers to the FBI's Data Intercept Technology Unit, which handles liaison to U.S. companies from the National Security Agency. Microsoft became PRISM's first corporate partner in May 2007. Apple demonstrated the most resistance to State intervention for approximately five years (Tsotis, 2013).

The Release of Information: Edward Snowden

Edward Snowden released secret and top secret documents that he procured while working for the U.S. government that exposed the collection of bulk data by the National Security Agency. Edward Snowden was able to collect these documents during his time working as a sub-contractor for the National Security Agency. He released the bulk of his documents on June 5, 2013, to a journalist from the news publication *The Guardian*. After the documents and the information was released to the public, Edward Snowden was charged with stealing government documents and is seen by the United States government as a traitor, as well as a whistleblower by advocates for privacy and groups against government overreach.

Edward Snowden was employed by the University of Maryland as a security guard for a secretive NSA complex on the campus. According to Snowden it was during this time in 2006 that he was recruited into the Central Intelligence Agency and worked for them in the field of information-technology security and was stationed in Geneva, Switzerland. After leaving the CIA in 2009, Snowden then worked for the private sector of IT security with Dell and then with Booz Allen as a contractor with the NSA for three months in Hawaii. It was during this time that Snowden started copying classified information from the NSA.

Snowden compiled a large amount of documents while employed by Booz Allen on the NSA's domestic surveillance practices. After three months of collecting documents, Snowden told his superiors that he needed time off for medical reasons and on May 20, 2013, he embarked on his journey to Hong Kong, China, where he set up a meeting with a reporter from the United Kingdom-based news source *The Guardian. The Guardian* then released secret documents on the NSA's spying techniques compiled by Snowden on June 5, 2013. The first documents released were on the NSA's bulk data collection by the actions of the Foreign Intelligence Surveillance Court that ordered the telecommunications company Verizon to release information on their customers on a daily basis to the NSA. Verizon was ordered to release bulk data on tens of millions of Americans.

The Guardian and other news sources around the world continued to release more of the secret files acquired from Snowden. These include:

(1) The NSA's surveillance program known as PRISM. This program was used to directly store information gathered from Internet servers such as Facebook, Google, Microsoft, and Yahoo to track online communication by bulk data collection.
(2) The United Kingdom's eavesdropping agency GCHQ program codenamed TEMPORA. This agency tapped fiber optic cables that are used for international communications that they shared with the NSA. This program gathered and stored over 600 million communications every day and stored the information for thirty days to be analyzed.
(3) The NSA's hacking program that infiltrated over 61,000 hacking operations worldwide that allowed them to infiltrate governments, public universities, and businesses all over the globe to acquire information.
(4) The NSA spied on European Union offices in the United States and in Europe using electronic eavesdropping operations.

(5) Thirty-Eight embassies and UN missions were spied on by the NSA. These countries included European and non-European members of the United Nations.
(6) The bulk collection of communication data of U.S. allies in Latin America.
(7) Documents that showed the NSA bulk collection was used on average citizens with no ties to terrorism hundreds of times a year and that the programs had budgets exceeding 53 billion dollars a year.
(8) The NSA acquires and stores 200 million text messages a day from individuals around the world, including U.S. citizens. This data was used to determine an individual's location, contacts, and financial data.

It has been suspected that Snowden may have leaked over 50,000 classified files to news sources and journalists. These files were secret, top secret, and Special Intelligence stamped. The United States Justice Department has charged Snowden with theft of government property, unauthorized communication of national defense information, and willful communication of classified communications intelligence information to an unauthorized person. The last two charges fall under the U.S. Espionage Act. Snowden is now in Russia, where the Russian government has granted him asylum.

Section 702 of the Foreign Intelligence Surveillance Act

The Office of the Director of National Intelligence provides an assessment of Section 702 of the Foreign Intelligence Act. "Section 702 refers to part of the Foreign Intelligence Surveillance Act (FISA) Amendments of 2008, and Section 702 (50 USC 19881a). This provision of FISA allows for foreign intelligence information concerning non-U.S. persons located outside the United States to be acquired" (2016). This allows for a more specific, broadened, and efficient procedure to collect the communications of targets.

Limited Targeting under the Law

The Office of the Director of National Intelligence takes the position that the government cannot target anyone under the court-approved procedures for Section 702 collection unless there is an appropriate, and documented, foreign intelligence purpose for the acquisition and the foreign target is reasonably believed to be outside the United States. Section 702 cannot be used to intentionally target any U.S. citizen, or any other U.S. person, or to intentionally target any person known to be in the United States. Section 702 cannot be used to target a person outside the United States if the purpose is to acquire information from a person inside the United States.

How Data Is Obtained and Used

The Office of the Director of National Intelligence argues that "Section 702 involves the assistance of electronic communications service providers, a dynamic that is explicitly laid out in the statute itself. However, under Section 702 of FISA, the United States Government does not unilaterally obtain information from the servers of U.S. electronic communication service providers. All such information is obtained with FISA court approval and with the knowledge of the service provider based upon a written directive from the Attorney General and the Director of National Intelligence" (2016).

Oversight, Compliance, and Minimization

The Office of the Director of National Intelligence argues that "collection under Section 702 does not require individual judicial orders authorizing collection against each target. Instead, the FISA court approves annual certifications submitted by the Attorney General and the Director of National Intelligence that identify categories of foreign intelligence that may be collected, subject to Court-approved 'targeting' procedures and 'minimization' procedures" (2016). Here, it becomes clear that it renders oversight to fall within the FISA court, not a regular court, and certifications are provided by the Attorney General and Director of National Intelligence, rather that outside checks and balances. By doing this, it affords greater discretion to itself. While the Office of the Director of National Intelligence cites oversight by FISC, it also contends that the executive branch and Congress serve as an internal system of checks and balances. It states that only non-U.S. persons outside the U.S. are targeted, and that it minimizes the acquisition, retention, and dissemination of incidentally acquired information about U.S. persons.

Section 215 of the Foreign Intelligence Surveillance Act

The Office of the Director of National Intelligence argues that "after the 1978 passage of the Foreign Intelligence Surveillance Act (FISA) it became apparent that the law left significant gaps in intelligence collection authority. While the Government had the power in a criminal investigation to compel the production of records with a grand jury subpoena, it lacked similar authority in a foreign intelligence investigation" (2016).

The Office cites that Section 215 of the USA PATRIOT Act enables requests to the FISA court for orders requiring production of documents relevant to an authorized national security investigation to protect against international terrorism or clandestine intelligence activities.

Under Section 215, the details of FISA-related investigations, including requests for business records, are classified. The only way they can be produced is if they are the type of records that could be obtained pursuant to a grand jury subpoena or other court process. This is an important power asset for the State, as it allows for the collection, storage, and assessment of data for investigations with limited public accessibility and potential oversight.

Safeguards Protecting Civil Liberties

Section 215 contains a number of safeguards that protect civil liberties, beginning with its narrow scope. It can only be used to obtain foreign intelligence information not concerning a United States person or to protect against international terrorism or clandestine intelligence activities. It cannot be used to investigate ordinary crimes, or even domestic terrorism. The Office of the Director of National Intelligence further defends stated safeguards to civil liberties by arguing that Section 215 grants greater protections than ordinary grand jury subpoenas. "A court must explicitly authorize the use of section 215 to obtain business records. By contrast, a grand jury subpoena is typically issued without any prior judicial review. Section 215 expressly states that a U.S. person cannot be investigated solely on the basis of activities protected by the First Amendment to the Constitution of the United States." While this may be true in terms of granting such protections, Section 215 can only be used to obtain foreign intelligence information not concerning a United States person. There is also congressional oversight, with the Attorney General informing Congress on how Section 215 has been implemented every six months.

Robert S. Litt, ODNI General Counsel, sets the general framework to defend the scope of mass surveillance by the State where national security interests prevail. He argues, "I want to make a few points about the Fourth Amendment. First, under established Supreme Court rulings a person has no legally recognized expectation of privacy in information that he or she gives to a third party. So obtaining those records from the third party is not a search as to that person. [...] Second, the Fourth Amendment doesn't apply to foreigners outside of the United States. Third, the Supreme Court has said that the 'reasonableness' of a warrantless search depends on balancing the 'intrusion on the individual's Fourth Amendment interests against' the search's 'promotion of legitimate Governmental interests'" (2013).

Litt further argues that the surveillance vis-à-vis telephony data is limited in scope and design. "The FISA Court has repeatedly approved orders directing several telecommunications companies to produce certain categories of telephone metadata, such as the number calling, the number being called, and the date, time, and duration of the call. It's important to emphasize that under this program we do not get the content of any conversation; we do not get the identity of any party to the conversation; and we do not get any cell site or GPS locational information" (2013) Under the surveillance program, large volumes of metadata are collected although only a small fraction of it is actually assessed, where there are suspicions of links between foreign terrorists and persons in the United States. One argument for the program's operational effectiveness is to have access to metadata to afford the State to identify narrowed and specific risks while still being able to assess broader risks and associations.

Given the program's emphasis on non-content data, Litt argues that there is low privacy value and it cannot violate the Fourth Amendment because it doesn't identify any individual. However, public concerns over privacy issues, in part due to its clandestine approach, have put the program's legitimacy in question. Litt's fundamental premise is built upon the fact that the Supreme Court has held that if individuals provide information to third parties, they have no reasonable expectation of privacy pursuant to that information. The metadata attained through such surveillance is information that the telecommunications companies obtain and store on their own. Litt argues that the State can obtain this information without a warrant. It is argued that the central difference between telecommunications companies and the State is what the State can do with that information. It is clear then that the State affords itself added power, albeit with some limitations. These limitations include, but are not limited to:

(1) The information must be stored in secure databases.
(2) The only intelligence purpose for which this information can be used is counterterrorism.
(3) Only a limited number of specialized analysts have access to databases.
(4) Such analysts are only allowed to search the database when they have a reasonable suspicion that a particular telephone number is associated with specific foreign terrorist organizations that have been identified to the Court. Specifics must be documented in writing and approved by a supervisor.

(5) Information can only be used in a limited manner such as connecting telephone numbers calling other telephone numbers.
(6) Information obtained in said manner is destroyed after five years. (Litt, 2013)

What is clear is that Section 215 affords the State additional powers, albeit limited. This has led to public concerns over privacy, and has led to some amendments to scale back such powers. These amendments suggest that the State has redefined the parameters, without sacrificing the bulk of its mandate. On January 17, 2014, the White House Office of the Press Secretary released President Obama's remarks on the review of U.S. signals intelligence program. Three areas of the release are focused on: (1) Section 702 of Foreign Intelligence Surveillance Act; (2) Section 215 of the USA Patriot Act; and (3) National Security Letters.

Section 702 of Foreign Intelligence Surveillance Act

The White House Office of the Press Secretary contends that "Section 702 is a valuable program that allows the government to intercept the communications of foreign targets overseas who have information that's important to our national security. […] To address incidental collection of communications between Americans and foreign citizens, the President has asked the Attorney General and DNI to initiate reforms that place additional restrictions on the government's ability to retain, search, and use in criminal cases, communications between Americans and foreign citizens incidentally collected under Section 702" (2014). This move was a symbolic overture to recognize public concern over privacy issues. No specific reforms were identified, which makes it difficult to gauge whether potential amendments would be peripheral, targeted, or holistic.

Section 215 of the USA PATRIOT Act

The White House Office of the Press Secretary contends that "under Section 215 of the PATRIOT Act the government collects metadata related to telephone calls in bulk. [… T]his is a capability that we must preserve, and would note that the Review Group turned up no indication that the program had been intentionally abused. […] For this reason, the President ordered a transition that will end the Section 215 bulk metadata program as it currently exists, and establish a program that preserves the capabilities we need without the government holding the data" (2014). Here, the State affords itself immunity by declaring that there was no evidence of abuse of such power. It also justifies the surveillance program's scope, albeit shifts the holding of data to a third party.

The White House Office of the Secretary states that the transition implements two specific phases. First, the State will now only pursue phone calls that are two steps removed from a number associated with a terrorist organization instead of three. Moreover, during this transition period, the database can be queried only after a judicial finding. Second, the intelligence community and the Attorney General have been tasked to use the transition period to develop options for a new program that can *match* the capabilities and address gaps that the Section 215 program was designed to address without the State being in possession of the metadata, and recommend alternative approaches before the program comes up for reauthorization. Section 215 then is not dismantled. Rather, it is amended to preserve its central scope without compromising its influence and reach. Similar to Section 702 the core concession was to have the metadata held by a third part, although it is unspecified as to (i) who that would be, (ii) to what degree third parties would guarantee safeguards, (iii) how third parties would be compelled to provide information to the State, and (iv) whether the State can shield itself from liability by introducing a third party in the process.

National Security Letters

In investigating threats, the FBI applies the use of National Security Letters (NSLs), which can be used to require organizations to provide certain types of information to the government without disclosing such orders to the party that is being investigated. This has been a principal concern of companies who want more transparency about such requests from law enforcement. As a result, the Attorney General has been tasked with amending how NSLs are used in two manners: (1) to ensure that non-disclosure is not *indefinite*, and (2) to ensure that NSLs are terminated within a *fixed time frame*, unless the State shows a need for further secrecy.

Although this appears to be significant in terms of scaled back power, the State actually controls the parameters of such amendments. First, it does not appear to have to disclose why the letters are issued, and continues to mandate compliance from companies. Cessation of non-disclosure can occur by simply ending the NSL tenure for a select party. It is not a guarantee that the company will be specifically privy to specific and further information. Second, the State preserves its own discretion, through its ability to declare that non-disclosure must continue as a result of any number of possible reasons that would necessitate further secrecy.

While legal challenges have been issued to limit the reach and scope of surveillance programs, much of the broader test to its legitimacy will come with constitutional challenge. To date, the federal Supreme Court has limited its involvement in specific matters of national security and more specifically surveillance programs. However, much of its standing rests on one case it did agree to hear, and clarify in terms of the metadata collection program's constitutionality.

Clapper v. Amnesty International USA (2013)

The Supreme Court affirmed many of the powers of mass surveillance by the State in *Clapper v. Amnesty International USA* (2013). It is important to examine this decision in context with the subsequent changes made as noted in the aforementioned. Those changes, albeit small, were intended to address public scrutiny, rather than address legal and/or constitutional concerns. In *Clapper*, several groups, including attorneys, journalists, and human rights organizations, brought a facial challenge to a provision of the Foreign Intelligence Surveillance Act (FISA). The provision creates new procedures for authorizing government electronic surveillance of non-U.S. persons outside the U.S. for foreign intelligence purposes. The groups argue that the procedures violate the Fourth Amendment, the First Amendment, Article III of the Constitution, and the principle of separation of powers. The new provisions would force these groups to take costly measures to ensure the confidentiality of their international communications. The District Court for the Southern District of New York granted summary judgment for the government, holding that the groups did not have standing to bring their challenge. The groups only had an abstract subjective fear of being monitored and provided no proof that they were subject to the FISA. The U.S. Court of Appeals for the Second Circuit reversed, holding that the groups had standing based on a reasonable fear of injury and costs incurred to avoid that injury.

The core question that came before the Court was whether respondents have Article III standing to seek prospective relief under the FISA. By way of a 5–4 majority, it was decided that they did not have Article III standing. The Court held that the respondents did not have standing under Article III of the U.S. Constitution because no injury occurred. Claiming a reasonable likelihood that their communications would be intercepted under FISA is not enough to show future injury for standing purposes. The Court also refused to acknowledge a present injury stemming from the respondents' choice to take costly measures to protect their confidential communications.

While there have been some lower level court rulings in terms of raising fundamental concerns over surveillance programs (e.g., the Second Circuit Court of Appeals in *ACLU v. Clapper* and in *Klayman v. Obama*, where the federal court also raised constitutional concerns). In a rare standoff of constitutional interpretation, we have federal district and appeals courts in direct contrast to the federal Supreme Court. This not only conveys the controversy, but also the complexity of the surveillance program and the allowable reach of the State in matters of national security.

Lower level court dissent does not go unnoticed but it has less standing than the federal Supreme Court ruling in *Clapper v. Amnesty* (2013). By setting precedent, the U.S. Supreme Court makes it difficult for future challenges to limit the power and reach of the State in matters of national security. While amendments have been made by either the federal government or the NSA itself in amending areas of the program, such alterations still preserve the surveillance program's central structure and design. What is most important is that the Supreme Court ruling will help ensure the program's tenure and potentially help expand the power of the State.

The Micro or Localized Level of Cyber Surveillance

Over 18,000 different governmental agencies in the United States can be classified as police agencies. Approximately 17,000 of these are within the jurisdiction of *local government* (counties, cities, and towns) (Israel et al., 2001, p. 15–16). Along with the fact that most agencies are local, come added powers of jurisdictional authority. Since the United States does not have a centralized system of policing, where a top-bottom approach would entail mandated policies and protocol, individual agencies will embark on their own concentrated efforts at addressing crime. Each agency will determine (in significant part dependent on resources) priorities. It would be unlikely smaller police agencies would engage in the same law enforcement models as larger police agencies, as the former would not have the resources to engage in more ambitious projects. In this vein, proactive policing (a staple of federal agencies engaged in surveillance and entrapment measures) would be limited to larger local agencies that have the resources to engage in such programs, and continue to lobby for increased resources from state and federal governments to maintain and expand such programs.

Much of the proactive policing initiatives (e.g., combating child pornography online, and addressing sexual exploitation of minors through child luring on the Internet) continue to be dealt with at the local level, but through the initiatives of larger police agencies. There may also be collaboration across local agencies where warranted to expand a program's coverage or reach. Sting operations, for example, could reach multiple jurisdictions, some of which have larger law enforcement agencies and others that have smaller ones. The bulk of costs remain with the larger agencies, even if others are collaborating. This requires significant resources (financial and expertise) to implement short- and/or long-term operations to combat stated crime in cyberspace. Law enforcement agencies at the local levels are influenced by legal precedent, particularly at the U.S. Supreme Court level. This provides the parameters for what they are able to engage in relative to surveillance and entrapment contexts.

Privacy continues to be asserted as a fundamental right, although no specific mention of it exists within the body of the Constitution or its amendments. Landmark cases that involved selective incorporation of specific amendments in the 1960s were largely won not so much on *privacy issues*, but rather a *due process approach*. Where there were abuses or more specifically actions that violated the constitutional rights of an individual, limits were imposed onto the State. *Mapp* and *Miranda* are, therefore, civil liberty matters of due process and equal protection of the individual, specifically embedded within the context of the Bill of Rights. The liberal emphasis on privacy is more influenced by evolving standards of a changing society and interpretation.

Despite landmark cases in the 1960s limiting the powers of the State, resistance toward expanding selective incorporation and total incorporation of the Bill of Rights has been profound. The liberal shift went from limiting State power to championing privacy concerns vis-à-vis abortion. The concentration of conservative ideology on the Court since this time has slowly afforded law enforcement greater power and discretion (*Cardwell v. Lewis*, 1974; *United States v. Cortez*, 1987; *Whren v. United States*, 1996). Government has expanded both State and law enforcement power through national security legislation.

The distinction between civil and criminal matters of privacy can be made at this point. In matters of evolving moral standards such as those related to birth control, abortion, and sexual practices, the Courts have permitted the expansion of such civil privacy parameters. In matters of criminal jurisdiction, there has been a resistance to accepting privacy as an entrenched right. This is evidenced in how the Court has decided matters pertaining to search and seizure laws. These cases have incrementally shifted the balance of power from civil liberties to the State. They have done this through a timeline of Supreme Court cases that have served as guiding precedent to influence both legislative policy and future constitutional challenges.

While it is true that most cases that have come before the U.S. Supreme Court have not involved issues relative to the Internet, the rulings in these cases have created greater power to law enforcement agencies as well as greater immunity. The expansion of power then has afforded law enforcement to further expand its reach to cyber policing. The move toward proactive policing of cyberspace has allowed for expanded reach of surveillance, entrapment, and information gathering, which more effectively allow for search warrants to be obtained, arrests made, charges laid and greater evidence to be used against defendants during legal proceedings.

Conclusion: Spatial Policing and Cyberspace

The move toward proactive policing model is not a theoretical possibility, but rather a staple of the current U.S. criminal justice system. This can be observed at the global level, with Interpol serving as a centralized system for information sharing, databases, and collaboration across countries. This is evidenced at the federal level, where select federal agencies engage in surveillance, collection, and analysis of telephony and Internet content and metadata. The expanded powers are advanced through provisions contained within the USA PATRIOT Act, other legislation, and government directives. The expanded reach of the State has largely been given constitutional legitimacy through U.S. Supreme Court rulings. Even at the local levels of police agencies, the larger ones that have greater resources have moved toward proactive model of law enforcement practices.

In the next 10 to 50 years, the criminal justice system will operate more aggressively, invasively, and proactively in matters of addressing crime. Each level of law enforcement (global, federal, and local) will concentrate on different areas of crime control, but all three will incorporate the proactive model as a matter of policy.

References

Anheier, H. K., & Juergensmeyer, M. (Eds.). (2012). *Encyclopedia of global studies*. Sage Publications.

Electronic Privacy Information Center (2016). Retrieved from https://www.epic.org/privacy/surveillance/#.

Electronic Frontier Foundation. (2016). Electronic surveillance manual. Retrieved from https://www.eff.org/document/electronic-surveillance-manual.

Gellman, B. (2008). *Angler: The Cheney Vice Presidency*. Penguin.

Gellman, B., & Poitras, L. (2013, June 7). US, British intelligence mining data from nine US Internet companies in broad secret program. *The Washington Post, 6*.

Interpol. (2013). *Annual report 2013*. Retrieved from https://www.interpol.int/News-and-media/Publications2/Annual-reports/2013.

Israel, J., Kamisar, Y., & LaFave, W. (2001). *Criminal procedure and the Constitution: Leading Supreme Court cases*. St. Paul, MN: West Group.

Lichtblau, E. (2009). *Bush's law: The remaking of American justice*. Anchor Books.

Litt, R. S. (2013). Privacy, technology and national security: An overview of intelligence collection. *Brookings Institution, 19*.

Office of Director of National Intelligence. (2016). *Semiannual Assessment* of *Compliance* with *Procedures* and *Guidelines Issued Pursuant* to *Section 702* of the *Foreign Intelligence Surveillance Act, Submitted* by the *Attorney General* and the *Director* of *National Intelligence*. Retrieved from https://www.dni.gov/files/documents/icotr/15th-702Joint-Assessment-Nov2016-FINAL-REDACTED1517.pdf.

RT. (2016, January 29). Canada halts intelligence sharing with Five Eyes after 'accidentally' sending over Canadians' data. Retrieved from https://www.rt.com/news/330530-canada-halts-intelligence-sharing-nsa/.

Tsotis, A. (2013). Why was Apple late to the PRISM party? Retrieved from https://techcrunch.com/2013/06/17/apple-nsa/.

Washington Post. (2013). President's surveillance program worked with private sector to collect data after Sept. 11, 2001. Retrieved from https://www.washingtonpost.com/investigations/presidents-surveillance-program-worked-with-private-sector-to-collect-data-after-sept-11-2001/2013/06/27/2c7a7e74-df57-11e2-b2d4-ea6d8f477a01_story.html?utm_term=.b0746c16e24f.

4

Minorities, Space, and Policing

Charles E. Crawford

Nearly 50 years ago, American novelist, essayist, and civil rights advocate James Baldwin's *Esquire* magazine essay captured the anger, frustration, and mistrust of policing in the Black urban inner-city space:

> The only way to police a ghetto is to be oppressive. None of commissioner Kennedy's policemen, even with the best will in the world, have any way of understanding the lives led by the people they swagger about in two's and three's controlling. Their very presence is an insult, and it would be, even if they spent their entire day feeding gumdrops to children. They represent the force of the white world, and that world's real intentions are, simply, for that world's criminal profit and ease, to keep the black man corralled up here, in his place. (Baldwin, 1960)

Despite vast improvements in police-minority relations over the decades, Baldwin's words ring true in some of our nation's cities today. One tragic incident sparked a movement that has become synonymous with policing the minority community and that is the creation of #BlackLivesMatter after the shooting death of Trayvon Martin. On February 6, 2012, 17-year-old African American Trayvon Martin was walking home after purchasing items at a local convenience store when Retreat at Twin Lakes Community Neighborhood Watch Captain George Zimmerman observed him. Zimmerman called 911 and reported seeing suspicious activity and a suspicious guy who looked like he was up to no good or on drugs. Zimmerman then told the dispatcher the individual was starting to run. The dispatcher asked Zimmerman if he was following the individual, he replied yes, and was told it was not necessary for him to do so. The call ended, and minutes later Trayvon Martin was dead. The exact details have been disputed, but when Martin, who was talking with his girlfriend on a cell phone, began to run from a man who was following him in a vehicle, Zimmerman exited his vehicle, followed Martin, who was unarmed, and a confrontation and struggle took place. Zimmerman ended with Martin on top of him and he fired a single shot into Martin's chest, killing him. Zimmerman would claim self-defense under the Florida "stand your ground" law (Barry, 2012). Zimmerman was charged with second-degree murder and his criminal trial would cause America to reflect on race, gun use, and the law. On July 14, 2013, George Zimmerman was found not guilty.

In response to the verdict and the attempt to place Martin's character on trial after death, Alicia Garza, Patrisse Cullors, and Opal Tometi created #BlackLivesMatter as a form of "ideological and political intervention in a world where Black lives are […] targeted for demise" (#Blacklivesmatter, 2017). Although the start of #BlackLivesMatter was not connected to a policing incident, the movement would take on a new purpose within a year with the 2014 death of 43-year-old Eric Garner captured on video as an NYPD officer applied a chokehold during a confrontation over selling loose cigarettes. Less than a month later in Ferguson, Missouri, Officer Darren Wilson encountered 18-year-old African American Michael Brown walking in the middle of the street. Wilson asked Brown to move to the sidewalk. There were statements from witnesses that conflicted with Wilson's testimony about the interaction with Brown; nonetheless, a violent confrontation ensued while Wilson was still in the vehicle. Brown fled, Wilson exited the vehicle, and the end result was that Wilson shot the unarmed Brown at least six times. Wilson claimed self-defense and that Brown was a threat and charging toward him (Robles & Bosman, 2014). The grand jury did not indict Wilson for the shooting death. The Brown shooting and decision of the grand jury would divide the nation and send waves of protest across Ferguson and the country. The shooting in Ferguson thrust issues of race, policing, deadly force, and the #BlackLivesMatter movement into the national spotlight. Furthermore, Ferguson focused research attention on the numbers of minorities killed by police, revealing a disturbing pattern and the fact that there is no national data collection on police involved shootings.

These cases are not isolated and unfortunately there are numerous examples in recent history that have involved police actions in a minority neighborhood context with similar tragic consequences. On August 11, 1965, Black motorists Marquette and Ronald Frye were pulled over by White California Highway Patrolman Lee W. Minikus in a predominately Black neighborhood. Marquette Frye failed a field sobriety test and was told he was being placed under arrest and his car would be impounded. Frye's mother was contacted, and a crowd of 200 to 300 bystanders gathered. The once-compliant Marquette resisted arrest, and a struggle ensued with the police. In the end, the entire Frye family that was present and two bystanders were arrested and removed from the scene. By this time, the crowd had grown to 1,000 and became increasingly hostile. Rumors began to spread about mistreatment of the Frye family during their arrest. By 8 PM the crowd began throwing rocks and pulling White drivers from their vehicles and beating them. By the end of what became known as the Watts Riots, there were nearly 2,000 National Guard troops and 1,500 Los Angeles police officers and sheriff's deputies deployed to the area, 34 people were killed, 600 buildings were destroyed, and more than 3,000 arrests were made (Governor's Commission on the Los Angeles Riots, 1965).

Recent generations cannot forget the 1991 video that captured the beating of Black motorist Rodney King at the hands of LAPD officers. King suffered severe injuries, including skull fractures, broken teeth, and brain damage. A total of 23 officers responded to the chase, but ultimately only four officers were charged. The now infamous trial of officers Stacey Koon, Lawrence Powell, Timothy Wind, and Theodore Briseno was held in the predominately White community of Simi Valley. This move was significant, not only because of the racial composition of the space but the fact that many LAPD officers also resided there (Oliver et al., 1993). In 1992, the four officers were acquitted, and the response in Los Angeles was an eerie parallel to the Watts Riots nearly a quarter of a century earlier. The riots lasted for six days, and the city paid a heavy price with 4,000 businesses destroyed, $1 billion in property damage, nearly 8,000 arrests, and 52 deaths (Oliver et al., 1993). One of the more disturbing revelations about the original beating came from Koon's own book, in which he suggested that the incident was not extraordinary but just a typical night on the LAPD (Koon & Deitz, 1992, p. 22).

This chapter is not intended to be a retelling of the numerous tragic examples of violent encounters between the police and minority citizens, or the history of urban civil unrest in the United States. My purpose is to explore several themes that may give some insight into how these events were shaped in part by the spatial context of a minority neighborhood. Furthermore, this chapter investigates some of the legal and political history that has allowed such conduct to occur with a tacit assent. To reiterate from Chapter 1, this is not to suggest a spatial determinism or that space alone explains the strained relationships between the police and minorities. The minority neighborhood contains a history, one that reflects the heart of policing, which is ultimately about controlling space and people.

Controlling Space and People

The use of a police force to control people is an ancient concept in stratified societies. One early example can be found in ancient Rome. The conditions of the Roman Empire eventually led to the creation of a more formal style of policing, breaking away from the citizen as policeman that was present in many societies of the time. As Rome grew in wealth and power, so did divisions, classes, and factions. These circumstances, combined with the ease of purchasing slaves, led Rome to become crowded with populations of homeless, poor, and discontented citizens who possessed the frightening tool of insurrection. As Reith (1975) points out, the only thing holding back these increasingly hostile classes was the power of oratory, but the only way to truly stop the activities of these swarms were repressive measures (p. 214).

In this turbulent mix of class strife and organized political violence, Augustus Caesar (63 BC–14 AD) created a strong and effective police system. Although Augustus created his own elite guard, it was the Vigiles, a force he created in 6 AD, that had the most direct law enforcement connection. The Vigiles were a force of 7,000 men originally created to deal with fires, but their duties were expanded to fight street crime in Rome's 14 administrative districts (Stead, 1983). A traditional interpretation of this need for a police force is that there was rising crime in the streets of the city, along with fugitives and runaway slaves. Rome at times was a dangerous city; as Roman poet and satirist Juvenal put it, only a fool would go out to dinner without having made a will (Durant, 1944, p. 341). Perhaps the interpretation that is most relevant for this discussion is that the crimes and actions most feared came from slaves and other oppressed people. Given the massive inequality that was present, a major function of the police was to protect the property and positions of the elite (Sheldon, 2001).

Slave Patrols

Perhaps the most direct historical connection for this chapter on minorities, space, and policing is the peculiar American development of the slave patrol. The literature reviewing the development of American policing often overlooks the role of the slave patrol. The fears of mob violence, protest, and disorder in England and the United States were real in their consequences and are a part of the history of developing an urban police force. These factors, along with the history of older systems, such as militias, sheriffs, and night watches, may explain the rise of modern policing in Northern urban cities. However, the institution of slavery in the United States contained its own problems, including needs for control of people and space. Considering that 80% of Blacks lived in the rural South during the antebellum period (Williams & Murphy, 1990), the slave patrol played a role in not only developing police forces of the South but also creating racial and social turmoil. To help understand the creation of slave patrols, records from supportive state governments can be examined. For example, the state government of South Carolina expressed the collective fears of the region and the need for control:

> Foreasmuch as many late horrible and barbarous massacres have been actually committed and many more designed, on the white inhabitants of the Province, by negro slaves, who are generally prone to such cruel practices, which makes it highly necessary that constant patrols should be established. (Cooper, 1839, p. 568)

Such sentiments and laws were passed in all Southern states based on the belief that greater surveillance of Blacks was necessary. The state of Georgia provides an example of how the basic slave patrol would have been manned and operated. All urban White men between the ages of 16 and 60 had to conduct patrols each night. In rural areas, slave patrol members were required to visit every plantation in their districts, searching all Black households for weapons and ammunition and any houses suspected of harboring runaway slaves (Wood, 1984). The intrusion of the patrol into the slaves' private spaces was a regular and unwelcomed occurrence and illustrates the conflict at the heart of this discussion. Probable cause for the patrol to initiate a search often had little logic supporting it.

For example, if there was too much noise or music coming from a cabin, this could prompt an investigation from patrollers. Conversely, quiet homes with the lights out would also be searched. Slaves and free persons who cooperated and were passive would still be threatened with physical violence. Those who appeared to be asleep were struck lightly with a whip to see if they were truly tired. Patrollers were also encouraged to investigate and break up gatherings of slaves, although what constituted a violation in terms of size and purpose of the gatherings was never specified. Furthermore, these investigations frequently brought the patrollers into the most intimate part of the slaves' quarters, where female slaves faced the possibility of sexual assault (Hadden, 2001).

The prevailing belief of the period was that slaves should not be left unsupervised at any time, which created a problem for plantations where the owner was either away or a White person could not be present. This made control of the slaves' private space of the utmost importance for Whites in the antebellum South due to real fears of insurrection from a captive group. Also of critical importance for the control of what was viewed as a dangerous class was restricting the movement of slaves in public spaces. The laws of the time required slaves to carry passes authorized by their masters whenever they were away from the plantation. In South Carolina, for example, the law stated that no slave could be away from a plantation without written permission unless they were accompanied by a White person, even a child as young as ten, who could vouch for the slave (Henry, 1968). Stopping Blacks and checking passes became one of the key duties of the slave patrol. However, possessing a valid pass did not ensure the patrol would recognize it. Slaves with a general pass that did not specify a destination or time of return were sometimes harassed and punished if the patrol felt the slave had overstayed his or her welcome (Hadden, 2001).

Controlling the movement of slaves in an urban environment created unique problems for a slave-owning society. It was often difficult to discern who was a runaway, free person, or a slave sent on errands. Slave patrols in the rural environment were often mounted, and much of the activity revolved around stopping Blacks on country roads and inspecting private homes and plantations. By contrast, city slave patrols were often on foot, which resulted in greater control of public spaces, such as taverns, and more frequent stops for inspecting papers on streets and in alleyways. One interesting public space that proved to be a challenge was that of the church. Slaves were required to carry passes to attend religious services, and for patrollers, the possibility existed that slaves were attending who did not possess legitimate passes, or runaways were being hidden. Consequently, church services became a frequent stop for patrollers to inspect papers; those caught without a proper pass (if they did not flee first) were whipped (Hadden, 2001).

Punishment at the hands of the slave patrol was something slaves tried to avoid at all cost. The punishments were often arbitrary, which served to increase the psychological torment of encountering a patrol. Former slave Ida Henry recounted when she and her mother were caught praying during a night service. Her mother was stripped and handcuffed, her shackled arms were raised over a tree limb, the patrollers raised her up onto her toes, and she was whipped (Foner, 1983, p. 103). Understandably, slaves used evasion, deception, and offensive tactics to avoid discovery by the patrols. If caught, many begged and pleaded for leniency, offering whatever meager goods they could trade for safe passage (Hadden, 2001). The whip was only one tool of punishment the patrols employed. They frequently carried binding ropes as well as firearms. Slaves were often fired on if they attempted to flee. Although slaves were rarely killed by gunfire, the shots along with the other tactics provided psychological and physical intimidation.

The movement of slave patrols also revealed an awareness of time and space—they would increase their activity on the weekends due to more slaves moving through public spaces, attending church, hunting, or taking care of personal affairs. Due to this knowledge, slave patrols did not conduct many weeknight rides; it appears as though the main purposes of the infrequent rides during the week were to have slaves believe patrols were omnipresent (Hadden, 2001, p. 125). In addition to altering patrols based on day of the week, patrols were also altered by months and seasons, with fewer rides during harvest season, as slaves would have less free time and were less likely to be given a pass.

The control of dangerous classes during the antebellum period included free Blacks as well. Being a free Black person did not prevent encounters with slave patrols, because skin color was equated with the status of being a slave. Free Blacks also had to carry papers proving their status, and failure to do so could result in the same severe punishments meted out to slaves. Although the slave patrol was a development of the American South, the issue of controlling the Black population extended to Northern American cities as well. Free Black populations represented a special challenge and need for control even in cities that did not have large slave populations. For example, the mayor of Philadelphia in the early 1800s issued an order stating that all people of color found on the streets after hours should be supervised by the officers of the night (Curry, 1981). Northern city officials appeared to have given little thought to preserving peace and order in Black neighborhoods, as the main concern was control of Blacks outside of their communities, especially as they came into contact with Whites (Hawkins & Thomas, 1991).

Hawkins and Thomas (1991) provide a powerful summary of the prevailing use of policing and control of Black populations in antebellum and postbellum America:

> Throughout the antebellum period, controlling blacks by any means necessary occupied most white urbanites in cities where significant numbers of blacks worked and lived. Southern cities developed elaborate policing systems to control both slaves and free blacks ... as thousands of former slaves flocked into the urban areas of the South and North, white municipal officials attempted to continue the pattern of racial dominance by using the police as the first line of defense against black freedom. (pp. 71–72)

The slave patrol was a unique response to the issue of controlling space and people. At first glance, it may be tempting to think of the patrol force as an unregulated militia. On closer review, their functions were specific compared to the watchmen, sheriffs, and constables of other areas that had non-policing duties. Reichel (1988) points out the key component of the system that made it closer to law enforcement as we know it today was accountability to a central government authority. Although there were variations from state to state, slave patrol members were appointed by local commissioners and had to obey orders issued by governors, county courts, and military commanders (p. 67).

The slave patrol is often an understudied aspect of the expansion of law enforcement. The development of the patrol preceded the formation of modern urban police forces in Northern cities and in many ways was more advanced than the watch systems of the time. For example, Sam Walker (1992) points out that in 1837 the City of Charleston had a slave patrol of nearly 100 officers, making it one of the largest police forces of the time (p. 6). The history and relationship between slaves and patrollers has left an undeniable imprint on the connection between Black Americans and the police. The slave patrol's control of movement in and through cities provides a framework in which policing the minority space can be examined today.

Policing the Minority Space: Theory and Practice

The creation of the minority space has been a story of conflict. On the exterior, it appears that distinctive neighborhoods are created due to the demands of class, ethnicity, and race, which in turn influence people's choices of housing. As we begin to examine the history and spaces of many of our nation's cities, we discover a fierce struggle. Forces such as entrepreneurial investment, redlining, transportation routes, and rapid suburban growth have all combined to worsen inequalities and spatial segregation, most notably between rich and poor and Black and White (Logan & Molotoch, 1987; Sung, 2002).

For the police, the minority space becomes territory, which is more than just geography. Territoriality is a central concept to understanding police actions in the minority neighborhood context. According to Sack (1986), territoriality "is a spatial strategy to affect, influence, or control resources and people, by controlling area" (p. 1). If we are to understand police actions, we must acknowledge the uniqueness of the minority space. Quite simply, the actions of police officers are often determined by where they occur and the people involved. Steve Herbert (1997) points out that spatial strategies are fundamental to police powers because they create and mark space and enforce boundaries. Although race and racism were not key variables explored with his research on the Los Angeles Police Department, Herbert offered some insight into how race and space can combine to shape policing actions. He feels that police officers may view the minority space as dangerous and somehow immoral. The people that occupy the space may be viewed more like foes than citizens, which may result in a more confrontational and aggressive style of policing (Herbert, 1997, pp. 5–6).

Police officers are aware of the people they encounter; the citizen's race, age, demeanor, and appearance can all be factors that condition their response. The larger playing field on which these encounters happen is equally important, as officers are sensitive to the surrounding environment. American society has frequently associated skin color with criminality. Therefore, as a city's minority population grows, so may public fear, which in turn may lead to greater segregation and calls for the police to expand hardline surveillance, crime control, and policing of minorities (Bursik & Grasmick, 1993; Skogan, 1990). Within this context, the perception of who is dangerous, fear of crime, and apparent incivility of the neighborhood all combine and are personified in the residents of these spaces, most notably poor, young Black males. Race and perception of a dangerous group is a factor in police operations in the minority space; however, class is another powerful aspect.

As Weitzer (1999) points out, there is a primacy of race in the research literature on policing minorities to the point that class may be completely ignored. It is often the case that Black and White lower-income areas are associated with higher crime rates, which in turn may generate more involuntary police-citizen contacts and more opportunities for misconduct and mistreatment. Although the body of literature is small compared to the studies on race or class alone, the interaction of racial and class compositions of neighborhoods on police actions has been explored (Alpert & Dunham, 1988; Klinger, 1997; Weitzer, 1995). For example, Weitzer (1999) studied the influence of race and class on the perceptions of police actions by interviewing residents of a Black middle-class area, a White middle-class area, and two adjacent lower-income Black areas.

The perception (and in some cases the observation) of police misconduct varied by the neighborhood's class position, in that the lower-class neighborhood residents reported observing and perceiving more unwarranted stops and physical abuse from the police compared to the Black and White middle-class neighborhoods. However, the more revealing finding was that once the residents of the Black middle-class neighborhood left their space or "safe haven," they experienced more suspicion and mistreatment. Conversely, Whites both in and out of their neighborhoods enjoyed a "racial halo effect" that reduced their chances of being mistreated by the police (Weitzer, 1999, pp.

843–844). Neighborhood, class, and race are all undoubtedly components of the minority space that need to be further explored if we are to fully understand the police function and relationships in our society.

What is imperative to understand is that Black Americans have always been policed, and in many cases it revolved around the extremes of overpolicing and underpolicing. David and Melissa Barlow discuss this history and extremes in their text *Police in a Multicultural Society*. Overpolicing, according to Barlow and Barlow (2000), involved brutal treatment and oppressive practices. In the past, this was typified by the use of slave patrols, discussed earlier. More recent history reveals a different approach to policing minority space, as Rabinowitz succinctly puts it: "The white community and its law enforcement were responsible for the great mass of Negro arrests. For them the basic necessity was control, for most whites were convinced that Negroes comprised a criminal class which jeopardized the peace and security of the city" (Rabinowitz, 1980, p. 44). In many ways, White officers in the Black community represented the first line of defense against the perceived dangerous class of Blacks. Today the forms have changed somewhat, yet the closer scrutiny of Black citizens remains through excessive stopping such as the highly controversial New York City Police Department stop, question, and frisk program. There is a sizable body of research literature showing that Black citizens are more likely to be stopped by the police given their existence in the population, and they feel that they have been victims of racial profiling (Barlow & Barlow, 2000; Harris, 2002; Russell-Brown, 2004). Conversely, underpolicing within the Black community has an equally long and detailed history. Barlow and Barlow (2000) state that underpolicing involved denying equal protection by failing to safeguard Blacks and other minorities from White violence. The systematic failure to protect Black citizens and equally enforce the law is just as troubling if not more dangerous than the examples of overpolicing.

Race and Policing Today

The common thread that runs through the extremes of over and underpolicing is the awareness of the minority neighborhood or space. As Sung (2002, p. 44) points out, the policed world is essentially composed of highly organized human settlements, and the police today are not impervious to the neighborhoods they serve. Clearly, neighborhoods and homes within in them can vary greatly in race, ethnicity, and income. A part of having a heterogeneous society is that diversity can influence where people want to live or can live. With immigrant populations, there can be waves of succession and spatial assimilation, particularly as these populations close the income gaps with the majority group. The most relevant exception would be for Black Americans. Black Americans today remain one of the most segregated racial and ethnic groups (Sung, 2002).

Brunson and Miller (2006) provide much needed insight into policing in the minority space from the perspective of the young men who frequently find themselves the targets of aggressive police tactics. The authors conducted a qualitative study on 40 young African American men between the ages of 13 and 19 in the city of St Louis. As the authors point out, St. Louis typifies distressed urban areas, with concentrations of disadvantaged people, segregation, and aggressive styles of policing often found in such locations in the United States. This makes Brunson and Miller's research highly relevant for this discussion. The majority of the respondents in the study (83%) reported being harassed by the police and more than half of those who were never involved in serious delinquency also reported being harassed by the police. Subsequently, the respondents held less positive views of the police and felt targeted not simply because of their race, but due to the fact they lived in a distressed neighborhood (p. 634). The respondents in the study were keenly aware of the race and space connection for police actions.

As Brunson and Miller point out, it is often the visibility of illegal activity in distressed spaces that makes aggressive police tactics acceptable to some and justifiable to police administrators. However, police may not take the time to distinguish between law abiding and criminal residents due to the perceptual framework officers may bring to the task, and when such attempts are made they may be imperfect. All residents may be viewed as potential suspects due to ecological contamination and subjected to heavy-handed police tactics. The young men in the study reported they felt the police besieged their community and they all felt the stain of a unilateral suspicion tied to their race and space, which made them question the legitimacy of the police (2006, p. 636).

From the historic Black Belt of Chicago to current racially segregated urban environments like Brownsville Brooklyn, and suburban areas such as Ferguson, Missouri, in America race, space, and class are intertwined and policing responds to each. There are complex forces at work that create these communities and the questionable police practices conducted within. Further complicating factors for studies that try to disentangle race, policing, and space is the fact there are very few comparable White communities with the same factors that face disadvantaged minority communities. Often the research on police actions in the minority space focus on large urban areas but as recent events have shown us, the troubled relationship between police and minority communities may play out on different stages, and the consequences may be just as dire. Consider the recent police shootings in South Carolina of Walter Scott and Levar Jones.

On April 4, 2015, in North Charleston, South Carolina, Officer Michael Slager stopped Walter Scott for a traffic violation. The stop was initially captured on dash cam and there was a struggle in which officer Slager was heard yelling "taser, taser, taser!" Later there was a second confrontation that was recorded by a bystander that showed the unarmed 50-year-old Scott fleeing from Slager, who pulled his duty weapon and fired rounds into Scott's back, killing him (Berman, 2016a). Slager was terminated and faced a criminal homicide trial in which his testimony that he felt total fear as Scott came towards him was at odds with the video evidence. The jurors were unable to reach a unanimous decision, resulting in a mistrial.

A little more than 100 miles away, in September 2014, African American motorist Levar Jones pulled into a convenience store parking lot, and South Carolina Trooper Sean Groubert approached Jones under the pretense of enforcing a seatbelt violation. Groubert's dash cam recorded the encounter as he asked Jones for his driver's license. The unarmed Jones turned back to retrieve his license and registration from his vehicle. Groubert shouted at Jones to get out of car while firing four rounds from his pistol, striking Jones in the leg (Berman, 2016b). Officer Groubert was fired, and was charged with assault and battery, to which he pled guilty.

Each of these cases reflects not only a heightened perception of threat from an unarmed minority subject, but the excessive stopping, questioning, and frisking that occurs in many minority spaces both urban and suburban. Seven months after the shooting of Michael Brown in 2014, the Department of Justice (DOJ) released a scathing and eye-opening report on the police practices in Ferguson, Missouri. The report found that the Ferguson Police Department focused on generating revenue and not public safety. This resulted in changing the character of the department and creating a pattern of unconstitutional practices. The department also used aggressive enforcement of municipal codes as benchmarks for productivity and promotions. These practices had a direct impact on Ferguson's African American population. African Americans comprised roughly 67% of the city's population and yet were 85% of vehicle stops, 90% of citations, and 93% of arrests. Most disturbing in the context of the Michael Brown shooting was the fact that African Americans were 95% of those charged with Manner of Walking in Roadway, and were 90% of those who had documented officer use of force against them. All of which led to an understandable community distrust of the police (Department of Justice, 2015).

Andrea Boyle has conducted what may be one of the most detailed examinations of race, space, and policing to date in her 2015 book *Race, Place, and Suburban Policing: Too Close for Comfort.* Boyle conducted detailed fieldwork over a two-year time period in Meacham Park, a suburb of St. Louis and less than 30 miles from Ferguson. Boyle not only traces the annexation of large parts of Meacham Park's land by the affluent suburb of Kirkwood to create a strip mall, but also conducts in-depth interviews with 30 adult residents about their experiences with police contact. African Americans in the newly formed space were subjected to aggressive police practices that were often fueled by stereotypes, and two high-profile shootings of police officers that rocked the community. These experiences and perceptions of the police led to feelings of distrust and being overwhelmed by the police. Boyle's research further challenges one-dimensional notions of disadvantage that characterizes the urban space as bad, and the suburban space as better for African Americans. Quite simply there are Black experiences and interactions with police that are similar regardless of space to a degree. She acknowledges there are differences connected to place, particularly when minorities live in close proximity to Whites and represent an economic and political threat, which brings about greater police scrutiny.

This is by no means an exhaustive review of the complex economic, social, and racial relations within the United States that have led to the creation of unique minority spaces, whether urban, suburban, or rural and how these spaces condition police practices. My intent is to provide a glimpse into the history of some minority spaces and to urge stakeholders to listen the voices of the residents that are often ignored or quieted in the face of economic and political opposition. These spaces often contain citizens who due to perceptions of being a member of a stereotypical dangerous group may become what Jerome Skolnick (2011) has labeled a "symbolic assailant" warranting greater police surveillance.

Can the Police Make a Difference?

After reviewing a portion of the turbulent history of policing the minority space, searching for solutions appears to be an arduous task at best. The combination of class, race, and space are challenging for researchers and practitioners. As I have noted at several points, police officers are aware of space and have a perception of the inhabitants as being either hostile or supportive, dangerous or safe. This is a form of spatial recognition that leads to action. There are current police strategies that may be useful in improving the police-minority relationship once the spatial awareness is increased. For example, community policing in many ways is a catchall for various law enforcement programs with many differing definitions. However, the core element is involving the community as a partner, not just a group that something must be done to, or for.

Weitzer and Tuch (2006) defined community policing as "police officers working with community members to address the causes of crime and to prevent crimes from occurring, rather than just respond to crimes after they occurred" (p. 169). This attempt at crime prevention, open channels of communication with the police, and mutual respect are what minority respondents found desirable. The authors conclude that Blacks more than any other group see community policing as a way to reduce tensions between citizens and the police as well as build trust (Weitzer & Tuch, 2006).

As a philosophical approach, community policing holds a great deal of promise. It is a transformation of policing that has been going on for nearly two decades, with some claiming community policing represents a "quiet revolution" as citizens and police join together to defend communities (Kelling, 1988). There have been successful community policing experiments using a variety of strategies to fit the needs of particular neighborhoods, as well as programs that have dealt with specific problems, such as hate crimes, gangs, and drugs (Palmiotto, 2000). In addition to problem solving, community policing appears to hold promise for addressing and reducing police misconduct (Terrill & Mastrofksi, 2004). Community policing has been embraced and implemented not only in the United States but also globally. American police departments have begun to share their practices and programs with agencies from diverse international cities in Russia's Sakhalin Islands, Lviv, Ukraine, Ghana, Indonesia, and El Salvador (Brogden & Nijhar, 2005).

In some instances, other strategies that many departments are currently using may be adapted and the goals altered to improve the police-minority relationship. For example, Willis (2011) points out how COMPSTAT, which is viewed traditionally as a data-driven police strategy focusing on index offenses and clearance rates, can move beyond the concentration on crime and include other measures of police performance and success. Willis suggests that these weekly meetings that are typically a part of COMPSTAT may do well to include community input on quality of life issues, less serious crimes, and how the police treat people that may not be captured in traditional information. Furthermore, the type of information and problems addressed in COMPSTAT reveal the importance police departments place on these issues as they attempt to develop solutions. Including the community and applying the same level of focus on their concerns shows a commitment to the residents, and problem solving, both of which will enhance the legitimacy of the police.

This attempt to expand COMPSTAT to solicit citizen information and input is closely connected to the actions that are typically seen as part of traditional community policing. As Willis illustrates, the use of both policing strategies may be an approach that fits well with procedural justice and the suggestions of a recent presidential task force report. The final report of the President's Task Force on 21st Century Policing offered several recommendations to strengthen police-community relations within the context of recent events. In addition to the recommendation of community policing efforts, the report suggested police departments adopt a "guardian" rather than a "warrior" mindset and use procedural justice as a guiding principle (President's Task Force on 21st Century Policing, 2015). Procedural justice revolves around the perceptions of fairness in the process of conflict resolution and at the core of the concept is transparency and communication. Tyler (2004) identified four key concepts for procedural justice: participation, neutrality, dignity and respect, and motives. Each of these fits well with enhancing the police-minority relationships and spatial awareness.

Community policing, modified COMPSTAT, and procedural justice may appear to be the utopia of harmony, safety, and positive police-minority relations that we all desire. However, I do not wish this to be a Pollyanna view of these programs. As wonderful as the concepts of inclusion, community partnership, and crime prevention are, even if pursued with vigor, challenges remain to repair the relationship between the police and some minority communities. Consider the brief history of the minority space that was outlined earlier, and the nuances of the theories discussed, and research insights into police contact with minorities. The forces of segregation, economic isolation, poverty, and the perception of dangerous classes are all part of the spatial framework that face police departments as they attempt to transform law enforcement practices. As Sung (2002) points out, recent history and experiences with community policing suggest that it has not been a transforming problem-solving strategy but is ameliorative at best (p. 139).

The constraints of the minority space are intertwined with issues of race and class, which are simply beyond the police department's control. These same issues also place minorities at a severe disadvantage when it comes to negotiating and improving police practices in their neighborhoods. Perhaps the most difficult transition for police and society to make are the beliefs about dangerous classes and crime that are bound to the people who reside in the minority space. As Chamblis (1994) illustrates, it is Black males particularly and minorities generally who pay the price in the form of intense police surveillance.

There are other changes that are of equal importance if police practices are to improve in the minority space. Weitzer and Tuch (2006) noted several reforms that garnered support in their survey. The prominent suggestions from the respondents were that the police department should match the racial composition of the city, require officers to explain their actions to citizens, and require them to apologize to people whom they have stopped and found to be innocent of any criminal activity. In addition to these reforms, respondents also recommended citizen oversight of police behavior and punitive actions for officers who violate citizens' rights (p. 174). From the point of view of citizens, there is much work to be done to truly reform policing and achieve the quiet revolution. There are practical suggestions that come from the voices of people of color who have been subjected to police misconduct and a criminal justice system that has targeted and marginalized communities.

For example, Solis et al. (2009) provide some recommendations based on the LatCrit framework and their interviews with Latino/a citizens on their experiences with the police. The authors found a missing piece in the discussion of police strategies are youth voices, despite the fact they are more likely to come into involuntary contact with officers. When departments have tried to implement youth programs they may not attract large numbers of Latino/a youth, and the lines of communication are damaged. The authors further suggest that police should focus on helping communities and residents solve daily problems rather than those directly related to crime. Learning how to deescalate tense situations and increasing awareness of culture may all help in the efforts to create a better police response in minority spaces.

In my attempt to show the reality of the difficult work ahead if police departments are to recognize the distinctiveness of the minority space for law enforcement practices, I do not suggest or argue that current efforts should be discarded, or that reframing older strategies are not worthwhile pursuits for both citizens and the police. As we learn more details about conditions and police practices in our nation's cities, particularly those within the minority community, it is disheartening to say the least. Perhaps the core concepts of neighborhood partnership and crime prevention that embody community policing are what gives hope that things can change. Progress has been made; our police forces include more minorities among their ranks and leadership, and officers are held accountable for their actions in many cases. There are also cities across the nation where police departments engage in creative and rewarding projects with the communities they serve. Frequently they have taken the time to understand the profound histories and pressures that have created the minority spaces in which they patrol. Police departments must also cope with the limitations they face in accomplishing the larger structural changes that would empower the residents in our nation's most disadvantaged areas. For a truly successful reform and transformation of policing, policy, and practices, we must address and recognize the importance of the minority spatial context.

References

#BlackLivesMatter. (2017). Herstory. Retrieved from http://blacklivesmatter.com/herstory/.

Abu-Lughod, J. (2007). *Race, space, and riots in Chicago, New York, and Los Angeles.* New York: Oxford University Press.

Alpert, G., & Dunham, R. (1988). *Policing multi-ethnic neighborhoods.* New York: Greenwood.

Anderson, E. (1990). *A place on the corner* (2nd ed.). Chicago: University of Chicago Press.

Anderson, E. (1999). *Code of the street: Decency, violence and the moral life of the inner city.* New York: Norton.

Baldwin, J. (1960). Fifth Avenue, uptown. *Esquire.* Retrieved from http://www.esquire.com/features/fifth-avenue-uptown.

Barlow, D., & Barlow, M. (2000). *Police in a multicultural society.* Prospect Heights, IL: Waveland Press.

Barry, D. (2012). In the eye of the firestorm: In Florida, an intersection of tragedy, race and outrage. *The New York Times*, A1.

Berman, M. (2016a). Mistrial declared in case of South Carolina officer who shot Walter Scott after traffic stop. *The Washington Post.* Retrieved from https://www.washingtonpost.com/news/post-nation/wp/2016/12/05/mistrial-declared-in-case-of-south-carolina-officer-who-shot-walter-scott-after-traffic-stop/?utm_term=.484eb641b9f9.

Berman, M. (2016b). Former South Carolina trooper pleads guilty to shooting unarmed driver during traffic stop. *The Washington Post.* Retrieved from https://www.washingtonpost.com/news/post-nation/wp/2016/03/14/former-south-carolina-trooper-pleads-guilty-to-shooting-unarmed-driver-during-traffic-stop/?utm_term=.7cb8595e4cdb.

Boyles, A. S. (2015). *Race, place, and suburban policing: Too close for comfort.* Oakland, CA: University of California Press.

Brogden, M., & Nijhar, P. (2005). *Community policing: National and international models and approaches.* Portland, OR: Willan Publishing.

Brunson, R. K., & Miller, J. (2006). Young black men and urban policing in the United States. *British Journal of Criminology*, *46*(4), 613–640.

Bursik, R., & Grasmick, H. (1993). *Neighborhood and crime: The dimensions of effective community control.* San Francisco: Lexington Books.

Chamblis, W. (1994). Policing the ghetto underclass: The politics of law and law enforcement. *Social Problems, 41*, 177–194.

Cooper, T. (1839). *Statutes at large of South Carolina* (vol. 5). Columbia, SC: A. S. Johnston.

Curry, L. (1981). *The free blacks in urban America, 1800–1850: The shadow of a dream.* Chicago: University of Chicago Press.

Department of Justice. (2015). Investigation of the Ferguson Police Department. United States Department of Justice Civil Rights Division. Retrieved from https://www.justice.gov/sites/default/files/opa/press-releases/attachments/2015/03/04/ferguson_police_department_report_1.pdf.

Dorsey, J. (1986). *Up south: Blacks in Chicago's suburbs, 1719–1983.* Bristol, IN: Wyndham Hall Press.

Durant, W. (1944). *The story of civilization, Vol. II: Christ and the Caesar.* New York: Simon & Shuster.

Foner, P. (1983). *History of black Americans: From Africa to the emergence of the cotton kingdom to the eve of the compromise of 1850.* Westport, CT: Greenwood.

Gallup. (1993). *The Gallup poll monthly*, no. 339. Princeton, NJ: Gallup.

Governor's Commission on the Los Angeles Riots. (1965). *Violence in the city: An end or a beginning?* Retrieved from http://watts.library.lmu.build/cms/files/original/3963ddd7ca7834f3b1b4f01b19c469fa.pdf.

Greenberg, D. (1981). *Crime and capitalism: Readings in Marxist criminology.* Palo Alto, CA: Mayfield.

Hadden, S. (2001). *Slave patrols: Law and violence in Virginia and the Carolinas.* Cambridge, MA: Harvard University Press.

Harring, S. (1977). Class conflict and the suppression of tramps in Buffalo, 1892–1894. *Law & Society Review, 11*(5), 873–911.

Harris, D. (2002). *Profiles in injustice.* New York: New Press.

Hawkins, H., & Thomas, R. (1991). White policing of black populations: A history of race and social control in America. In E. Cashmore & E. McLaughlin (Eds.), *Out of order: Policing black people* (pp. 65–86). New York: Routledge.

Henry, H. (1968). *The police control of the slave in South Carolina.* New York: Negro University Press.

Herbert, S. (1997). *Policing space: Territoriality and the Los Angeles police department.* Minneapolis: University of Minnesota Press.

Jaynes, G., & Williams, R. (Eds.) (1989). *A common destiny: Blacks and American society.* Washington, DC: National Academies Press.

Kelling, G. (1988). Police and the communities: The quiet revolution. *Perspectives on Policing*, 1.

Kennedy, R. (1997). *Race, crime, and the law.* New York: Pantheon Books.

Klein, A. (2008, June 5). D.C. police to check drivers in violence-plagued Trinidad. *The Washington Post.* Retrieved from http://www.washingtonpost.com/wpdyn/content/article/2008/06/04/AR2008060402205_pf.html.

Klinger, D. (1997). Negotiating order in patrol work: An ecological theory of police response to deviance. *Criminology, 35*, 277–306.

Koon, S., & Deitz, R. (1992). *Presumed guilty: The tragedy of the Rodney King affair*. Washington, DC: Regnery Gateway.

Logan, R., & Molotoch, H. (1987). *Urban fortunes: The political economy of place*. Berkeley: University of California Press.

Lynch, M., & Groves, B. (1989). *A primer in radical criminology* (2nd ed.). New York: Harrow and Heston.

Massey, D. (1985). Ethnic residential segregation: A theoretical synthesis and empirical review. *Sociology and Social Research, 69*, 315–350.

Monkkonen, E. (1981). *Police in urban America: 1860–1920*. Cambridge: Cambridge University Press.

Oliver, M., Johnson, J., & Farrell, W. (1993). An anatomy of a rebellion: A political economic analysis. In R. Gooding-Williams (Ed.), *Reading Rodney King: Reading urban uprising* (pp. 119–120). New York: Routledge.

Palmiotto, M. (2000). *Community policing: A policing strategy for the 21st century*. Gaithersburg, MD: Aspen.

President's Task Force on 21st Century Policing. (2015). *Final report of the president's task force on 21st century policing*. Washington, DC: Office of Community Oriented Policing Services.

Rabinowitz, H. (1980). *Race relations in the South 1865–1890*. Urbana: University of Illinois Press.

Reichel, P. (1988). Southern slave patrols as a transitional police type. *American Journal of Police, 7*(2), 51–78.

Reith, C. (1975). *The blind eye of history: A study of the origins of the present police era*. Montclair, NJ: Patterson Smith.

Richardson, J. (1974). *Urban police in the U.S.* Port Washington, NY: Kennikat Press.

Robles, F., & Bosman, J. (2014). Autopsy shows Michael Brown was struck at least 6 times. *New York Times*. Retrieved from https://www.nytimes.com/2014/08/18/us/michael-brown-autopsy-shows-he-was-shot-at-least-6-times.html?_r=0.

Russell-Brown, K. (2004). *Underground codes: Race, crime, and related fires*. New York: New York University Press.

Sack, R. (1986). *Human territoriality: Its theory and history*. Cambridge: Cambridge University Press.

Sheldon, R. (2001). *Controlling the dangerous classes: A critical introduction to the history of criminal justice*. Needham Heights, MA: Allyn and Bacon.

Skogan, W. (1990). *Disorder and decline: Crime and the spiral of decay in American neighborhoods*. New York: Free Press.

Skolnick, J. H. (2011). *Justice without trial: Law enforcement in democratic society*. New Orleans: Quid Pro Books.

Solis, C., Portillos, E. L., & Brunson, R. K. (2009). Latino youths' experiences with and perceptions of involuntary police encounters. *The Annals of the American Academy of Political and Social Science, 623*(1), 39–51.

Sowell, T. (2005). *Black rednecks and white liberals.* San Francisco: Encounter Books.

Spitzer, S. (1981). The political economy of policing. In D. Greenberg (Ed.), *Crime and capitalism: Readings in Marxist criminology* (pp. 214–240). Palo Alto, CA: Mayfield.

Stead, P. (1983). The Roman police. *Policing: An International Journal of Police Strategies & Management, 6*, 3–7.

Sung, H. (2002). *The fragmentation of policing in American cities: Toward an ecological theory of police-citizen relationships.* Westport, CT: Greenwood.

Terrill, W., & Mastrofski, S. (2004). Working the street: Does community policing matter? In W. Skogan (Ed.), *Community policing: Can it work?* Belmont, CA: Wadsworth.

Wacquant, L., & Wilson, W. (1989). The cost of racial and class exclusion in the inner city. *Annals of the American Academy of Political and Social Science, 501*, 8–25.

Walker, S. (1992). *The police in America: An introduction* (2nd ed.). New York: McGraw-Hill.

Weitzer, R. (1995). *Policing under fire: Ethnic conflict and police-community relations in Northern Ireland.* Albany: SUNY Press.

Weitzer, R. (1999). Citizens' perceptions of police misconduct. *Justice Quarterly, 16*(4), 819–846.

Weitzer, R., & Tuch, S. (2006). *Race and policing in America: Conflict and reform.* New York: Cambridge University Press.

Williams, H., & Murphy, P. (1990). The evolving strategies of policing: A minority view. *Perspectives on Policing,* 13.

Williams, K. (2004). *Our enemies in blue.* New York: Soft Skull Press.

Willis, J. (2011). Enhancing police legitimacy by integrating Compstat and community policing. *Policing: An International Journal of Police Strategies & Management, 34*(4), 654–673.

Wood, B. (1984). *Slavery in colonial Georgia.* Athens: University of Georgia Press.

5

Policing Borders: Immigration, Criminalization, and Militarization in the Era of Social Control Profitability

Martin Guevara Urbina and Ilse Aglaé Peña

> *Law enforcement is a mixed bag. Some officers are lazy and could care less. It's almost a sense of the Wild, Wild, West. Officers ... don't seem to think the Fourth Amendment applies. They are used to autonomy with little oversight. They know how to keep people in check and the cops use these tactics to their advantage. I don't like to see how many young kids are treated. I want to see respect, but XYZ happened. There is a massive disillusionment. The police departments around here have serious issues and are underpaid and overwhelmed. We all know who killed so and so. Everyone knows who killed this kid, but the police won't investigate ... Everything here is hearsay. The Judge rules it doesn't matter. What you need here is a genealogy chart rather than rules of evidence.*
>
> —State Public Defender (cited in Durán & Posadas, 2015)

As in no other time in U.S. history, policing the southern border involves a wide variety of local, state, and federal law enforcement agencies, with a unified mission of patrolling the 2,000-mile U.S.-Mexico border and securing communities. As the frontline agents of the law, police officers are the gatekeepers controlling who enters and exits the country and who is funneled into immigration facilities, the criminal justice system, or juvenile courts. However, historically, law enforcement has been characterized as a hierarchy reinforcing institution, recruiting and hiring individuals who held anti-egalitarian beliefs (Sidanius, Liu, Shaw, & Pratto, 1994; Sidanius & Pratto, 1999; Skolnick, 2011; Urbina & Álvarez, 2015). Geographically, the U.S.-Mexico border has been a central place for socioeconomic inequality, injustice, and violence (Álvarez & Urbina, 2016; Andreas, 2000; Chacon & Davis, 2006; Dunn, 2009; Jimenez, 2009; Phillips, Rodriguez, & Hagan, 2002). Douglas Massey, Jorge Durand, and Nolan Malone (2002, p. 7) compared the Gross National Product of Mexico and the United States and stated that "nowhere else on earth is there such a sharp contrast along a land border, much less one that is two thousand miles long." Consequently, different living conditions involving ethnic, racial, and economic segregation have shaped police officer strategies for interacting with border communities and people entering or leaving the country. If policing decisions are in any way racially biased, minorities (undocumented and documented) may be more at risk during the later processing stages.

As a culturally and socially diverse geographic setting, the U.S.-Mexico border has intertwined notions of ethnicity, race, and skin color with citizenship, community safety, and national security. As the Southwest shifted from Indigenous to Spanish, Mexican, and then U.S. control, racialized border tensions have heightened or intensified. For instance, people of Mexican descent, who constitute the great majority of minorities along the border, have often walked an ambiguous line in terms of racial categorizations by government officials (Almaguer, 2008; Bender, 2003; De León, 1983; Gomez, 2007; Lopez, 2006; Mirandé, 1987; Urbina, Vela, & Sanchez, 2014). Tracing the contours of race, citizenship, law, and social control along the border region, Law Professor Laura Gómez (2007) illustrates the centrality of colonialism for the Mexican American experience, and the paradoxical *legal* construction of Mexicans as racially White, with the *social* construction of Mexicans as racially inferior. In effect, the border has demonstrated a socially constructed political line, where the ground itself cannot tell us which part is Mexico and which part is the U.S., that continues to escalate a militarized physical geographic separation, turning the international border into a militarized war zone (Andreas, 2000; Dunn, 1996; Heyman, 1999; Nevins, 2010; Urbina & Alvarez, 2015). Josiah Heyman (2008) documents that this separation has become a "virtual wall" because of wide surveillance using highly advanced computer technologies along with the massing of police forces. Invariably, this geographic, economic, political, and social boundary has the power to shape the experience of not only law enforcement officers, but also border communities. The multiple issues that exist along the U.S.-Mexico border provide a more nuanced view of the challenges and complexities involved in patrolling the border, policing communities, and securing the border region. Subsequently, with pressing shifts in border security, in the midst of globalization, the central objective of this chapter is to further delineate, through analysis of existing data and face-to-face interviews with police administrators, the dynamics of border policing in the twenty-first century.

Situating the Contours of Policing Borders

For almost two decades, critics from all walks of life have passionately and sometimes aggressively charged that the U.S.-Mexico border is porous; unsafe; a safe haven for "illegal aliens," drug traffickers, narco-terrorists, and international terrorists; and that additional federal agents and military personnel are needed to secure the borders, along with high-tech military equipment for national security. In 2014, for instance, various lawmakers and other government officials quickly capitalized on the increase of unaccompanied children arriving on the U.S.-Mexico border trying to cross into the U.S. to make a tenuous connection to an insecure border and grave lack of border enforcement. Some politicians even suggested that Central American children could be disease carriers or terrorists. More recently, during the second GOP debate in September 2015, Carly Fiorina charged, "The border's been insecure for 25 years," Donald Trump declared the need to "build a wall, a wall that works," and Ben Carson proclaimed that "If we don't seal the border, the rest of this stuff clearly doesn't matter."

Reality, however, is far from highly charged political rhetoric, which is propagated and sensationalized by conservative media. In actuality, the 2,000-mile U.S.-Mexico border is not only heavily guarded but already a testing region for domestic militarization where wartime technologies are not just stockpiled in warehouses in case of a foreign invasion, but are being deployed on immigrants and people like you and us. The militarization of the southern border has been unfolding for years (Dunn, 1996; Kraska & Kappeler, 1997), but drastically escalated after September 11, 2001 (Balko, 2013; Golash-Boza, 2012a, 2012b; Miller, 2014; Welch, 2002, 2006, 2009), as has been vividly captured by Michael Welch in "Immigration Lockdown before and after 9/11: Ethnic Constructions and Their Consequences" (2007). The Department of Homeland Security constructed 649 miles of high-tech fencing along the U.S.-Mexico border in 2011, adding federal agents, radio towers, flood lighting, mobile surveillance, and other advanced military technology. Not surprisingly, by 2012, there were 21,370 Customs and Border Protection agents, targeting "high-risk areas and flows" and prepared to act on any given *threat*, including the apprehension of children from Central America. By some accounts, the United States already has 60,000 border guards, more than double the size of Ecuador's army, illustrating that the U.S. government has strategically militarized the U.S.-Mexico border, funneling $17.9 billion into more "boots-on-the-ground" and infrastructure by fiscal year 2012. As Americans tend to see walls, fences, and war zones around the world with indignation, what is going on in America, in our own backyard? After all, we tend to envision war in foreign lands, but not in America and certainly not in our neighborhoods.

Policing America in the Age of Globalization: The Militarization of the U.S.-Mexico Border

As is vividly detailed by Radley Balko in *Rise of the Warrior Cop: The Militarization of America's Police Forces* (2013) and Todd Miller in *Border Patrol Nation: Dispatches from the Front Lines of Homeland Security* (2014), along the border the American police are looking more reflective of an occupying army than a "protect and serve" law enforcement agency. While the army metaphor might seem far-fetched, the border region is in fact looking more and more like a war zone. Consider, for instance, about 700 miles of wall have *remarked* the landscape of the borderlands, backed by sophisticated surveillance equipment, like cameras, towers, and more than 12,000 motion sensors.

Customs and Border Protection (part of U.S. Department of Homeland Security) has its own air and marine forces, a special operations branch, and a separate tactical unit, with rapid-response teams of 500 federal agents ready for deployment within 48 hours, anywhere. The federal agency also has armored personnel carriers and uses operating bases like those used in U.S. involved-wars to secure positions in remote areas along the border. In fact, its Blackhawk helicopters and Predator B drones have been patrolling areas of the border region as if they were in a war zone, like Afghanistan. Subsequently, for decades government spending has astronomically increased (Urbina & Álvarez, 2016), but since 9/11 the government has funneled $100 billion into border armament and high-tech surveillance systems. In the words of Drew Dodds, a salesperson trying to cash in on the border security gold rush at the 2012 Border Security Expo, "we are bringing the battlefield to the border," now that U.S. intervention in Afghanistan, Iraq, and other places is winding down (Miller, 2014, p. 129).

Parallel to Customs and Border Protection, Border Patrol agents (also part of the U.S. Department of Homeland Security), who can easily and quickly be spotted along the border, are also increasingly being up-armored with a military-style combination of military hardware, assault rifles, helicopters, drones, and surveillance technologies. The once somewhat "open" border region is being transformed into what Timothy Dunn in *The Militarization of the U.S.-Mexico Border* (1996) characterizes as a state of "low-intensity warfare." A new warfare which, contrary to the argument of it only existing in certain areas, is not restricted to the desert or the Arizona border, but all along the river. In the Rio Grande Valley of Texas, for instance, federal agents are using a surplus military aircraft once used to safeguard U.S. soldiers in Afghanistan from Taliban attacks or other targets. Stationed on the U.S. side of the international divide, the aerostat (moored balloon) is an unmanned, high-altitude sentinel carrying sophisticated cameras that enable U.S. Customs and Border Protection to look deep into Mexican territory and "spot" people from 12 miles away in the darkness of the night, allowing immigration officials to detect mobility and mobilize forces.

In fact, with less U.S. involvement in Iraq and Afghanistan, more than 70 Defense Department aerostats are now available for use along the U.S.-Mexico border. Reportedly, along the Rio Grande Valley, four balloons are currently flying the skies, overlooking the Mexican state of Tamaulipas.

The Palestine-Mexico Border: America's Constitution-Free Zone

Until recently, war zones, airstrikes, police-community confrontations or riots, and even police brutality have been associated with so-called third-world countries lacking democracy and civility and in terrorist countries. However, in the twenty-first century, no foreign travel or television set is required to witness the frontline of warfare dividing, intimidating, and sometimes brutalizing communities, in operations that resemble testing grounds for federal agents, military personnel, and tech companies. The American Civil Liberties Union, for instance, reports that like the Gaza Strip for the Israelis, the U.S.-Mexico border region has been transformed into a "Constitution-free zone," an open-laboratory for exploration, exploitation, and profit.

Under the new border regime, almost any type of security, surveillance, and equipment can be developed, tested, and showcased, like in a *militarized shopping mall*, for politicians, law enforcement officials, and other nations to see and buy. In fact, border security is increasingly becoming a globalized industry, where corporate venders like Israel's Elkabetz are revolutionizing transnational boundaries. In February 2014, before Donald Trump's Great Mexican Wall idea, Customs and Border Protection (CBP), in charge of policing U.S. borders, contracted with Israel's giant private military manufacturer Elbit Systems to build a "virtual wall," a highly technologically advanced physical divide set back from the actual international boundary in the Arizona desert. The Israeli company (through Elbit Systems of America), whose U.S.-traded stock increased by six percent during Israel's massive military operation against Gaza in the summer of 2014, will utilize the same databank of advanced technology used in Israel's border region (Gaza and the West Bank) in Arizona (Miller, 2014; Miller & Schivone, 2015). With possibly up to one billion dollars at its disposal, CBP has tasked Elbit with building a "wall" of "integrated fixed towers" utilizing the latest and most advanced equipment, including radars, cameras, motion sensors, and control rooms, making Arizona the mecca of border enforcement, for other states to follow. Wall construction will begin in the rugged, desert canyons around Nogales, Arizona, be evaluated, and once DHS determines that part of the multi-million dollar wall project is effective, the rest of the wall will be built to monitor and patrol the entire state's border with Mexico.

To be sure, these towers are only part of a much broader border operation, the Arizona Border Surveillance Technology Plan. The Arizona wall project is simply a *blueprint* for a historically unprecedented infrastructure of high-tech border battlements, which has attracted various companies and the attention of lawmakers and other government officials for several years. In fact, this is not the first time Israeli corporations have been involved in border build-up in the United States. Soon after 9/11, in 2004, Elbit's Hermes drones were the first so-called unmanned aerial crafts to patrol the U.S.-Mexico border. Then in April 2007, details Naomi Klein in *The Shock Doctrine: The Rise of Disaster Capitalism* (2007, p. 438), another Israeli consulting company (Golan Group) composed of former officers of IDF Special Forces, provided an intensive eight-day course for special DHS immigration agents working along the Mexican border, covering "everything from hand-to-hand combat to target practice to 'getting proactive with their SUV.'" Beyond federal immigration agencies, the Israeli company NICE Systems also supplied "America's toughest sheriff," Joe Arpaio, with a surveillance system to monitor one of his "infamous" Arizona jails. Exploring America's transformation of the southern region, journalist Jimmy Johnson (2012) characterizes the border as the new "Palestine-Mexico border," illustrating America's new *Constitution-free zone*, where law becomes illusive and law enforcement practice highly questionable.

America's New Battlefield: The U.S.-Mexico Border Region

Pointing to the surveillance industry "synergy" between two distant places, Naomi Weiner, project coordinator for the Israel Business Initiative, proclaims "We've chosen areas where Israel is very strong and Southern Arizona is very strong," further indicating that Arizona possesses the "complete package" for Israeli companies (Miller & Schivone, 2015, p. 5). Her language is quite telling, "We're sitting right on the border, close to Fort Huachuca," a nearby U.S. military base where technicians maneuver the drones surveilling the U.S.-Mexico borderlands, and "We have the relationship with Customs and Border Protection, so there's a lot going on here. And we're also the Center of Excellence on Homeland Security" (Miller & Schivone, 2015, p. 5). Along the way, as an additional layer of "legitimacy," DHS designated the University of Arizona the lead university for the Center of Excellence on Border Security and Immigration in 2008, incorporating selected universities into the global border security enterprise, enabling schools to receive millions of dollars in federal grants. Conducting research, while developing border-policing technologies and related equipment, engineers in the Center for Excellence are analyzing locust wings in order to develop miniature drones equipped with high-tech cameras that can move into the tiniest areas near ground level, while large military drones (like the Predator B) continue to patrol over the U.S.-Mexico border region at 30,000 feet. With growing interest in the Arizona-Israeli border security and economic venture, officials from Tech Parks Arizona see Global Advantage (collaboration between the University of Arizona Tech Parks and the Offshore Group) as the ideal collaboration to strengthen the U.S.-Israel "special relationship," exposed in military operations around the world.

As reported by Todd Miller and Gabriel Schivone (2015, p. 6), "that mammoth security firm is ever more involved in finding 'civilian applications' for its war technologies," aggressively pushing to bring the battlefield to borderlands around the world, where the notion of *national security* serves as a prime justification for increased border enforcement, neutralizing laws, while redefining borders and justice systems (Golash-Boza, 2012a, 2012b, 2015; Welch, 2002, 2007), as documented by Welch in *Crimes of Power & States of Impunity: The U.S. Response to Terror* (2009) and in *Scapegoats of September 11th: Hate Crimes and State Crimes in the War on Terror* (2006). In "Scenes from an Occupation" (2011), demographer Joseph Nevins documents that although there are multiple differences between the political, economic, and social situations of the United States and Israel, Israel-Palestine and Arizona *share* the common target of keeping out "those deemed permanent outsiders," Palestinians, undocumented Mexicans, unauthorized Latinos from Central or South America, indigenous people from remote areas of the world, or Black people from unwanted countries.

The notion of national security, however, tends to by-pass the human element—violations of international law and human rights—along with ethnic/racial profiling and police brutality by immigration agents and local law enforcement (Golash-Boza, 2012a, 2012b; Urbina & Álvarez, 2015; Welch, 2006, 2007, 2009; Whitehead, 2013). Of course, as the saying goes, *blood is thicker than water and money is thicker than both.* Invariably, violations seem to matter little when there is great profit to be made, as Brigadier General Elkabetz indicated in a 2012 border technology conference. As charged by Miller and Schivone (2015, p. 6), considering the aggressive move that the U.S. and Israel are taking in "securing" borders and patrolling borderlands, "the deals being brokered at the University of Arizona look increasingly like matches made in heaven (or perhaps in hell)." Or, as characterized by journalist Dan Cohen and colleagues, "Arizona is the Israel of the United States," and with great profits to be made, borders are being redefined to maximize profitability (Urbina & Álvarez, 2016), not only in Arizona but other border states that are likely to follow.

Redefining Borders and Police Mission: National Security or Dividing Communities?

In this new era of border security, where borders are being redefined to further expand "border enforcement," we must also question if the ultimate mission of the new regime is in fact for national security; or to create an environment of fear, instilling mentally an us-versus-them (the enemy) mentality, which then calls for even more security? If we spend a little time along the U.S.-Mexico border, we soon realize that "in the name of safeguarding the nation" (Fernández, 2014, p. 2) the border has expanded far beyond the river, where militarized immigration enforcement is exacerbating a climate of fear and impunity. Officially, for instance, the jurisdiction of Custom and Border Protection (CBP) extends 100 miles inward from not only the U.S.-Mexico border, but any U.S. external boundary, which includes the 2,000-mile southern border and the 4,000-mile long northern border. In fact, 197.4 million people live within the specified zone; that is, 66 percent of Americans live in areas where they are, essentially, stripped of basic constitutional rights (Kagel, 2014).

As one example, Miller (2014) utilizes the 2010 Super Bowl at Sun Life Stadium in Miami, Florida, to illustrate the rapidly expanding operations of border enforcement. Using the security service of the Border Patrol, the agency showed how it can quickly "mobilize international boundaries ... to any part of the homeland for any given reason" (Miller, 2014, p. 19). Similarly, in *Lockdown America: Police and Prisons in the Age of Crisis* (1999, p. 141), Christian Parenti details how "militarized immigration enforcement ... has been repatriated, piece by piece, to the U.S. interior." Working with local law enforcement agencies across the country, Border Patrol anti-immigrant sweeps often involve "heavily armed tactical raiding parties backed up by helicopters and dogs" (Parenti, 1999, p. 141; Urbina & Álvarez, 2015), intimidating and harassing both undocumented and documented citizens, as documented by John Whitehead in *A Government of Wolves: The Emerging American Police State* (2013).

Clearly, militarized border security functions, including surveillance and operations, are strategically designed for *mass* social control (Urbina & Álvarez, 2015), as a governing mechanism to not only easily manage the population but also to maintain total control and dominance, while oppressing and silencing the poor and minorities (Urbina & Álvarez, 2016). Parenti (1999, p. 159), for instance, reports that racialized law enforcement practices (like the profiling of *brown* people, "Mexican" looking people, or the harassment of anyone who looks Latino) have fueled a system of "apartheid by other means," a "de facto criminalization and political marginalization of documented and undocumented immigrants alike." Miller (2014, p. 260) documents how mass surveillance, intimidation, and aggressive operations amount to a "process of self-segregation" that "results in a white monopoly on public space" (Fernández, 2014, p. 2); and subsequently, "cleansing" to ensure that "public space—parks, libraries, streets, and hospitals—will be largely reserved for those privileged by citizenship, wealth, and, most important, whiteness" (Golash-Boza, 2012a, 2015; McDowell & Wonders, 2010, p. 68; Romero, 2006).

David Lyon (1994, 2015) illustrates how the design and implementation of surveillance and social control technologies always start by targeting society's most disadvantaged population, the weakest and most marginalized groups, which normally tend to be the poor and people of color. From international boundaries and side margins, high-tech technologies, along with militarized immigration enforcement officers, move inward across the country. Beyond selected segments of society, reports Craig Whitlock and Craig Timberg (2014, p. 1), law enforcement agencies are "increasingly borrowing border-patrol drones for domestic surveillance operations," creating "novel privacy challenges" (Finn, 2011) for all citizens. In truth, as charged by some critics, "whether it's gunning down rock throwers on Mexico's side of the border or racially profiling residents of Arizona, you don't need a video-equipped drone to see that the Border Patrol is overstepping its bounds" (Fernández, 2014, p. 3).

Since militarized immigration officials are *free* to patrol in the border zone and far into the county's interior, with the right to violate the Fourth Amendment, agents within this zone may enter private property, search vehicles and private possessions, and stop people without a warrant or probable cause (Golash-Boza, 2012a, 2012b; McDowell & Wonders, 2010; Michalowski, 2007; Romero, 2006; Stephen, 2004). In 2009, for example, U.S. Senator Patrick Leahy was forced out of his vehicle a little more than 100 miles from the New York State's border, and in 2012, 96-year-old former Arizona Governor Raul Castro, was detained by CBP agents, who forced him out of his vehicle to stand in 90-degree heat for nearly 30 minutes because the immigration agents detected radiation from his pacemaker. In a more recent case, Shena Gutiérrez (a U.S. citizen) was detained for five hours, experiencing a traumatizing encounter, as CBP agents interrogated and searched through her possessions. Reportedly, agents trampled her and cuffed her so tight that Gutiérrez was left with bruises (Kagel, 2014). Therefore, as immigration reform is being debated and borders redefined in the name of national security, with civil liberties being push to the margins, U.S. militarized zones reveal that human rights violations are becoming the challenge of our times (Salinas, 2015), in our own backyard.

Social Control Movements: Beyond the Border

A comprehensive analysis of the immigration discourse also requires an appreciation of international forces shaping modern immigration laws and enforcement, along with corresponding ramifications, for structural, political, cultural, and ideological forces governing immigration laws, deportations, the criminalization process, and punishment intertwine with the globalization movement (Álvarez & Urbina, 2016). As documented by Sofia Espinoza Álvarez (2012), starting in the early 1980s, the advent of a series of punitive social control movements, like *the war on drugs*, *the war on immigrants*, and *the war on terrorism*, not only has significantly influenced the nature of social control, but it has situated it within a global scale (Bosworth & Flavin, 2007), while redefining the legal, political, and social parameters of social control.

Towards the end of the twentieth century, Jonathan Simon (1997, p. 173) proposed that advanced industrial societies were actually "governed through crime," with the over-developed societies of the West and North Atlantic "experiencing not a crisis of crime and punishment but a crises of governance that has led [them] to prioritize crime and punishment as the preferred contexts of governance," redefining the limits of criminal and immigration laws, while socially reconstructing the confines of race and ethnicity. Then, at the turn of the century, Tony Fitzpatrick (2001, p. 220) argued that as "global capital becomes apparently unmanageable" and "as the polity and the economic detached after a century of alignment," the state must give itself, particularly its agents, something to do, and so the state "socially and discursively constructs threats that only it can address through ... punitive responses to the chaos it has [helped facilitate]," as in the case of the war on drugs, the war on terrorism, and the war on immigrants. With crime and criminal justice systems becoming increasingly transnational, assisted by advanced technological innovations and a highly charged American media, "at once totalizing and individualizing," such strategies congeal in appealing political formations that can govern "all and each" with stealthy precision (Gordon, 1991, p. 3), giving the state a notion of absolute control, legitimacy, and justice, and to a feared and mal-informed society, an appearance of global power and solidarity.

These social control movements, though, have been driven just as much by a historical desire for revenge, conquest, control, dominance, and global expansion, than a defined mission for unity, safety, equality, and justice; subsequently, yielding grave consequences for certain segments of society (Álvarez & Urbina, 2014; Urbina, 2012). As documented by various scholars, social control movements fuel border militarization, ethnic/racial profiling, intimidation, harassment, and violence against immigrants, violations of civil rights, widespread deportations and detentions, and intrusive government surveillance on both undocumented and U.S. citizens. In fact, both the war on terror and the war on drugs have increasingly become a war against immigrant and minority communities (Álvarez & Urbina, 2016; Salinas, 2015; Urbina, 2012). Kelly Lytle (2003, p. 5), for instance, reports that the war on drugs led to the militarization of the U.S.-Mexico border, and a change in focus from *wetbacks* to *border violators*: "... the day of the Wetback was over ... the day of the border violator, a fugitive in a foreign country had arrived ... the beginnings of rhetoric within the U.S.-Mexico borderlands that criminalized undocumented Mexican immigrants." According to Law Professor David Cole (2001, p. 248), "racial profiling studies ... make clear that the war on drugs has largely been a war on minorities. It is, after all, drug enforcement that motivates most racial profiling." As for the war on terrorism, the American Civil

Liberties Union reports that "the war on terror has quickly turned into a war on immigrants." The resulting implications and consequences, however, are often washed aside as unavoidable "side effects" or the price of doing business for keeping "illegals" out to secure our borders.

Use of Excessive or Deadly Force

Until recently, Americans tended to associate police harassment, brutality, or deadly force with police forces in foreign counties, like our neighbor to the south, but not U.S. police forces. In truth, contrary to the popular notion of *not our police forces*, police brutality and deadly force have been routine practices since the advent of the police in America (Alpert & Dunham, 2004; Bayley & Mendelsohn, 1969; Escobar, 1999; Fyfe, 1981; Morales, 1972; Skolnick & Fyfe, 1993; Urbina & Álvarez, 2015), as historically documented by Samuel Walker in *Popular Justice: A History of American Criminal Justice* (1998) and Jerome Skolnick in *Justice Without Trial: Law Enforcement in Democratic Society* (2011). Some critics, though, charge that we are not only hearing more about police practice nowadays due to technological advances, including the social media, but that police violence has increased against certain segments of society and that in some cases it has become out of control (Aguirre-Molina, 2014; Applebome, 2012; Balko, 2006; Barlow & Barlow, 2012; Durán, 2009, 2015; Holmes, 1998, 2000; Human Rights Watch, 1998; Jacobs & O'Brien, 1998; Kane & White, 2013; Pew Research Center, 2014; Russell, 1998; Smith & Holmes, 2003; Urbina & Álvarez, 2015; Whitehead, 2013).

In May 2013, Arpaio's office was found by a judge to have racially profiled Latinos in regular traffic and immigration patrols. Yet, on September 4, 2015, U.S. District Judge Susan Bolton upheld part of Arizona's controversial immigration law, rejecting claims that the so-called "show your papers" provision of the law discriminates against Latino immigrants and Latinos in general. As such, the law allows police in Arizona to check the immigration status of anyone they stop. The federal judge also upheld a provision that allows police to check the legal status of detainees in the U.S. Ironically, Judge Bolton's ruling came two days after a federal judge approved a deal between the U.S. Department of Justice and Maricopa County to resolve accusations of civil rights violations and dismissed the department's lawsuit against Arizona Sheriff Joe Arpaio and his deputies.

Nationally, we have been seeing a xenophobic hysteria—centered on illegals, Mexicans, terrorists, ISIS, the border crisis, the child immigrant crisis, Syrian refugees, and Ebola—mashed together to instill public fear, provoke public sentiment, and influence public opinion. The reality is that our highly militarized border is more secure than ever before.

The Contours of Border Enforcement: Underneath It All

Created in 1924 to secure U.S. borders, the Border Patrol, now part of the Department of Homeland Security's Customs and Border Protection agency, has been active in its defined mission for almost 100 years, with its agents, as the frontline agents of border enforcement, the most visible upholders of national security, patrolling the 2,000-mile southern border. In effect, according to the department's website, its "priority mission" is "preventing terrorists and terrorists [sic] weapons, including weapons of mass destruction, from entering the United States." Its "primary mission," though, is "to detect and prevent the illegal entry of aliens" into the country. Critics, however, charge that the formally defined objectives, mission, and vision of some institutions are often more a reflection of political rhetoric and manipulation than the realities of life, often serving as a smokescreen to what Urbina and Álvarez (2016) characterize as *underneath it all*—the hidden motives of social control. From an economic standpoint, while we are dealing with a *comparatively* small percent of undocumented people, about $12 billion is spent annually on border security, more than all other federal security agencies (apart from the Pentagon) combined (Tirman, 2015; Urbina & Álvarez, 2015, 2016), under the passionate and aggressive argument that we are under attack by dangerous immigrants, narco-terrorists, international terrorists, even children from Central America, and most recently Syrian refugees. Yet in fiscal year 2012, 364,000 "aliens" were reported to have been arrested, but not a single international terrorist (Fernández, 2014). Sadly, immigrants have been demonized by some with highly charged and xenophobic language to justify aggressive enforcement tactics and achieve political ends while ignoring the underlying issues of reasonable immigration policy, racism, fear, and shifting global populations.

Voices from the Border: Police Administrators

To gain insight into the "world of policing" in communities along the border by local police departments, we interviewed four police administrators in two different cities/counties, each with more than 20 years of experience in law enforcement. The participants were Maverick County Sheriff Tom Schmerber, Lt. Aldo Escamilla with the Eagle Pass Police Department, Val Verde County Sheriff Joe Frank Martinez, and Captain Fred Knoll with the Del Rio Police Department. In face-to-face interviews (November/December 2015), the four highly experienced law enforcement administrators shared, with vivid detailed, their views and concerns regarding major problems, challenges, barriers, obstacles, and other issues in policing the border, local communities, and the region. Beyond the noted specific issues, the shared information enables us to situate the "local police experience" within a broader context, ultimately enhancing our ability to design sound policy recommendations.

Major Challenges in Policing the Border and the Region

The participating police administrators reported that among the various challenges, government officials (policymakers, state congressman, representatives, and other public officials) have limited knowledge of the realities of policing borders, and subsequently the federal government does not allow the necessary flexibility to utilize resources, particularly federal dollars to hire additional officers. According to Sheriff Martinez,

> Somebody in Washington, DC, is making decisions as to what I need here in Val Verde County. When somebody comes visit from Washington, they come to the border to visit, everybody comes along, you have DPS, Border Patrol, Parks and Wildlife, National Park Service, and they put on a show for the congressman, and that's what they see, but not the actual picture.

As such, Sheriff Martinez reported constantly facing a major challenge in properly managing the department; stating "I'd rather have the flexibility of the dollars they're giving me and use them in manpower vs. overtime ... what I spend in one year in overtime, I can probably hire 4 deputies full-time in a year." In the neighboring county, Sheriff Tom Schmerber expressed similar concerns with state and federal grants, which are awarded with rigid "strings attached; they want to tell us what to do and how to work," and thus not allowing him as the sheriff to perform the things he needs to do to more effectively and efficiently patrol our border communities. As an example, declared Sherriff Schmerber, "if I want to buy certain vehicles I need to work on the border, the grants will not allow me to get certain vehicles, they say the money is for overtime, or to work on the highway."

Another issue involves a nationwide shift in policing, where respect for law enforcement has diminished over the years; or perhaps the *way the law is applied.* According to Captain Fred Knoll, we are seeing a higher use of excessive force and a much higher rate of police-involved shootings. Seeking to illustrate a historical shift, Captain Knoll proclaimed,

> People have become more defiant of the law, you have more people that are radicalized, they don't seem to agree with the system, and so I feel it's a more dangerous society than it was 15 or 20 years ago and when you add other criminal elements like the increased drug trade, the shift in mentality and no respect for the law, it just leads to a dangerous combination.

Another issue is the topography of the border region, in that unlike major urban areas or metro cities around the country where boundaries are "defined," most border cities are small or rural, desolate areas, with an international river that makes it almost impossible to police without "running into other issues." Pointing to the significance of the international boundary, Captain Knoll reported, "here, the next 'door' is another city, with their own laws and police departments, creating a divide, a kind of no-man's land between us and Mexico, yet we still have to be neighbors."

Police administrators also mentioned shifts in the nature of illegality over the years. Captain Knoll reported that 20 years ago, a major police function was "dealing" with undocumented people (i.e., detaining them for the Border Patrol). In recent years, the illicit drug industry has become the central issue, forcing business on both sides of the border to restructure their operations for security, with some business owners on the Mexican side relocating to the U.S. side. Worse, criminal groups have created fear on both sides, increasing mobility in the border cities. Increased violence and fear along the border, for example, brings more traffic from Mexico and therefore the "illegal elements try to hide with the legitimate traffic." Drug cartels have affiliations with people on both sides of the border, and thus "security is always a concern nowadays, in ways not experienced before." Regarding the nature of crime along the border, Captain Knoll reported "we hardly see any illegal alien trafficking anymore, most of what we see is weapon smuggling, and drug smuggling, these are the big issues, the little human trafficking has moved farther north." Alluding to the war on terrorism along the border, Captain Knoll remarked,

> To me those are the issues that we face right now, that to me personally threaten the security of our country because these illegal cartels, if you pay them the right price, who are they going to do business here to get their stuff to the United States whether its bombs or people from other countries who want to come to the U.S.

Another major challenge involved the bureaucracy, multiple channels to address, and the high volume of paperwork. Therefore, with limited manpower, for some assignments, it takes too long to get them done. According to Lt. Escamillia, anything that needs to get done that requires documentation or assistance from the Department of Public Safety, Border Patrol, Customs, or any other law enforcement agency, before his department can act they need a memo of understanding, an MOU between the agencies, because of liability concerns. For instance, in order for his department to assist Border Patrol, there has to be a memo of understanding between both agencies stating, "we are doing this and what's going to happen, if we are doing this, these are the steps we are going to take." Showing his frustration, Lt. Escamillia commented,

> If I assign a detective and they go out to conduct an investigation my biggest concern is that if for any reason the detective gets hurt, is the city going to say, "well you shouldn't have been there in that part of the county, the insurance is not going to cover and we cannot do anything."

In sum, as reported by the participating police administrators, their departments are regularly confronted with various challenges, problems, barriers, obstacles, and related issues, including lack of knowledge by government officials in Washington, limited flexibility with federal funding, lack of finances and manpower, bureaucracy, high volume of paperwork, liability concerns, shifts in the nature of crime (e.g., different types of crime and more violence), shifts in mentality (less obedience) toward the law, drug industry and cartels, topography, mobility, and the international boundary. Regarding their single biggest challenge in policing the border region, they reported that every city/county and their agencies have different needs. Sheriff Martinez remarked, "I think the single biggest challenge is probably manpower." Similarly, Sheriff Schmerber reported that his "biggest challenge is manpower, not enough deputies to cover a wide area," a concern also shared by Lt. Escamilla, "The single biggest challenge is financing and the support (like more personnel, vehicles, and other equipment) that we need to get the job done." For Captain Knoll,

> the biggest challenge is the illicit drug trade ... and, broadly, we are a lot more complex than other inner cities in the United States because of course you have a border with another nation whose rules,

laws, and policies are totally different from those we have in our own country.

The Biggest Problems that Remain to Be Addressed in Policing the Border, Local Communities, and the Region

According to Sheriff Martinez, the biggest *problem* is the fact that Washington does not want to change existing procedures to give his department and other departments along the border more autonomy. Seeking to illustrate a crucial geographical difference, Sheriff Martinez noted that here in Texas we have a river that divides two countries, and there is also significant difference along the U.S. side. Sheriff Martinez noted that in New Mexico and Arizona, as an example, they have a fence along the border, so their issues are totally different than the ones in Texas. Beyond these areas, each of the 31 border sheriffs from San Diego, California, to Brownsville, Texas, has his or her own problems; "the counties are not the same, we all have our own issues, concerns, and various problems." Therefore, for Sheriff Martinez, "the biggest problem that remains to be addressed is the lack of flexibility to prioritize the specific issues that pertain to our area."

For Captain Knoll, the "biggest problem that remains to be resolved is the threat of border violence." Captain Knoll reported not experiencing the "spillover on the same scale" as supposedly occurring in other border areas, but "I always feel that the threat is right there because when you are miles or even feet away, it's hard to ignore and say, 'it's on the other side of the river, on the other side of the country.'" Summarizing his views and concerns on *spillover terror* or perhaps *fear* (actual, imagined, or exaggerated), Captain Knoll declared,

> We're not talking the issues that are going on in Afghanistan or Iraq where we are continents away, here we have the criminal element feet away in some cases. Just knowing that criminal elements exist, the stories that we get to hear or read about how many times there's deaths in the border cities a day, how many times rounds are being fired, sometimes we can hear them over here, it's really too close for comfort in my opinion, that is a big concern. I've heard stories in the city of El Paso, Texas, because of its close proximity to Juarez, Mexico, how they've taking stray bullets that come across the border that have actually gone in the City Hall building of the city … folks in San An-

> tonio are not catching stray bullets like we are here and that makes it very unique because of where we are located.

Similar to Sheriff Martinez, for Sheriff Schmerber "the biggest problem that remains to [be] seriously discussed and addressed is flexibility so that I can more effectively mobilize my officers, particularly in certain areas." The sheriff reported that since several neighborhoods are close to the international river, officers have to work "by the river ... on the frontline of patrolling." Though, according to Sheriff Schmerber, it's "more the possibility of danger and possible accidents. Wild stories aside, how many times do we hear about police officers actually being hurt or killed along the border? So, it's really not a problem, but a matter of being prepared." As for everyday patrol, the sheriff reported relying on Border Patrol agents patrolling along the river, but sometimes immigration agents are not along the river or sometimes they move away, in which case, it could result in possible problems if an accident was to happen. Further, with so much law enforcement mobility along the border, coordination among agencies needs to be well-designed. For instance, reported Sheriff Schmerber, the DPS also works on the border and "they hired 250 troopers that got sent to the border to help out so we really need to get together to make sure we don't bump into each other." Therefore, with so many local, state, and federal agents working the border, coordination is crucial for well-structured everyday functioning and special operations.

Differences between Police Practices along the Border and Other Non-Border Areas

Participating police administrators reported that one of the more significant differences is that border towns function as ports of entry for people, undocumented and documented, coming into the country. As such, border cities are areas in transition, with traffic moving in both directions from both countries. As for traffic moving north, a high volume of people pass through border towns and continue to bigger cities up north, back to their destination, or in the case of undocumented people, establishing their residence further north. As such, if undocumented people engage in some type of illegal behavior in those communities, it's those departments that have to address those issues. Geographically, Sheriff Martinez remarked, "I would imagine there is a big difference between what we see here and what they see there." Similarly, Captain Knoll reported that "combined with local mobility and traffic from two very large countries, topography along the border region forces police departments to be a little more innovative with the way that we patrol our communities." Unlike officers in large cities like Houston and San Antonio who normally patrol residential areas, border agents are exposed to an "open-field" kind of "international" environment. "While safety is universal," reported Captain Knoll, "we have to train for a never constant environment, wildlife, natural waterways, an international lake, a lake we share with Mexico, with several bass tournaments during the year, we have a military base, a junior college, and a university."

Regarding the notion promoted by the conservative media, politicians, and other government officials that the border is ripped with crime and violence, Lt. Escamillia declared,

> in border cities, the high majority (or a substantial amount) of the population is Latino, Mexican, sometimes close to 100%. In fact, in cities like Del Rio, Eagle Pass, El Paso, Laredo, and all the way to Brownsville on the Atlantic to San Diego on the Pacific, Latinos constitute a significant amount of our population. However, people in Austin and Washington don't understand our communities, they just see it as border violence. So to do a good job, we have to police differently, we need to consider ethnic issues, like language and culture.

To complicate matters, reported Lt. Escamillia, some federal agencies expect local police departments to collaborate with them "in securing the border and in apprehending illegals," but it's "difficult to differentiate a U.S. citizen from illegal immigrants, without having to rely on racial profiling, which then might lead to violations of civil liberties." Similarly, Sheriff Schmerber remarked, "we all know that the majority are Hispanics including myself," but some "agents are not familiar with our communities so it causes friction when agents cannot distinguish between residents, undocumented people (who are only 'illegal' because they are unauthorized to be in the U.S.) and actual criminals." Illustrating some frustration, Sheriff Schmerber continued, "Yes, we have multiple issues to resolve, and some very serious issues, but not what some media and some people report, like Donald Trump has argued."

Additionally, according to Lt. Escamillia, some people tend to see border towns as "too Mexican," "too violent," or cities in transition, people going north. However, transition goes both ways, but some people would rather not talk about it, for the "obvious reasons." If we study the movement,

> border towns are a gateway, drugs are moving north, weapons are moving south through the same border and guess what, we have (stash) houses on both sides of the border, we have corruption on

> both sides of the border, not just on one side, we have stash houses going up westbound and going eastbound, coming in and going out, it's insane when people talk that illegals are bringing the drugs. While they do bring in a few pounds here and there, drugs in the U.S. are being moved by U.S. citizens with the help of, well you know who.

Therefore, "these illusive operations," reported Lt. Escamillia, "make border policing a daily challenge and a constant fear for our communities, the fear of cartel members not found in other areas of the country." Regarding the violence we regularly hear on the news media, Captain Knoll reported, "we are seeing a lot of violence, shootings, officer involved incidents at least on my experience compared to what I'm used to in my career," and "during the last two years, every time we turn on the TV there are officer-involved shootings whether it's on our state or somewhere else almost every day, I just think the numbers have gone too high." Another police administrator, Lt. Escamillia reported,

> I also worry about possible spill-over from Mexico, but then I remind myself that border towns are some of the safest cities in the country. In fact, if we listen to the news, we hear about shootings every day, and just about all of them take place in cities up north, east, or west ... seldom do we hear about killings along the border on the U.S. side.

Mechanisms Currently Being Put in Place to Resolve Existing Problems in Border Policing

Police administrators reported that the "uniqueness of the border" requires multiple mechanisms to be situated to effectively patrol the border region, from communication with Washington to coordination among agencies to securing federal grants. Further, mechanisms need to be properly situated for everyday policing and long-term operations, which require "manpower and funding." For instance, since the majority of border patrol agents are located along the U.S.-Mexico border, grant money from the Department of Homeland Security is awarded to local law enforcement agencies along the border to "help cover gaps that border patrol cannot cover"; for example, border patrol agents are scattered along the border every quarter mile or half a mile, but if local departments put additional "boots on the grounds" it kind of "creates a police-chain."

Sheriff Martinez reported that his department is getting grant money for additional equipment and to pay deputies for overtime, allowing him a little flexibility to direct resources to areas that require immediate attention and the ability to more efficiently work with Border Patrol. Similarly, Captain Knoll reported that about a decade ago (post-9/11) the federal government realized that the southern border was having "unique problems versus other cities inside the United States," and subsequently the federal government has designated various different grants for law enforcement in border counties. As for his department, Captain Knoll commented, "We take advantage of these grants to implement special operations, joint operations with Border Patrol, and work with Customs on outbound operations" (the point of exit where border agents inspect vehicles leaving the U.S.), "it kind of increases manpower, it doesn't give us extra manpower, it just kind of gives them technical assistance," and even though "arrests that are made it's under their authority, when they stop folks for federal reasons, sometimes we also find that some people have warrants, so if the offenses don't fall within their authority, we take those people into custody." Sharing his excitement, Captain Knoll explained,

> Let me tell you, when we go to meetings in cities more inland and we talk about these border operations and the grants we have, they kind of look at us and say, 'hey I've never heard of that'… that's because these moneys and projects are available for border counties rather than inner cities or metro cities … so these resources we have been entitled, allowing us to design and implement mechanisms, are essential for policing borders and the results have been good.

Lt. Escamilla also mentioned having grants awarded by the U.S. Department of Homeland Security, resources which are used to assist border patrol agents, "where a lot of times what border patrol officers cannot do police officers can or vice-versa, particularly with probable cause to stop a vehicle or conduct a search." Unlike police officers, Lt. Escamilla informed us, "border patrol agents do not need probable cause to stop a vehicle, all they need is a reason for suspicion, that's enough to stop a vehicle and conduct a search"; for instance, "all they need to see is a car leaning on the back that looks like its leaning on something." Therefore, it is more difficult for police officers to make a stop, but it's easier for border patrol agents, enabling agencies to work together and readjust mechanisms as deemed necessary to patrol the border and secure communities. However, "if we look at the bigger picture with some intelligence and honesty," continued Lt. Escamilla, "let me tell you something else, in my opinion, everything tends to revolve around finance … everybody wants money."

Vested in communication and understanding, Sheriff Schmerber referenced a coalition, where sheriffs meet every 12 months in different places along the border. Reportedly, they invite government officials, like congressmen and senators, to attend, learn about border issues, and dialogue about possible avenues for addressing specific issues within individual border cities, counties, and states. These meetings, charged Sheriff Schmerber, "are not to be taken as working vacations, but arrive at the meetings with a well-planned agenda for serious discussion"; ultimately, "designing and implementing long-term mechanisms to patrol the border and secure cities, but also to improve our communities, particularly when it comes to juveniles, many of them with great need for good mentors and role models."

Future Challenges in Securing the Border and Policing Communities and the Region

Police administrators were asked about future challenges in policing the border. Sheriff Martinez reported that the biggest challenge will be getting everyone on the same page, where local, state, and federal agencies jointly collaborate to more effectively patrol local communities, secure the border, and better serve the public. Another major challenge will be convincing policymakers in Austin and Washington that cities along the U.S.-Mexico border have different issues and concerns, and therefore their "propositions or mandates do not work as a cure-all; border agencies need flexibility to implement specific needs." Pointing to the current political climate, particularly the "presidential race," Captain Knoll mentioned that future challenges will greatly depend on the political environment, "depending on whose president and whose governor who have political motives, which may or may not be in tune with reality." For instance, declared Captain Knoll,

> if we have a president or a governor that really has a strong sentiment against illegal immigration, weapons issues, drug issues, you're going to get an administration who is going to set the tone for how things are going to operate for four to eight years or longer, but if we get somebody who is a little more liberal, a little more open-minded, a little more flexible, those aggressive efforts are going to be tamed down a bit.

Of course, continued Captain Knoll, this does not necessarily mean that because politicians have a liberal way of thinking they do not believe in social control, but enforcement is simply less aggressive, often focusing on other issues and diverting resources to those issues. Pointing to possible shifts in border crime, Lt. Escamilla remarked, "we haven't had any type of serious spillover from Mexico, but I think that the biggest challenge is going to be preventing spillover violence, especially since we are hearing about issues in Laredo." According to Lt. Escamilla, "last time there was a homicide, we found two bodies out in the county, possibly killed by a Mexican criminal organization, but that is the only case of spillover in the past 17 years." As an international issue, continued Lt. Escamilla, "If we seriously think about it, until the U.S. government and the Mexican government decide on alternative approaches to deal with the drug trade, spill-over is always a concern." As for a possible solution, Lt. Escamilla charged,

> let's face it, no matter how many laws are passed, how many people get arrested, how many people get indicted and prosecuted, how many people get convicted, or how many people are sentenced to prison, the drug trade coming north and the weapons going south will continue. Simple economics, supply and demand.

Consistent with the other police administrators, Sheriff Schmerber anticipates that the biggest challenge will be securing funding, with flexible conditions, so that local agencies can properly plan and implement innovative mechanisms without having to rely on politically favored but ineffective strategies. As one example, Sheriff Schmerber mentioned that "at one point they started building fences across the river but fences don't resolve our problems, they just create more problems and divide our communities." A strong advocate of communication and collaboration, for him the challenge will be to put the local politics aside and have communication with Mexico, so that projects, ideas, and efforts are not counter-productive. An approach not supported by some critics, Sheriff Schmerber mentioned that he has established communication with the government of Piedras Negras to secure both cities, prevent possible spill-over violence, gain the trust of both communities who travel back and forth, and avoid dividing communities. Sharing his border police strategies, Sheriff Schmerber continued,

> When I was elected, there was no communication, and this was a big issue for me, so I established communication. I asked the governor for permission to make Maverick County and our neighbor city in the state of Coahuila an example for other counties along the U.S.-Mexico border to do the same and communicate with each other.

Sheriff Schmerber also noted that we need to approach the border for what it is, an "international border," which requires bilateral communication. "Frankly, if our President and governors meet regularly with Mexican officials to converse on various issues, why can't we communicate with our neighbor cities to converse, plan, design, and implement comprehensive safety reforms, beneficial to both communities?" Captain Knoll also illustrated the importance of communication with their neighbors in Mexico,

> I think the one thing I miss from my previous years in my career, which was very positive, we had a lot more relation with our counterparts over in Mexico on a local and non-bureaucratic level where we used to be able to resolve some of these problems real quick between us and them because of agreements and alliances we had. No need to rely on Washington, Austin, or Mexico City. But when the drug corruption issue came up some years back especially within the last 10 years, it really diminished our ability to have one-on-one contacts across the border. Since the military took over in Mexico because of the corruption issue, we no longer have that one-on-one contact where we could either meet in our office or theirs to discuss issues at hand. Now if we want to meet with somebody it has to be more formal, and who knows when you're going to be able to actually meet with their captain in charge of this area to really sit down and talk on a local level about our specific issues. Before, our officers used to go over there, we had detectives that we used to know over there, we had people at the prosecutor's office that we knew over there from the *Aduana* (Mexican customs) so it was a lot easier for us to go over there and talk about our problems and theirs, and we had a good relationship, a level of respect, and so it was in our best interest to resolve our border issues jointly, it really was great.

Conclusion

As the U.S. intervention abroad in places like Afghanistan and Iraq is winding down, the federal government in multi-million dollar joint ventures with transnational corporations are bringing the battlefield to the American border—of course, conveniently and strategically, the U.S.-Mexico border. Pragmatically, borders and accompanying walls or fences between people, whether it is in a neighborhood, city, state, or international boundary, depends on society's internalization of an us-versus-them mentality that justifies increased border enforcement, a militarized border, violations of civil liberties, ethnic/racial profiling, displacement of immigrants, exploitation of undocumented people, oppression of immigrants (undocumented and documented), and the perpetuation of political, military, and corporate power structures.

Broadly, the influx of federal immigration agents and high-tech surveillance systems, with their aggressive national security mission, is not limited to the U.S.-Mexico border, where the Department of Homeland Security (joined by local police departments and the state police) presence is becoming an occupying army, stretching inland into both sides of the international boundary. What we normally only saw on television in foreign lands, as immigration laws become more *illusive* along the border, the federal government is strategically bringing the battlefield to our states, our cities, our neighborhoods. Anti-immigrant critics, particularly those vested in public office or economic profits, passionately try to justify their proposed actions by using sensationalizing terms, like *illegals*, *wetbacks*, *criminal aliens*, *terrorists*, *narco-terrorists*, *they take our jobs*, and *they don't pay taxes*, charges that are further sensationalize by the conservative media and intellectual racists. In truth, politics and profits aside, as documented in various studies, high levels of immigrants often equate with lower levels of violence (Martinez, 2015; Morín, 2009; Salinas, 2015). Yet along the 2,000-mile U.S.-Mexico border, the border region continues to be a militarized area with numerous fears (Álvarez & Urbina, 2016; Andreas, 2000; Dunn, 1996; Heyman, 1999, Nevins, 2010; Urbina & Álvarez, 2015), despite lower levels of violence and property crime (U.S. Government Accountability Office, 2013).

In fact, as the current transatlantic joint border security operations indicate, along with the unprecedented number of deportations and criminalization of immigrants (Álvarez & Urbina, 2016; Urbina & Álvarez, 2016), the militarization of the southern border is not only rapidly advancing into the Mexico interior but also the U.S. interior. Yet, since everything seems to indicate that Americans will never be satisfied with increased levels of policing or security along the U.S.-Mexico border region, the security empire will continue to grow, like a well-grounded organism, swallowing anything and everything that gets in the way. Already occurring in Arizona and other areas along the border (and even in the interior), if you are, or simply appear, foreign (because of skin color, language, accent, clothing, music, type of vehicle, or simply being "out of place"), watch out for *la migra* (Border Patrol), ICE, the state police, local police, and officers from multiple other agencies, including the DEA and FBI. As the saying goes, when all you have is a hammer, everything looks like a nail.

As for the future of border policing, social control, and police reform, we need to confront the stereotypes, prejudice, racism, discrimination, and oppression against immigrants (undocumented and documented) and border communities. To be sure, while some critics aggressively argue that ethnicity/race is not a significant factor (or even a factor) in immigration laws, border enforcement, criminalization, incarceration, or discourse, ethnic and racial minorities are already "wearing" a *racial uniform*—skin color—which itself has become the mark of illegality; ultimately, illegality is equated with *brownness* and *browness* is equated with illegality. In essence, as one of the biggest "clienteles" of local, state, and federal agents, immigrants are "guilty" of being *undocumented*, they are "guilty" of being *brown* people, they are "guilty" of being *Mexican* immigrants, and, in a sense, they are "guilty" for simply existing or having been born. Of course, underneath it all, there is a more devastating motive—the continued legacy of hate, exploitation, oppression, and marginalization of society's most vulnerable people, while seeking to maintain total control, dominance, and silencing of immigrants, ethnic/racial minorities, and the poor (Urbina, 2012, 2014; Urbina & Álvarez, 2016; Urbina et al., 2014), as documented by Sofia Espinoza Álvarez and Martin Guevara Urbina in *Immigration and the Law: From Conquest to the War on Terrorism* (2016).

Beyond the 2,000-mile U.S.-Mexico border, we need to ensure that local, state, and federal agencies address not only the racial profiling, brutality, and violence against immigrants, minorities, and poor people (Salinas, 2015; Urbina, 2012; Urbina & Álvarez, 2015), but also the injustices during arrest, detention, and incarceration throughout the country (Salinas, 2015; Álvarez & Urbina, 2016). However, with the political economy of the criminal justice system now being a major component of the U.S. economic system (Álvarez & Urbina, 2016; Urbina & Álvarez, 2016), reform will be the challenge of our times, as it will harm the criminal justice system's multi-billion dollar enterprise and the billions of dollars in revenue for private corporations, from companies running private prisons to corporations providing high-tech equipment to the criminal justice system. For those who are benefiting (directly or indirectly) from the multi-billion dollar criminal justice enterprise, reform is the bottom line. Or, as the saying goes, reform is like taking the bone away from a dog.

Lastly, in face-to-face interviews with local police administrators, we gained insight into the world of policing borders, gaining perspective about the multiple problems, challenges, barriers, obstacles, and other issues in policing the border, local communities, and the region. Their shared views, concerns, and recommendations are vital not only for better understanding border policing, but also for situating mechanisms to more effectively patrol the border and secure our communities and the border region. It should be noted that even though the information shared was consciously or unconsciously *filtered through their police lens*, it allows us to better decipher, conceptualize, and situate the information within a broader context, as detailed in the first part of this chapter. Not surprisingly, no polemic issues, like police brutality, profiling, sexism, or racism, were referenced as issues of concern or even mentioned. Taken together, though, the rich, vivid, and consistent shared information enables us to obtain an appreciation for the everyday security of our borders and communities, providing us a baseline for future research, specific ideas and strategies for police reform, and recommendations for policymakers.

References

Aguirre-Molina, M. (2014). Police aggression: A social determinant of health (and death). Información al Desnudo. Retrieved from http://informacionaldesnudo.com/police-aggression-a-social-determinant-of-health-and-death/.

Almaguer, T. (2008). *Racial fault lines: The historical origins of white supremacy in California*. Berkeley: University of California Press.

Alpert, G., & Dunham, R. (2004). *Understanding police use of force: Officers, suspects, and reciprocity*. Cambridge: Cambridge University Press.

Álvarez, S. E. (2012). Latinas and Latinos in the U.S.: The road to prison. In M. G. Urbina (Ed.), *Hispanics in the U.S. criminal justice system: The new American demography* (pp. 203–224). Springfield, IL: Charles C Thomas.

Álvarez, S. E., & Urbina, M. G. (2014). Capital punishment on trial: Who lives, who dies, who decides—A question of justice? *Criminal Law Bulletin, 50*, 263–298.

Álvarez, S. E., & Urbina, M. G. (2016). *Immigration and the law: From conquest to the war on terrorism*. Springfield, IL: Charles C Thomas.

Andreas, P. (2000). *Border games: Policing the U.S.-Mexico divide*. Ithaca, NY: Cornell University Press.

Applebome, P. (2012, January 24). Police gang tyrannized Latinos, indictment says. *The New York Times*. Retrieved from http://www.nytimes.com/2012/01/25/nyregion/connecticut-police-officers-accused-of-mistreating-latinos.html.

Balko, R. (2006). *Overkill: The rise of paramilitary police raids in America*. Cato Institute. Retrieved from http://object.cato.org/sites/cato.org/files/pubs/pdf/balko_whitepaper_2006.pdf.

Balko, R. (2013). *Rise of the warrior cop: The militarization of America's police forces*. New York: PublicAffairs.

Barlow, D., & Barlow, M. (2012). Myth: The core mission of the police is to fight crime. In R. M. Bohm & J. T. Walker (Eds.), *Demystifying crime and criminal justice* (2nd ed.) (pp. 73–80). Los Angeles, CA: Roxbury Publishing Company.

Bayley, D., & Mendelsohn, H. (1969). *Minorities and the police: Confrontation in America.* New York: Free Press.

Bender, S. W. (2003). *Greasers and gringos: Latinos, law, and the American imagination.* New York: New York University Press.

Bosworth, M., & Flavin, J. (Eds.). (2007). *Race, gender, and punishment: From colonialism to the war on terror.* Piscataway, NJ: Rutgers University Press.

Chacon, J., & Davis, M. (2006). *No one is illegal: Fighting racism and state violence on the U.S.-Mexico border.* Chicago: Haymarket Books.

Cole, D. (2001). Formalism, realism, and the war on drugs. *Suffolk University Law Review, 35,* 241–255.

De León, A. (1983). *They called them Greasers: Anglo attitudes toward Mexicans in Texas, 1821–1900.* Austin, TX: University of Texas Press.

Dunn, T. J. (1996). *The militarization of the U.S.-Mexico border 1978–1992: Low-intensity conflict doctrine comes home.* Austin: University of Texas Press.

Dunn, T. J. (2009). *Blockading the border and human rights: The El Paso operation that remade immigration enforcement.* Austin, TX: University of Texas Press.

Durán, R. J. (2009). Legitimated oppression: Inner-city Mexican American experiences with police gang enforcement. *Journal of Contemporary Ethnography, 38*(2), 143–168.

Durán, R. J. (2015). Mexican American law enforcement officers: Comparing the creation of change versus the reinforcement of structural hierarchies. In M. G. Urbina & S. E. Alvarez (Eds.), *Latino police officers in the United States: An examination of emerging trends and issues* (pp. 128–147). Springfield, IL: Charles C Thomas.

Durán, R. J., & Posadas, C. E. (2015). The policing of youth on the U.S.-Mexico border: A law enforcement perception of leniency. *Race and Justice, 6*(1), 1–27.

Escobar, E. (1999). *Race, police, and the making of a political identity: Mexican Americans and the Los Angeles Police Department, 1900–1945.* Los Angeles, CA: University of California Press.

Fernández, B. (2014, May 7). The creeping expansion of the Border Patrol. Aljazeera. Retrieved from http://america.aljazeera.com/opinions/2014/5/border-patrol-immigrationmilitarizationhomelandsecurity.html.

Finn, P. (2011). Domestic use of aerial drones by law enforcement likely to prompt privacy debate. *The Washington Post.* Retrieved from http://www.washingtonpost.com/wp-dyn/content/article/2011/01/22/AR2011012204111.html.

Fitzpatrick, T. (2001). New agenda for social policy and criminology: Globalization, urbanization and the emerging post-social security state. *Social Policy and Administration, 35*, 212–229.

Fyfe, J. (1981). Who shoots? A look at officer race and police shooting. *Journal of Police Science & Administration, 9*(4), 367–382.

Golash-Boza, T. M. (2012a). *Immigration nation: Raids, detentions, and deportations in post-9/11 America*. New York: Routledge.

Golash-Boza, T. M. (2012b). *Due process denied: Detentions and deportations in the United States*. New York: Routledge.

Golash-Boza, T. M. (2015). *Deported: Policing immigrants, disposable labor and global capitalism*. New York: New York University Press.

Gómez, L. E. (2007). *Manifest destinies: The making of the Mexican American race*. New York: New York University Press.

Gordon, C. (1991). Governmental rationality: An introduction. In G. Burchell, C. Gordon, & P. Miller (Eds.), *The Foucault effect: Studies in governmentality* (pp. 1–52) Chicago, IL: University of Chicago Press.

Heyman, J. M. (1999). Why interdiction? Immigration control at the United States-Mexico border. *Regional Studies, 33*(7), 619–630.

Heyman, J. M. (2008). Constructing a virtual wall: Race and citizenship in U.S.-Mexico border policing. *Journal of the Southwest, 50*(3), 305–334.

Holmes, M. (1998). Perceptions of abusive police practices in a U.S.-Mexico border community. *The Social Science Journal, 35*(1), 107–118.

Holmes, M. (2000). Minority threat and police brutality: Determinants of civil rights criminal complaints in U.S. municipalities. *Criminology, 38*(2), 343–367.

Human Rights Watch. (1998). *Shielded from justice: Police brutality and accountability in the United States*. Retrieved from http://www.hrw.org/legacy/reports98/police/index.htm.

Jacobs, D., & O'Brien, R. (1998). The determinants of deadly force: A structural analysis of police violence. *American Journal of Sociology, 103*(4), 837–862.

Jimenez, M. (2009). *Humanitarian crisis: Migrant deaths at the U.S.-Mexico border*. American Civil Liberties Union. Retrieved from https://www.aclu.org/files/pdfs/immigrants/humanitariancrisisreport.pdf.

Johnson, J. (2012). A Palestine-Mexico border. North American Congress on Latin America. Retrieved from https://nacla.org/blog/2012/6/29/palestine-mexico-border.

Kagel, J. (2014, July 20). There's something scary happening on the left side of this picture. Mic. Retrieved from http://mic.com/articles/94032/there-s-something-scary-happening-on-the-left-side-of-this-picture#.paI2MbnMb.

Kane, R., & White, M. (2013). *Bad cops, police misconduct, and the New York City Police Department.* New York: New York University Press.

Klein, N. (2007). *The shock doctrine: The rise of disaster capitalism.* New York: Picador.

Kraska, P. B., & Kappeler, V. E. (1997). Militarizing American police: The rise and normalization of paramilitary units. *Social Problems, 44*(1), 1–18.

Lopéz, I. F. H. (2006). *White by law: The legal construction of race.* New York: New York University Press.

Lyon, D. (1994). *The electronic eye: The rise of surveillance society.* Minneapolis: University of Minnesota Press.

Lyon, D. (2015). *Surveillance after Snowden.* Cambridge, UK: Polity Press.

Lytle, K. (2003). *Constructing the criminal alien: A historical framework for analyzing border vigilantes at the turn of the 21st century* (Working Paper 83). San Diego: University of California-San Diego Center for Comparative Immigration Studies.

Martinez, R. (2015). *Latino homicide: Immigration, violence, and community.* New York: Routledge.

Massey, D. S., Durand, J., & Malone, N. J. (2002). *Beyond smoke and mirrors: Mexican immigration in an era of economic integration.* New York: Russell Sage Foundation.

McDowell, M., & Wonders, N. A. (2010). Keeping migrants in their place: Technologies of control and racialized public space in Arizona. *Social Justice, 36*(2), 54–72.

Michalowski, R. J. (2007). Border militarization and migrant suffering: A case of transnational inquiry. *Social Justice, 34*(2), 60–72.

Miller, T. (2014). *Border Patrol nation: Dispatches from the front lines of homeland security.* San Francisco, CA: City Lights Publishers.

Miller, T., & Schivone, G. (2015). Gaza in Arizona: The secret militarization of the U.S.-Mexico border. *Salon.* Retrieved from http://www.salon.com/2015/02/01/gaza_in_arizona_the_secret_militarization_of_the_u_s_mexico_border_partner/.

Mirandé, A. (1987). *Gringo justice.* Notre Dame, IN: University of Notre Dame.

Morales, A. (1972). *Ando sangrando: A study of Mexican American-police conflict.* La Puenta, CA: Perspectiva Publications.

Morín, J. L. (2009). *Latino/a rights and justice in the United States: Perspectives and approaches* (2nd ed.). Durham, NC: Carolina Academic Press.

Nevins, J. (2010). *Operation gatekeeper and beyond: The war on "illegals" and the remaking of the U.S.-Mexico boundary.* New York: Routledge.

Nevins, J. (2011). Scenes from an occupation. *Dissident Voice.* Retrieved from http://dissidentvoice.org/2011/05/scenes-from-an-occupation/.

Parenti, C. (1999). *Lockdown America: Police and prisons in the age of crisis*. New York: Verso.

Pew Research Center. (2014). *Stark racial divisions in reactions to Ferguson police shooting*. Washington, DC: Pew Research Center.

Phillips, S., Rodriguez, N., & Hagan, J. (2002). Brutality at the border: Use of force in the arrest of immigrants in the United States. *International Journal of the Sociology of Law, 30*(4), 285–306.

Romero, M. (2006). Racial profiling and immigration enforcement: Rounding up of usual suspects in the Latino community. *Critical Sociology, 32*(2–3), 447–472.

Russell, K. (1998). *The color of crime: Racial hoaxes, white fear, black protectionism, police harassment, and other macroaggressions*. New York: New York University Press.

Salinas, L. S. (2015). *U.S. Latinos and criminal injustice*. East Lansing, MI: Michigan State University Press.

Sidanius, J., Liu, J. H., Shaw, J. S., & Pratto, F. (1994). Social dominance orientation, hierarchy attenuators and hierarchy enhancers: Social dominance theory and the criminal justice system. *Journal of Applied Social Psychology, 24*(4), 338–366.

Sidanius, J., & Pratto, F. (1999). *Social dominance: An intergroup theory of social hierarchy and oppression*. New York: Cambridge University Press.

Simon, J. (1997). Governing through crime. In L. Friedman & G. Fisher (Eds.), *The crime conundrum* (pp. 171–185). Oxford: Oxford University Press.

Skolnick, J. (2011). *Justice without trial: Law enforcement in democratic society*. New Orleans, LA: Quid Pro Books.

Skolnick, J., & Fyfe, J. (1993). *Above the law: Police and the excessive use of force*. New York: Free Press.

Smith, B., & Holmes, M. (2003). Community accountability, minority threat, and police brutality: An examination of civil rights criminal complaints. *Criminology, 41*(4), 1035–1064.

Stephen, L. (2004). The gaze of surveillance in the lives of Mexican immigrant workers. *Development, 47*(1), 97–102.

Tirman, J. (2015). The immigration debate is not about legality, it's about crime. Huffington Post. Retrieved from http://www.huffingtonpost.com/john-tirman/the-immigration-debate-is-not-about-legality_b_6876910.html.

U.S. Government Accountability Office. (2013). *Southwest border security: Data are limited and concerns vary about spillover crime along the southwest border*. Retrieved from http://trac.syr.edu/immigration/library/P7176.pdf.

Urbina, M. G. (Ed.). (2012). *Hispanics in the U.S. criminal justice system: The new American demography*. Springfield, IL: Charles C Thomas.

Urbina, M. G. (Ed.). (2014). *Twenty-first century dynamics of multiculturalism: Beyond post-racial America.* Springfield, IL: Charles C Thomas.

Urbina, M. G., & Álvarez, S. E. (Eds.). (2015). *Latino police officers in the United States: An examination of emerging trends and issues.* Springfield, IL: Charles C Thomas.

Urbina, M. G., & Álvarez, S. E. (2016). Neoliberalism, criminal justice, and Latinos: The contours of neoliberal economic thought and policy on criminalization. *Latino Studies, 14*(1), 33–54.

Urbina, M. G., Vela, J. E., & Sánchez, J. O. (2014). *Ethnic realities of Mexican Americans: From colonialism to 21st century globalization.* Springfield, IL: Charles C Thomas.

Walker, S. (1998). *Popular justice: A history of American criminal justice* (2nd ed.). New York: Oxford University Press.

Welch, M. (2002). *Detained: Immigration laws and the expanding I.N.S. jail complex.* Philadelphia: Temple University Press.

Welch, M. (2006). *Scapegoats of September 11th: Hate crimes and state crimes in the war on terror.* New Brunswick, NJ: Rutgers University Press.

Welch, M. (2007). Immigration lockdown before and after 9/11: Ethnic constructions and their consequences. In M. Bosworth & J. Flavin (Eds.), *Race, gender, and punishment: From colonialism to the war on terror* (pp. 149–166). Piscataway, NJ: Rutgers University Press.

Welch, M. (2009). *Crimes of power & states of impunity: The U.S. response to terror.* New Brunswick, NJ: Rutgers University Press.

Whitehead, J. (2013). *A government of wolves: The emerging American police state.* New York: SelectBooks.

Whitlock, C., & Timberg, C. (2014). Border-patrol drones being borrowed by other agencies more often than previously known. *The Washington Post.* Retrieved from https://www.washingtonpost.com/world/national-security/border-patrol-drones-being-borrowed-by-other-agencies-more-often-than-previously-known/2014/01/14/5f987af0-7d49-11e3-9556-4a4bf7bcbd84_story.html.

6

Rural Law Enforcement: Real Police Work?

Robert Hartmann McNamara

When one thinks of rural policing, it is easy to evoke images of life as depicted on *The Andy Griffith Show,* a popular sitcom in the 1960s. The show characterized rural life as slow paced, with little or no crime, and the relationships formed by citizens with each other were personal and long lasting. Otis, the town drunk on the show, even knew where the key to "his" cell was so that when he staggered into the jail, he would simply take the key, unlock the cell, and proceed to sleep off a heavy night of drinking. The sheriff did not even need to find Otis to make an arrest—Otis "arrested" himself. Life in Mayberry was easy, friendly, and generally without conflict. The role of the sheriff, Andy, was to mediate minor conflicts between people, to represent a peaceable kind of order, and to spend a good deal of time fishing with his son.

Barney Fife, the generally well-meaning, but quasi-competent and only deputy in the sheriff's department, often attempted to bring a legalistic law enforcement style into an otherwise service style department and town. In fact, much of the show was dedicated to having Andy repairing problems within the community that Barney created. In fact, because of his concerns about Barney's competence, Andy gave him only one bullet for his sidearm, and that was to be kept in his shirt pocket (The Andy Griffith Show Wiki, 2017).

These images of rural life as depicted in the show have an enduring quality despite numerous changes that have taken place along the American landscape. The U.S. Census Bureau estimates that about 80% of Americans live in cities and suburban areas, the latter of which is a modern-day creation as cities have grown in size (United States Census, 2013). Still, the fact that nearly 20% of the population is living in rural areas suggests that rural issues are important ones. For our purposes, we will focus on the changes in rural areas as they relate to crime and policing. Compared to urban areas, life may take on a more fixed pattern in rural communities but they are hardly insulated from larger social problems like crime. This means that policing in rural areas is unique in some ways given the nature of social life there, but it is changing to some degree as well. For instance, while it remains the case that rural police officers generally receive less training than their urban counterparts, and while departmental policies in rural police agencies tend to be less rigid or clearly established, the introduction of gangs and methamphetamine labs requires rural police officers to receive more training in these areas.

Recent incidents with police officers involved in use of deadly force, particularly as it relates to White officers shooting Black suspects, which has led to riots and community uprisings, raises many questions about police officers' fears about the performance of their duties. As of this writing, in a recent incident involving a police detective who was pistol whipped by a suspect, the detective stated that he was afraid to use his weapon, despite being justified in doing so, because he feared a public backlash since he was White and the suspects were Black (Chan, 2015).

The nature of these problems also suggests that departments establish new policies on how to deal with challenging problems and populations. This chapter begins with a discussion of the issues surrounding rural life and then offers insight into the life of rural police officers.

What Is Rural?

Defining rural areas seems, at first glance, to be a rather simple matter—it is the opposite of urban. But that does not solve the problem since defining "urban" is just as difficult a task. To some, rural is a geographical area; to others it might be a set of values, attitudes, and beliefs about a way of life. For still others, even if agreement is reached that rural constitutes a geographic location, the boundaries are often subjective. This makes any assessment of "rural" a difficult task. One might think to look to federal agencies for help in defining a rural area. This seems logical, but there is great variability there as well. The General Accounting Office (2008) offers a report that discusses the three most common federal definitions of rural: the one used by the Census Bureau; the White House's Office of Management and Budget's definition, and the one used by the Department of Agriculture's Economic Research Service.

The Bureau of the Census defines an urbanized area (UA) by population density. According to this definition, each UA includes a central city and the surrounding densely settled territory that together have a population of 50,000 or more and a population density generally exceeding 1,000 people per square mile. Incidentally, a "county" is not incorporated in the Bureau of the Census' classification scheme, so one UA may cover parts of several counties. Under this definition, all persons living in UAs and in places (cities, towns, villages, etc.) with a population of 2,500 or more outside of UAs are considered the urban population. All others are considered rural.

The White House Office of Management and Budget (OMB) designates areas as "metro" or urban, on the basis of standards released in January 1980. According to this definition, each metropolitan statistical area (MSA) must include at least one city with 50,000 or more inhabitants or an urbanized area (defined by the Bureau of the Census) with at least 50,000 inhabitants and a total MSA population of at least 100,000. These standards provide that each MSA must include the county in which the central city is located (the central county) and additional contiguous counties (fringe counties), if they are economically and socially integrated with the central county. Any county not included in an MSA is considered "non-metro" or rural.

U.S. Department of Agriculture's Economic Research Service (USDA) uses a rural-urban continuum code to distinguish metro and non-metro counties by their degree of urbanization or proximity to metro areas. This coding scheme consists of 0–3 for metro areas and 4–9 for non-metro areas. For example, a code of 4, the closest to an urban area, would be an urban population that contains a population of 20,000 or more and is adjacent to a metro area. A code of 9, the other end of the continuum, would be considered completely rural with a population of fewer than 2,500 not adjacent to a metro area.

These differing definitions create confusion in categorizing a given area and it also affects the estimated size of rural America. For example, The Census Bureau classifies 61.7 million (25%) of the total population as rural, while the OMB classifies 55.9 million (23%) of the total population as rural. The differing definitions used by the federal government also impact how researchers who study rural areas define them. This creates a significant problem with regard to estimating the extent of a problem in a given area as well as how many people it affects.

As Weisheit, Falcone, and Wells (2006) have noted, while most people would not define areas with large populations as rural, some studies have used samples of cities consisting of 175,000 people or even 500,000 people as rural areas. The moral of the story is that it is very important to assess how researchers de-

Table 6.1: Distribution of Police Agencies and Population in the U.S., 2013

Population Group	Number of Agencies	Population Covered
I (250,000 inhabitants and more)	78	58,379,497
II (100,000 to 249,999 inhabitants)	217	32,344,679
III (50,000 to 99,999 inhabitants)	484	33,381,466
IV (25,000 to 49,999 inhabitants)	889	30,734,287
V (10,000 to 24,999 inhabitants)	1,918	30,507,058
VI (Less than 10,000 inhabitants)	9,633	26,639,602
VIII (Nonmetropolitan County)	2,915	27,876,167
IX (Metropolitan County)	2,281	76,266,083
Total	18,415	316,128,839

Source: Department of Justice, Federal Bureau of Investigation. 2013. *Crime in the United States, 2013.* Washington, DC: U.S. Government Printing Office.

fine "rural" in order to evaluate their findings. Because there is no universal or agreed-upon definition, the study of rural life is fraught with difficulty and the patterns that have emerged should be viewed and interpreted with caution.

For our purposes, as it relates to the measurement of crime, the Uniform Crime Reports uses the following categories to identify urban and rural areas. If one were to take only the extreme ends of the population category, rural residents make up about 57 million people or about 18% of the population (Groups V and VI). What Table 1 also shows is that of the 18,415 law enforcement agencies in this country, about 63%, or 11, 551, serve those two population groups. This suggests that much of policing in America is of a rural variety. While the images of the NYPD or the LAPD are common ones for people to think about in terms of law enforcement, much of the work of police officers is conducted in small agencies.

Rural Crime

In perhaps the seminal work on the topic of rural policing and rural crime, Weisheit, Falcone, and Wells (2006) offer insight into the differences between urban and rural crime as well as some of the unique challenges facing rural police officers. Since the original publication in 1994, much of the research on this topic, although limited, is consistent in identifying a number of trends in terms of the characteristics of rural life as well as the challenges presented to policing in those areas. For instance, while many might think of traditional crimes such as gangs, drugs, and drunk driving (DUI) as urban crime problems, rural areas have been significantly affected by these problems as well.

Gangs

It would be difficult to avoid the discussion of gangs in any reference to the crime problem in the United States. The research on gangs has primarily focused on urban, inner-city areas and placed an emphasis on its relationship to drugs, crime, and violence (see McNamara & Burns, 2008). While the peak period for gang activity appeared to be in the mid-1990s, gang experts have noted that gangs have spread to suburban and rural areas as well.

While the presence of gangs has been documented in rural areas, with police departments participating in training and task forces to address gang-related problems, the real question is whether or not gangs have actually migrated or if the recent national attention paid to gangs has made them more noticeable in rural areas. Part of the difficulty in answering this question is the lack of data available about rural gangs as well as the methodological difficulties of charting gang activity.

An added difficulty in the study of gangs has been the motivation for gang membership appears to be changing. Some evidence exists that many of the reasons for joining a gang, e.g., the sense of belonging, pseudo-family structure, and loyalty to one's in-group as well as social cohesion among its members, has shifted to more economically based reasons. Some studies have identified an increasing tendency for youth to form what are called **hybrid gangs**, which consist of members of different gangs who come together for a particular activity, such as the drug trade. While this tendency has occurred in the past, it was sporadic and relatively rare. Gang experts are now asserting that there is an increasing trend within gangs, even arch rivals such as Bloods and Crips, to interact and work together in various ways (see for instance, Starbuck, Howell, & Lindquist, 2001).

According to the National Gang Youth Survey, conducted by the National Youth Gang Center, the number of cities and towns that report a gang presence was more than 3,400 in 2008. In 2012, that number decreased to 3,100. This higher rate of reporting by law enforcement agencies is consistent with other estimates, which show an increase in the number of gangs and gang members in urban areas and a decrease in rural ones; the latter showed a ten percent decrease in smaller cities and towns. In contrast, gang activity seems to be increasing in urban areas in recent times. Nationally, in 2012 there were an estimated 30,700 gangs and 850,000 members. This is in contrast to 2005, where there were 26,000 gangs identified with approximately 790,000 members.

The National Youth Gang Survey also asks each law enforcement agency to provide an overall general assessment of the current gang problem in their jurisdiction compared to previous years. In 2005, a slight majority (53%) of agencies that reported a gang problem also assessed their gang problem as "getting worse" compared to 2004. In contrast, in 2012, 55% of the responding agencies characterized their gang problems as "staying about the same," the largest percentage in the survey's history.

Taken as a whole, the results of the 2012 NYGS continue to emphasize the expansiveness and seriousness of the gang problem across the United States. Following a marked decline throughout the late 1990s, gang-prevalence rates, as well as estimated total gang membership size, have increased in recent years (Egley & O'Donnel, 2008).

Other findings relate to the increase in gang-related violence. Reports of homicides in general, and gang-related homicides in particular, are predominantly concentrated in the largest cities across the United States—approximately two-thirds of all homicides in the Uniform Crime Reports (UCR) and approximately three-fourths of all gang-related homicides recorded in the National Gang Survey occurred in cities with populations over 50,000 between 2002 and 2004. In 2005, law enforcement agencies reported that the gang problem appeared to involve more adults than juveniles. Law enforcement agencies report a greater percentage of adult (18 and over) gang members compared with juvenile (under 18) gang members (National Youth Gang Survey, 2005; Liederbach, 2007). In 2012, responding agencies reported a total of 2,363 gang-related homicides in the United States. According to the Uniform Crime Reports for that year, there were more than 14,800 homicides nationally. These findings suggest that gangs were involved in approximately 16% of all homicides in the United States in 2012, an increase of more than 20 percent from the previous five-year period (Egley, Howell, & Harris, 2012).

What the data suggested in 2005 was that, in general, the gang problem was growing, there was a greater level of gang violence, and that gangs seemed to be migrating to all areas of the country. The data from 2012 suggests a different trend, with less emphasis on rural gangs and a greater concentration of the problem in urban areas. However, it is important to note that while the gang problem continues to plague many cities across the country, the spread of gangs is not systematic or even. Gangs are found in all communities, but they are less common in smaller communities and rural counties. This is even true during the explosive growth seen in the mid-1990s, when gang membership peaked all across the country (Payne, Berg, & Sun, 2005).

This is not to say that gangs in rural areas do not pose problems for residents or the law enforcement community. However, the research suggests that gangs in rural areas tend to be less structured, smaller, and more transitory than gangs in urban areas. In general, gangs in small towns also tend to be more racially and ethnically diverse (Wells & Weisheit, 2004). This is likely given that smaller populations in rural areas, which tend to have lower rates of minority populations, tend to have fewer members of any one group to draw from in forming a gang. This also means that perhaps the tendency for the formation of hybrid gangs might be more common in rural areas than in urban ones. However, currently no empirical evidence exists to support this conclusion.

The research also shows that rural gangs are less likely than urban gangs to be involved in systematic crime, particularly as it relates to violence and drug trafficking (Weisheit, Falcone, & Wells, 2006; Brock, Copeland, & Scott, 2001). It is also the case that rural gangs are not simply satellite chapters of their more urban communities. Some of the research on the subject suggests that while some dispersion of urban gang members to rural areas occurs, it is less likely to be the reason for the increased attention to rural gangs. The popular image of the Crips and the Bloods sending recruiters to the Midwest to establish chapters of the gang may make for interesting headlines, but the reality is that the gang members in the Midwest were there long before the media images of gang migration occurred. While it is also true that gang members do migrate, the reasons for this stem largely from family decisions to move away from urban areas rather than a "corporate" decision of gangs sending members to new locations.

Granted, families move to rural areas for a number of reasons and if gang members are present in those families, it can lead to the development of gang chapters in those areas. However, that is a far cry from the conspiracy theorists who contend that urban gangs have planned and methodically targeted rural areas as locations for growth and expansion (Johnson, Hall, & Sabri, 2007).

Even with the existence of gang migration, both anecdotal and empirical, the fact that rural gangs are not as violent or as involved in criminal activities as urban gangs, suggests a number of fundamental differences between the two. While some urban gang members who move to rural areas may bring much of the gang culture with them, the evidence suggests that they do not have the kind of impact as portrayed in the media (Egley & Major, 2003; Wells & Weisheit, 2001).

Drugs

Perhaps the area in which rural communities have been given the most attention by the public and by the criminal justice system has been in the area of drugs, specifically their manufacture and distribution. While marijuana growers have long used rural areas, including state forests, to grow their crops and transport them to urban settings for distribution (see, for instance, Weisheit, 1992), recently the rise of methamphetamine, also known as "crank," has become particularly problematic for rural communities. While not new to rural areas, crank has become the drug of choice for both users and distributors in rural areas. As Weisheit and Fuller (2004) found, unlike most drugs, which initially become popular in urban areas and then find their way into rural communities, methamphetamine is one of the few drugs that became popular among users in rural areas and then spread to urban locations.

Like its urban counterpart, crack, methamphetamine is popular because it is cheap, relatively easy to make, and creates an intense high for users. What is particularly problematic about methamphetamine is the increased number of makeshift laboratories that have sprung up in rural areas to manufacture the drug. Rural areas are ideal locations for making crank, in part because of the privacy and isolation offered by a remote location. Additionally, the byproducts of producing the drug produce offensive odors and a significant amount of toxic waste product (up to five pounds of waste for every pound of methamphetamine produced). Often, this waste is dumped in rural areas and it contaminates the soil and water supply (Hertz, 2000).

In addition, one of the easiest ways of making methamphetamine involves the use of anhydrous ammonia, which is a common farm fertilizer stored in large tanks dotting the rural farmland. Thus, rural areas offer concealment, ample places to dump waste material from the manufacture of the drug, and easy access to chemicals without arousing much suspicion. Making crank is not difficult, does not require sophisticated processing equipment, and uses many common chemicals found in rural areas (Weisheit, Falcone, & Wells, 2006; see also Garriott, 2010). It is not surprising then that the number of people attempting to make this drug, both for personal use and for distribution purposes, has increased.

This is perhaps one of the most alarming trends in addressing crank in rural America: individuals who set up "meth labs" often do not have sufficient training, are users who get high while making the drug, or are simply careless in handling it since they do not understand the volatile properties of the drug, the chemicals, or the fact that the toxic waste generated from making the drug

Table 6.2: Rates of DUI Arrests by Population Size

UCR Grouping	Number of Arrests	Rate
Group I (Cities 250,000 or larger)	118,787	267.5
Group II (Cities 100,000–249,000)	72,207	272.3
Group III (Cities 50,000–99,999)	78,312	278.5
Group IV (Cities 25,000–49,999)	76,851	306.0
Group V (Cities 10,000–24,999)	88,885	368.6
Group VI (Cities less than 10,000)	97,687	512.0

Source: U.S. Department of Justice, Federal Bureau of Investigation. 2013. *Crime in the United States 2013*, Table 31. Washington, DC: U.S. Government Printing Office.

can result in explosions. The Drug Enforcement Administration (2003) refers to these small-time operations as "mom and pop" or "Beavis and Butthead" operations, but they represent the vast majority of meth labs across the country. According to the DEA's estimates, crank is the number one drug of choice in rural America and its manufacture is most common in rural areas.

DUI

Another feature of rural life is a greater use of alcohol. A consequence of higher levels of alcohol use in rural areas is driving while intoxicated arrests (DUI). In fact, arrests for DUI are much more common in rural areas. As Table 2 shows, according to the Uniform Crime Reports in 2013, the rate of arrest for DUI in cities of fewer than 10,000 people was nearly twice that of DUI arrests for cities with 250,000 people or more.

Some of this may be due to law enforcement practices, where rural officers, given the lower number of calls for service by residents, may focus more attention on drunk driving than in urban areas. Or rural officers may simply be more likely to be vigilant about DUI arrests than urban departments. The reason for this may stem from the very nature of rural life, where the geographic dispersion means greater distances between school, home, and recreational facilities. This, coupled with the lack of adequate public transportation, means that people, particularly youth, must travel great distances and spend considerable amounts of time in their cars.

In addition, the overall lack of traffic means that people who have been drinking (in addition to those who have not) are more likely to drive at excessive speeds while on the road. While this is normally a problem for all communities, add alcohol to the formula as well as the generally poor conditions of rural roads and the likelihood of an accident increases dramatically (Peters, Oetting, & Edwards, 1992). Thus, for many reasons, DUIs are a more common occurrence in rural areas than in urban ones.

Hate Crime

One of the general features of rural living, according to many estimates, is an overall mistrust of the government (see, for instance, Weisheit, Falcone, & Wells, 2006; 1994) as well as an emphasis on independence and freedom (Coates, 1987; Dyer, 1997). Hate groups and hate crimes thrive on the features of rural life in that the isolation found in such areas provide group members with a type of privacy not available in urban or suburban areas. In addition, the general climate of rural culture provides hate groups with an environment that might be more sympathetic to its causes than what might be found in urban or suburban communities. In fact, the origins of many hate groups can be traced to isolated rural communities for exactly this reason (Coates, 1987).

Given that many of these groups foment hate based on the distrust of the government, whom they say caters to minorities, immigrants, and others who might take jobs away from more deserving Whites, such groups can usually find like-minded people in rural areas since many policy changes impact semi-skilled and low-skilled workers, many of whom live in rural areas. Added to this is a willingness to use violence to solve problems, an important component to rural living. While rural residents are not necessarily violent by nature, rural culture, with its emphasis on personal freedom and a frontier justice mentality, makes a violent solution more likely to be accepted by more people in rural areas than in other sections of the country (Dyer, 1997; Watson, 2002; Coates, 1987; Weisheit, Falcone, & Wells, 2006).

Agricultural and Wildlife Crime: Only in Rural Areas

According to the U.S. Department of Agriculture, the overall value of crops, livestock, and poultry sold in the U.S. in 2015 was more than $432 billion, with a net income of $73.6 billion (U.S. Department of Agriculture, 2015). Interestingly, despite such a valued industry, little in the way of research has been conducted on agricultural crime. The theft of livestock, farm equipment, and product is a problem unique to rural areas. In fact, as one expert pointed out, the very nature of farm life leads to its susceptibility to victimization (Barcaly, 2001).

Large farms may be dispersed over a wide geographic area, making police patrol very difficult. Further, given the fact that neighbors live so far apart from each other, isolation is a much more a common feature of farm life. This means that crimes like theft, vandalism, and burglary are much more likely to either go unreported or unnoticed for extended periods of time.

Additionally, it is relatively common for farmers to leave expensive equipment in the fields or on the side of the road or to fail to properly identify their property in the event it gets stolen. This casual attitude about crime prevention often results in victimization (see Weisheit, Falcone, & Wells, 2006).

While simple theft and vandalism is a significant expense to farmers, the most lucrative area of agricultural crime is the theft of farming chemicals. Despite the fact that this crime is lucrative and relatively easy to carry out, particularly given the mobility and small size of chemicals, making them easy to transport, and given the general nature of farm life, which has a tendency to be lacking in crime prevention, very little research has been conducted on this subject. What is known are anecdotal stories in the news about such instances, but there has not been a definitive study of this type of crime (Weisheit, Falcone, & Wells, 2006).

Similar to agricultural crimes, which are clearly something unique to rural areas, poaching has become a highly profitable industry. According to the World Wildlife Fund as well as the Wildlife Alliance, poaching is a multi-billion dollar a year industry in the U.S. Poaching includes fish, deer, and other animals that are sold on the black market for a profit. While the international trade for things like ivory (of which U.S. is the world's largest importer and the second largest importer of illegal endangered species pelts, parts, and live animals), the local poaching of animals such hunting of deer and other animals out of season, as well as some forms of fishing, have historically been linked to poverty: illegal hunting was a means of survival. Today, poaching appears to be related to the challenge of evading wildlife officers as well as capturing trophies rather than profit (Forsyth & Marckese, 1993).

Other research on poaching suggests that most poachers are chronic offenders and have been arrested for other crimes. Thus, poaching is but one example of a long list of criminal activities. In addition, research on poaching suggests that drugs and alcohol are often involved, making the combination of drugs, guns, and the thrill and excitement of avoiding conservation officers a potentially deadly combination (Chitty, 1994).

Rural Policing vs. Urban Policing

Given the nature of rural life, it would seem that in some ways policing these areas would be qualitatively different than what occurs in urban communities. This is true, because the nature of social interaction is different as well as the relationship between the police and the public they serve. Additionally, the structure of policing is different as well. While urban or suburban areas typically consist of a local law enforcement agency for a given city or town, in rural areas the number and type of departments change considerably.

The central feature of rural law enforcement is the sheriff's office, which typically has jurisdiction over the entire county. Sheriff's offices in urban areas are usually confined in terms of their duties and operations, and in some places are restricted to serving summonses. Another feature of rural law enforcement is the state highway patrol, which is primarily responsible for traffic incidents on major thoroughfares. State troopers have also been used in very small towns where there is no police agency. Known in some circles as "resident state troopers" these individuals are the only representation of law enforcement in those areas.

In addition, rural areas typically have conservation officers to handle the poaching of wildlife as well as a federal law enforcement presence, particularly in border areas. At the local level, while it may appear that being a police officer in a rural area consists of fewer calls for service, a great deal of discretion in handling cases, and generally a lot of free time, as we have seen, the changing nature of rural life has brought with it a number of challenges for rural police departments. What is significant about this discussion is that, as was mentioned, most police departments are small in size, making it difficult for officers to specialize.

According to the most recent figures available, in 2013, nationally, about 46% of the nation's local police departments have fewer than 10 sworn officers. In addition, almost 89% of all local departments have fewer than 50 sworn officers. As Table 3 demonstrates, while it is interesting to consider departments such those in Los Angeles and the NYPD, it must be noted that departments of that size represent a very small percentage of most operations: less than 1% of all departments have more than 500 sworn officers and only 4% have between 100 and 500 officers. Thus, the standards used in those types of agencies are unrealistic for most departments in the United States.

What is interesting about the size of the departments around the country relates to the services they provide. In rural areas, the geographic dispersion requires officers to travel considerable distances on patrol and to answer calls for service. It also means that fewer officers provide general police coverage to

Table 6.3: Size of Police Departments—U.S. 2013

Number Sworn Personnel	Number of Agencies	Percentage
500 or more	106	.09%
100–499	539	4.4%
50–99	788	6.4%
25–49	1,653	13.4%
10–24	3,345	27.1%
5–9	2,996	24.3%
2–4	2,294	18.6%
1	605	4.9%
Total	12,656	100%

Source: Sedgwick, J. L. (2013). *Local police departments 2013.* Washington, DC: U.S. Department of Justice, Bureau of Justice Statistics.

a population that is already small and getting smaller, as more people move to suburban areas. Unlike their urban counterparts, who may have specialized divisions for certain activities, rural officers must be generalists and usually have a heavy workload due to the fact that handling any call for service typically takes more time due to the distance traveled.

It also means that rural departments' budgets are being strained since comprehensive services are required despite the fact that tax bases in rural areas are shrinking as more people move away. This is significant since local police departments, unlike other businesses, cannot simply cut back on the services they offer because of less funding.

Additionally, as was mentioned in the discussion on drunk driving, given the quality of the roads on which they travel, which are generally worse in rural areas than in urban ones, motor vehicle accidents and fatalities are higher in rural areas than in urban ones. According to the National Highway Traffic Safety Administration (2012), the fatality rate per 100 million vehicle miles traveled was 2.4 times higher in rural areas than in urban ones. This means motor vehicle deaths are more than twice as high in rural areas than in urban ones. Additionally, despite the fact that 19 percent of the U.S. population lived in rural areas in 2012, 54 percent of all traffic fatalities occurred in rural areas.

Table 6.4: Comparison of Clearance Rates for Violent and Property Crime: Urban vs. Rural Categories, 2013

Population Category	Violent Crime	Property Crime
Group I (>500,000)	38.4% (346,619)	13.8% (1,839,561)
Group II	43.6% (154,057)	17.6% (1,131,898)
Group III	47.9% (113,210)	20.2% (950,446)
Group IV	50.3% (84,484)	23.3% (827,833)
Group V	54.5% (74,008)	25.1% (773,096)
Group VI (<10,000)	56.7% (61,895)	22.7% (676,308)

Source: *Crime in the United States, 2013, Table 25, Percent of Offenses Cleared by Arrest or Exceptional Means.*

Geographic dispersion not only means it takes longer for officers to answer a call for service or to render assistance of some type, it also means that they are less likely to have other officers backing them up on a particular call. The danger involved in some types of calls is significant, particularly if the officer does not have assistance readily available. This is especially true in domestic violence cases or traffic stops, two of the most common situations in which officers are injured or killed.

Finally, given the broader scope required of rural police agencies in terms of providing services to the public, the relationships officers have within the community is often qualitatively different than what is seen in urban policing. This has an impact not only on police-community relationships, but also on the overall effectiveness of rural officers in general (Weisheit, Falcone, & Wells, 2006).

Effectiveness of Rural Police

The plots of *The Andy Griffith Show* depict Deputy Barney Fife as a bumbling and incompetent police officer. While it is true that the media has historically portrayed most police officers in this way (Inciardi, 1987), the general perception of rural police officers may be even worse in terms of whether or not they are effective in dealing with crime. However, if one looks at the data and uses a relatively standard criterion used to evaluate the effectiveness of police officers, clearance rates, the Uniform Crime Reports shows that rural agencies consistently have higher clearance rates than agencies in cities of 250,000 or more people (see Table 4).

Granted, some of this pattern may be explained by differing reporting rates, where people in rural areas are more likely to know the officer as well as the suspect, while the officers are also likely to have a smaller pool of potential offenders, which makes locating and arresting them easier than in urban areas. For whatever reason, the fact is that if clearance rates are used as a marker of police effectiveness, and they typically are, then rural police officers are actually more effective than their urban counterparts in addressing crime.

Additionally, another marker of police effectiveness relates to satisfaction levels by the customer: the public. Generally speaking, the research suggests that rural residents have greater levels of satisfaction with the police than do urban residents. Part of the reason for this may have to do with the relationships officers build with residents, with some officers having grown up in the area. Both of these factors may influence the officers' style of policing. This, in turn, helps officers tailor the services provided to meet the needs of community members (Weisheit, Falcone, 7 Wells, 2006). Thus, the way residents perceive the police is different in rural areas than in urban ones, which also affects their levels of satisfaction with the service they receive from officers.

Rural Policing Issues and Concerns

The research shows that there are a number of issues that rural officers face that are different in some ways and unique in others when compared to urban policing. While time does not permit a thorough examination of all the differences between rural and urban policing, there are three primary issues that serve as illustrations of many of the other problems. These include the unique types of stress rural officers face, violence perpetrated against officers, and the extent and type of police corruption in rural areas. Additionally, there is some debate about whether or not community policing actually occurs in any meaningful form in rural areas. These four issues will be discussed in greater detail.

Stress

According to Zhao, Thurman, and He (1999) stress is defined as "something that is imposed on a person usually from outside, that is, external or personal factors that bring about some degree of physical or psychological discomfort" (p. 153). The available research suggests that rural police officers face similar types of stress as urban officers, all of which are embedded in the nature of police work, such as fatigue, injury, inadequate training, etc. (Sandy & Devine, 1978).

However, Oliver and Meier (2004) offer insight into four unique stressors found in the nature of rural policing. First, because of geographical isolation and the limited number of officers on duty at any given time, rural police officers face more stress related to their personal safety and security. As was mentioned, some calls create particular hazards for officers, such as handling domestic violence calls or motor vehicle stops without the benefit of backup. However, in light of the isolation, one can argue that virtually every call answered by a rural police officer heightens stress levels. This is somewhat tempered by the relationships officers form with residents, making the risk to the lone officer potentially lower. However, this can also be a double-edged sword in that officers may be put in a difficult position *because* of their relationship with residents.

Second, there is a lack of anonymity in rural areas for officers. Officers in urban areas typically live outside of the community they serve and this can insulate them from complaints while off-duty, not to mention enhancing their ability to leave the stress at work. The same can't be said of rural police officers, who, given the remoteness of some areas, are forced to live in the communities they serve. In these cases, even off-duty officers are visible representatives of the department. In addition, given the small size of the department, there are fewer places officers can go to relax unnoticed and even fewer colleagues with whom to share their concerns about the job.

Third, the salaries and equipment and training opportunities are more limited in rural areas than in urban departments. This relates to the lower tax base as more residents move to suburban areas, but the problem is further complicated by the hiring crunch currently experienced in law enforcement across the country. As more departments begin to develop recruiting programs, including offering signing bonuses and low interest rate mortgages for new officers, rural departments find it increasingly difficult to compete with their larger and urban counterparts for the best candidates.

Finally, Sandy and Devine (1978) point to the nature of rural life as a problem for police officers: long periods of inactivity, low crime rates, and few calls for service. While some might see this as an advantage in that it reduces officers' risk of injury, boredom is a chronic problem in rural policing. At an extreme, officers can begin to feel as though what they do does not matter, grow apathetic, and leave the department.

Violence against Police

The evidence at first glance seems to suggest that violent crime occurs much more frequently in urban settings than in rural ones. Evidence also exists that violence in rural areas typically does not involve the use of guns, although they are more prominent than in urban areas (see Weisheit, Falcone, & Wells, 1994;

2006). Add the fact that officers often know the people involved in disputes and it would seem that the risks associated with handling these types of cases in rural areas would be lower. In general, this is true: according to one of the few studies on the subject, Weisheit, Falcone, and Wells, (2006) found that rural officers are four times less likely to be the victims of assault than officers in large urban areas serving 250,000 people or more and six times less likely than officers in urban areas of between 100,000 and 249,000 people. While this study is now nearly a decade old, and other more recent research is clearly needed, the findings even then were striking.

However, in very small towns of less than 10,000 people, officers are 1.5 times more likely to be killed than urban officers serving very large (250,000 or more) areas. The conclusion by Weisheit, Falcone, and Wells (2006) is that while rural officers are generally less likely to be assaulted, when that does happen, they are more likely to be killed. While the data does not offer any definitive answers as to why this trend occurs, the nature of rural life and the characteristics of rural policing (e.g., patrolling alone, no backup, long distances to obtaining medical attention, distrust of the police) may all play a part in the explanation.

Corruption

While many of the issues that focus on rural policing are under studied, the issue of corruption is not the exclusive domain of urban police departments. The lower wages paid to rural police officers, coupled with the interpersonal relationships officers form with residents, including criminals, can create a climate in which officers may feel pressured for a number of reasons to ignore certain criminal activity or to be more actively involved in it.

On the other hand, the nature of social relationships and interaction may mitigate officer involvement with corruption. Given the intimate nature of rural life, where people are more aware of the everyday events of residents, participation in corruption may be less likely since it is more easily revealed.

This is not to say that rural corruption does not exist. In fact, the salient question is not whether or not rural police corruption exists; rather, it is whether or not the community sanctions it. Weisheit, Falcone, and Wells (2006) make a distinction between two different types of corruption: *community-condemned corruption*, which is the kind that officers engage in for personal gain and *community-condoned corruption*, which has the support of community residents.

In the former, once discovered, there is usually a negative reaction by residents about the behavior. Community-condoned corruption, on the other hand, is the type of behavior which is approved or tolerated by residents. This is a more subtle and dangerous type of corruption because it serves to erode the ethical parameters of the entire justice system. Examples of community condoned corruption might be those instances in which officers are charged with taking bribes from marijuana growers or moonshiners or even crank lab owners, who provide a staple of jobs and boost to the local economy.

While the behavior is still inappropriate, the community response is not an angry one. In fact, jury members might be persuaded to acquit offenders in such cases (see Wiesheit, 1992). What is important to understand about community-condoned corruption or misconduct is that the relationships that officers form with residents may influence or color their reaction to what would normally be considered inappropriate behavior. This type of corruption is much more likely to occur in rural areas than in urban ones.

Community Policing and Rural Law Enforcement

Where does community policing fit into the discussion of rural policing? There are many experts who argue that little in the way of community policing occurs in rural areas. This is likely due to the fact that few rural departments have formalized programs or designated "community police officers." Part of the discussion also centers on how one defines community policing. The research suggests a wide range of definitions and programs that come under the category of community policing, but judging from what has been discussed thus far about rural life and Office of Community Policing Service's definition of community policing, it would be relatively easy to conclude that community policing as a philosophy and practice is identical to the nature of rural policing (Romesburg, 2005).

That is, if one defines community policing as a way to build bridges within a community, maintaining order within that community by developing personal and intimate relationships with residents so that they can collaborate to solve community problems, as well as integrating traditional policing methods where appropriate, then it seems likely that the very essence of rural policing embodies the parameters and issues surrounding what some are calling community policing.

Conclusion

Despite the fact that people are increasingly living in urban and suburban communities, a significant portion of the population represents rural America. The economic, political, and social aspects of life in these areas are, in many ways, different from their more sophisticated counterparts. However, as it relates to crime, a number of trends have been identified in rural and urban areas, including the presence of gangs, drug use and trafficking, and drunk driving. The nature of social life defines the particular features of these social problems as it does the nature of how police departments respond to them.

Rural policing presents a number of challenges for officers, both in terms of training, equipment, and lack of backup on calls, as well as the difficulty of managing the stress of working in isolated communities. Additionally, judging from the profile offered of police departments around the country, from an organizational standpoint the nature of policing in America is actually more of a rural variety—nearly 90% of all local police departments in this country have fewer than 50 officers. There are also some unique dimensions to rural policing, such as the close intimate relationships officers form with residents. While this topic is perhaps one of the most understudied in policing, the changing nature of society will require greater attention to it in the future.

References

Barclay, E. (2001). *A review of the literature on agricultural crime.* Institute for Rural Futures, Armidale, New South Wales: University of New England.

Brock, D., Copeland, M., & Scott, R. F. (2001). Rural policing in the Midwest: An examination of dissimilar regions and drug offending. *Journal of Contemporary Criminal Justice, 17*(1), 49–59.

Chan, M. (2015, August 14). Pistol-whipped Alabama cop didn't shoot attacker for fear of making headlines. *New York Daily News.* Retrieved from http://www.nydailynews.com/news/national/pistol-whipped-didn-shoot-suspect-fear-backlash-article-1.2325772.

Chitty, M. C. (1994). *Conservation police and wildlife poaching: An exploratory study.* Master's Thesis, Illinois State University.

Coates, J. (1987). *Armed and dangerous: The rise of the survivalist right.* New York: Hill and Wang.

Dyer, J. (1997). *Harvest of rage: Why Oklahoma City is only the beginning.* Boulder, CO: Westview Press.

Egley, A., Howell, J. C., & Harris, M. (2012). *Highlights of the 2012 National Youth Gang Survey.* Washington, DC: U.S. Department of Justice, Office of Justice Programs, Office of Juvenile Justice Delinquency Prevention.

Egley, A., & Major, A. K. (2003). *Highlights of the 2001 National Youth Gang Survey.* Washington, DC: U.S. Department of Justice, Office of Justice Programs, Office of Juvenile Justice Delinquency Prevention.

Egley, A., & O'Donnel, C. E. (2008). *Highlights of the 2005 National Youth Gang Survey*. Washington, DC: U.S. Department of Justice, Office of Justice Programs, Office of Juvenile Justice Delinquency Prevention.

Forsyth, C., & Marckese, T. A. (1993). Thrills and skills: A sociological analysis of poaching. *Deviant Behavior, 14*(2), 157–172.

Garriott, W. (2010). Targeting the local: Policing clandestine methamphetamine production in a rural U.S. community. *Canadian Journal of Law and Society*, *25*(1), 1–19.

Herz, D. C. (2000). *Drugs in the heartland: Methamphetamine use in rural Nebraska*. Washington, DC: U.S. Department of Justice, Office of Justice Programs, National Institute of Justice.

Inciardi, J. A., & Dee, J. L. (1987). From the Keystone cops to *Miami Vice*: Images of policing in American popular culture. *Journal of Popular Culture*, Fall 1987.

Johnson, H. W., Hall, J. A., & Sabri, B. (2007). Rural and urban criminal justice. In A. R. Roberts & D. W. Springer (Eds.), *Social Work in Juvenile and Criminal Justice Settings* (3rd ed.) (pp. 53–74). Springfield, IL: Charles Thomas.

Liederbach, J. (2007). Controlling suburban and small-town hoods: An examination of police encounters with juveniles. *Youth Violence and Juvenile Justice, 5*(2), 107–124.

McNamara, R. H., & Burn, R. (2008). *Multiculturalism and the criminal justice system*. New York: McGraw-Hill.

National Highway Traffic Safety Administration. (2012). *Traffic Safety Facts, 2012*. Washington, DC: U.S. Department of Transportation. Retrieved from http://www-nrd.nhtsa.dot.gov/Pubs/812050.pdf.

Oliver, M., & Meier, A. (2004). The four stress factors unique to rural patrol revisited. *Police Chief*. Retrieved from http://policechiefmagazine.org/magazine/index.cfm?fuseaction=display_arch&article_id=450&issue_id=112004.

Payne, B. K., Berg, B. L., & Sun, I. Y. (2005). Policing in small town America: Dogs, drunks, disorder and dysfunction. *Journal of Criminal Justice, 33*(1), 31–41.

Peters, V. J., Oetting, E. R., & Edwards, R. W. (1992). Drug use in rural communities: An epidemiology. In R. W. Edwards (Ed.), *Drug Use in Rural American Communities* (pp. 9–29). New York: Haworth Press.

Romesburg, W. H. (2005). *Law enforcement tech guide for small and rural police agencies: A guide for executives, managers, and technologists*. Washington, DC: U.S. Department of Justice, Office of Community Oriented Policing Services.

Sandy, J. P., & Devine, D. A. (1978). Four stress factors unique to rural patrol. *The Police Chief, 45*(September), 42–44.

Starbuck, D., Howell, J. C., & Lindquist, D. J. (2001). *Hybrid and other modern gangs.* Washington, DC: Office of Juvenile Justice Delinquency Prevention.

The Andy Griffith Show Wiki. (2017). Barney Fife. Retrieved from http://mayberry.wikia.com/wiki/Barney_Fife.

U. S. Census. (2013). *2010 Urban Areas FAQ.* Retrieved from http://www.census.gov.

U.S. Department of Agriculture, Economic Research Services. (2015). *Farm income and wealth statistics.* Retrieved from www.ers.usda.gov.

U.S. Drug Enforcement Administration. (2006). *Drug trafficking in the United States.* Retrieved from http://www.dea.gov/conern/drug_trafficking.html.

U.S. General Accounting Office. (2008). *Rural development: Profile of rural areas.* pp. 26–31. Retrieved from http://archive.gao.gov/t2pbat6/149199.pdf.

Weisheit, R. A. (1992). *Domestic marijuana: A neglected industry.* Westport, CT: Praeger.

Weisheit, R. A., Falcone, D. N., & Wells, L. E. (2006). *Crime and policing in rural and small-town America* (3rd ed.). Long Grove, IL: Waveland Press.

Weisheit, R. A., & Fuller, J. (2004). Methamphetamine in the heartland: A review and initial exploration. *Journal of Criminal Justice, 27*(1), 131–151.

Weisheit, R. A., & Wells, E. J. (2004). Youth gangs in rural America. *NIJ Journal, 251*, 2–6.

Zhao, J. S., Thurman, Q. T., & He, N. (1999). Sources of job satisfaction among police officers: A test of demographic and work environment models. *Justice Quarterly, 16*(1), 153–173.

7

Policing Urban Spaces

Kim Lersch

When I was asked to prepare this chapter, a number of thoughts ran through my head as important topics to cover. It is sometimes a difficult task to focus on a path when so much research has been conducted on a topic, especially in the wake of a number of highly publicized police shootings that have occurred over the past several years. According to the *Washington Post*, nearly 400 citizens were fatally shot by the police in the first five months of 2015, a rate that is more than double the level reported by the federal government over the past decade (Kindy, 2015). As of this writing, this number has climbed to over 800 (Brittain, 2015). Many of these incidents have occurred in large urban metropolitan areas. It seems like now, more than ever before, we need to have a better understanding of urban policing.

When we really take a hard look at policing, oftentimes we uncover trends and tendencies that go against our assumptions of what police officers actually do. For example, previous studies have found that the police really do not spend all that much time enforcing the law and that about half of all calls for service to the police do not involve criminal incidents. A typical police officer is more likely to spend time on routine traffic patrol than the investigation of violent crimes (Liederbach & Frank, 2006). And even though there has been much public outrage over several highly publicized accounts of citizens being killed at the hands of law enforcement officers, it should be noted that the vast majority of these fatal police shootings were, in fact, clearly justified and in some cases officers have been praised as heroes (Brittain, 2015).

So, what do we know about the behavior of the police? First, a good deal of what we know about policing is really focused on big city, urban policing. A cursory search in Criminal Justice Abstracts revealed nearly 300 journal articles based on data collected from the ten largest local police departments in the U.S. in the past decade: New York, Chicago, Los Angeles, Philadelphia, Houston, Washington, DC, Dallas, Phoenix, Baltimore, and Miami-Dade County. These ten agencies alone employ over 84,000 full-time sworn law enforcement officers (Reaves, 2015). Popular movies and television shows regularly portray fictional officers employed by these monstrous agencies, and the story lines tend to focus on violent crime, brutality, and questionable police practices. The life of the big city officer policing urban spaces is often painted as one of excitement, danger, and glory.

During our discussion of policing urban spaces, it is important to bear in mind that life for officers employed in these massive agencies is very, very different from the life of an officer in a "typical" agency. Nearly 75 percent of local police agencies in the United States employ less than 25 sworn officers. About 600 departments employ one single officer to maintain order throughout the entire jurisdiction (Reaves, 2015). Law enforcement officers in small, rural areas are often called upon to deal with a number of issues unheard of in larger, urban agencies, such as utility problems, checking homes while owners are out of town, barking dogs, or even controlling livestock wandering on the streets (Liederbach & Frank, 2006). While one can easily list multiple television shows based on larger agencies (such as *Law and Order*; *CSI: New York*, *Las Vegas*, etc.; *NYPD Blue*, etc.) one would struggle to name even a single television show that portrayed the life of a police officer in a small town other than *The Andy Griffith Show*, where the lead character was a sheriff in the small town of Mayberry, North Carolina. For many, the hustle and bustle of the big city seems much more intriguing than life on the farm.

What is it about an urban area that captures our imagination? What exactly do we mean when we say "urban areas"? Why is the nature of policing in urban areas different from the suburbs or more rural locales? And how is it different? These are the questions that we will be exploring in this chapter.

Defining Urban Areas

What do we mean, exactly, when we refer to an urban area? The answer can be much more complicated than one would expect. For example, I grew up in a city called Taylor, which is a suburb located about 15 miles from downtown Detroit, Michigan. There was virtually no end to the urbanization. If I drove from my home to a Tiger game in the downtown ball park, potentially I could pass through five different cities, each with their own police department. So, when we talk about an urban area, are we referring to the City of Detroit itself, or are we also including the surrounding suburbs, cities, towns, and unincorporated areas of the contiguous counties?

One important fact to keep in mind in our discussions is the fact that policing in the United States has evolved into an extremely decentralized enterprise. There are local municipal police agencies, sheriff's departments, state police departments, transit authority police, federal agencies, Native American Tribal Police, etc. In 2013, there were over 15,000 state and local law enforcement agencies in the United States (Reaves, 2015). My home state of Florida alone has nearly 400 different local and county-level law enforcement agencies. In a perfect world, neighboring police agencies would have an open, cooperative relationship with each other. Information on offenders, crime locations, and other forms of data could be easily shared and all would have the same crime mapping and analysis software, making cross-jurisdictional analysis a breeze. Unfortunately, we do not live in a perfect world. Expanding urban areas pose unique problems for highly territorial law enforcement agencies.

In early city development, there was a sharp break as one left the city limits and immediately entered rural areas. The city itself was a tight spatial cluster with a very distinct downtown area. This is no longer the case, as urban sprawl has become the norm. It is not uncommon for development to extent for 100 miles around the center of our largest cities (Gottdienter & Hutchinson, 2006). The city of Phoenix, Arizona, covers some 600 square miles, which is larger than the entire state of Delaware (Macionis & Parrillo, 2007). Fewer and fewer people actually live in the downtown, central city area but instead reside in what is known as a multicentered metropolitan region—a large geographic area with many separate centers for shopping, workplaces, and recreation.

As one might imagine, the experiences of growing up in the heart of Detroit can be much, much different than those of a child growing up in a surrounding suburb. I usually say that I am from Detroit until I meet someone who is actually from Detroit; then I quickly correct myself as I am not *really* from the city. This is important to keep in mind as an "urban area" can be quite heterogeneous depending on how this area is defined.

There are some official definitions that one could turn to for assistance. According to *Merriam-Webster's Dictionary* (2007), an urban area is defined as "of, relating to, characteristic of, or constituting a city." So, what is a city? A city is defined as "an inhabited place of greater size, population, or importance than a town or village" (*Merriam-Webster*, 2007). While these definitions provide a good starting point, they are not much use when one is trying to define where, exactly, an urban area begins and where it ends.

In 1949, the Office of Management and Budget and the U.S. Census Bureau developed standard definitions of what constituted a metropolitan area, or a standard metropolitan area (SMA). The need for this new definition was driven by the movement towards regional and suburban expansion. This sprawling growth was fueled in part by federal legislation that provided incentives for builders to develop suburban housing as well as programs to construct highways, making commuting from the suburbs into the urban areas much easier (Macionis & Parrillo, 2007). The new SMA was defined as a city with a population of at least 50,000 people plus the surrounding suburbs, smaller cities, and towns. The SMA was soon replaced by the standard metropolitan statistical area (SMSA), which allowed for growth in two or more adjacent counties. The SMSA was defined as a county or counties with a center city (or two) with a population of at least 50,000 plus adjacent counties that share common linkages with the central city (or cities).

The definitions continue to evolve over time. In 1983, the SMA became known as a metropolitan statistical area (MSA). The MSA is defined as a geographic entity that has a central, core area with a large population center plus the adjacent communities that share a high level of economic and social integration with the population center. The level of integration that the surrounding communities share with the central downtown region is measured by the number of commuters that travel to work from the counties to the urban center. In order for a region to be classified as a MSA, there must be a city with a population of at least 50,000 residents (Gottdienter & Hutchison, 2006; Office of Management and Budget, 2000). Micropolitan statistical areas have also been added to the classification scheme, which have at least one urban cluster with a population of 10,000–50,000 residents. In some cases, a MSA that has a single urban core with at least 2.5 million people may be divided into smaller groupings of counties that are known as Metropolitan Divisions. About 94% of the U.S. population lives in metropolitan or micropolitan statistical areas (Office of Management and Budget, 2013).

While these definitions from the Census Bureau may be useful to understand and employ for statistical descriptions of urban regions, the nuts and bolts nature of the classification schemes leave one with the impression that the nature and quality of life for residents of an urban area are relatively homogeneous. This is not the case. In a study comparing the level of mistrust held by residents of the City of Chicago to the views held by residents of the suburbs, smaller cities, and rural areas, Ross, Mirowsky, and Pribesh (2002) found that respondents living within the city reported significantly higher levels of mistrust. This form of alienation was a consequence of disadvantage and community disorder. There is something about the urban experience that results in weakened social ties and the feeling that other people are unsupportive, dishonest, and selfish. Strangers are viewed with suspicion, and urban residents are left with an inability to form effective relationships with others (Coleman, 1988; Mirowsky & Ross, 1983). Crime rates tend to be much higher in cities than in suburban areas, as are rates of poverty, disease, and overall disadvantage. Why? What it is about the urban experience that makes life so much different? What it is that encourages residents to become cynical, suspicious beings? And what are the implications for urban policing? To explore these questions, we will begin with a review of some of the classical theorists in the study of crime and urban life.

Defining Urban Life: The Classics

The first department of sociology was established at the University of Chicago in 1892 (Curran & Renzetti, 2001). Over the next several decades, the university was able to attract some of the most influential scholars in the study of urban life, including Robert Park, Earnest Burgess, Clifford Shaw, Henry McKay, and Louis Wirth. The writings of the Chicago School researchers continue to have a strong impact on contemporary analyses of the urban experience. These early faculty members were most likely shocked by the booming metropolis. Many of the early researchers had grown up in rural communities and several of their fathers had been ministers in their small hometowns (Greek, 1992).

Robert Park was a newspaper reporter for 25 years prior to beginning his career as a university professor. During his years as a journalist Park focused on urban problems, especially issues related to housing. Park used the tools of a journalist—personal observations, in-depth interviews, and an immersion in the area being studied—to chronicle the conditions in the city (Taylor et al., 1973). For a while, Park lived in New York City, where he was assigned as a police beat reporter. He investigated many aspects of urban life and even managed to infiltrate opium dens (Martin et al., 1990). As a result of his experiences, Park brought a rather unique reality-based perspective to the study of the city.

Park viewed the city as a kind of social organism. When taken together, the various business districts and neighborhoods that make up a city begin to take on the character of a living, breathing organism. Within the city itself, Park identified a number of "natural areas," or clusters that were somehow different or set off from the larger organism. These areas could be based on the race or ethnicity of those residing within the cluster (such as China Town or Greek Town) or they may be based on the concentration of factories or other businesses. Similar to how plants and animals compete in their natural environment, humans residing within these natural areas struggle to survive.

In a pattern that continues today, some areas within the city are simply more desirable to live in than others. Less powerful groups within the racial and ethnic mix of the city are forced to make do with life in the urban slums and ghettos (Shaw & McKay, 1969). Park applied the ecological concept of invasion, dominance, and succession to describe the process whereby a group of people "stuck" in a poorer area may seek out a better territory in which to live. Commercial businesses and industry as well as groups of people (such as the Irish, Italians, etc.) could also be involved in the process of invasion, dominance, and succession.

Ernest Burgess was an office mate of Park's. Burgess combined Park's ideas concerning invasion, dominance, and succession with a concentric model of city growth and change. Burgess recognized that the city of Chicago appeared to expand and grow in a series of concentric circles that moved outward from the central business district. Each circle or zone had distinct characteristics that set it off from the other zones (Burgess, 1925). Zone I, which was the innermost circle, was the central business district of the city. In Chicago, this area was (and still is) known as the Loop. Few people actually lived in Zone I, as factories and other commercial enterprises dominated the area.

Moving outward, Zone II was known as the Zone in Transition. Generally speaking, Zone II was the least desirable area to live in the city. Ever expanding businesses and factories attempted to invade and dominate Zone II from the Loop. The apartment buildings and other housing units were in poor repair. A dilapidated apartment building may be located directly next to a factory or other business. Landlords ignored repairs of rental units as the value of the property was in commercial value of the land itself and not in the housing units (Bursik & Grasmick, 1993). Only the poorest, least powerful groups resided in the Zone in Transition. However, as one moved outwards from the Loop and into the outer circles comprising the suburbs, living conditions improved greatly. Burgess noted that as the city continued to grow and expand in an outward, sprawling manner, the inner zones would begin to invade, dominate, and succeed into the neighboring outer zone (Vold et al., 2002).

Louis Wirth was a student of Park's. Wirth was rather pessimistic about urban life. In an essay titled "Urbanism as a Way of Life," Wirth (1938) examined the impact of the city on individual behavior. In Wirth's writings, he argued that the characteristics of the city—specifically the size, density, and heterogeneity of the residents—resulted in a way of life he described as "urbanism." While urbanism did have some positive attributes, such as greater heterogeneity leading to greater tolerance for diversity, there was a definite dark side to the impact of urban life.

For Wirth, high levels of population density led to heightened levels of friction and irritation with others, which may result in higher levels of anti-social behavior (Macionis & Parrillo, 2007). Wirth also argued that as the size of the population in a city grew, people would become more and more isolated from primary relationships with others. For example, if one goes into a store in an urban area, more than likely one does not know (nor care to know) the salesperson working at the counter. It is also likely that an urban resident does not know his or her own neighbors. In contrast, if one lives in a rural area, it is likely that close, primary relationships are shared with those who work and live nearby. You know the owner of the market, the mechanic, the police officer in your neighborhood, and you can recognize your neighbors' children. Wirth felt that the lack of primary relationships that exist in urban environments would result in higher levels of crime and other social problems. For Wirth, an important mechanism of social control was lost in an anonymous, impersonal world (Gottdiener & Hutchison, 2006).

Clifford Shaw and Henry McKay's work represents a culmination of the foundations set by Park, Burgess, Wirth, and other sociologists interested in the study of crime and place. Shaw and McKay were interested in the geographic distribution of juvenile delinquency and other social problems. Without the use of computers or other sophisticated mapping software, the researchers individually plotted the home addresses of male juvenile offenders who had been brought before the Juvenile Court in Cook County. Working with several different waves of data, Shaw and McKay manually located and plotted the home addresses of nearly 25,000 youths! In addition to the data on the juveniles, the researchers also examined various neighborhood characteristics including economic conditions, community stability, infant mortality, tuberculosis, and mental disorders.

What Shaw and McKay found was that juvenile delinquency was not evenly distributed throughout the city of Chicago. There was a regular decrease in the level of juvenile delinquency as one moved outward towards the suburbs from the center of the city. Shaw and McKay viewed juvenile delinquency as an indicator of some level of pathology or "sickness" within a neighborhood. This higher level of pathology found in the inner zones was not restricted to juvenile crime; the rates for tuberculosis, mental disorders, and infant mortality were all higher in the inner-most zones. Additionally, the inner zones were characterized by higher levels of poverty and a greater proportion of residents who rented their homes. Shaw and McKay felt that the social ills that prevailed in the inner zones were linked to a condition called social disorganization.

Social Disorganization versus Collective Efficacy

Just what is social disorganization? Sampson and Groves (1989, p. 777) defined the term as the "inability of a community structure to realize the common values of its residents and maintain effective social controls." The inner zones were marked by little residential stability, as renters came and went within the neighborhoods following the pattern of invasion, dominance, and succession. As new faces moved into an area, the stabilizing ties that had been established prior to their arrival were destroyed. Children did not identify with a single over-arching conventional order. Instead, the high degree of neighborhood diversity led to the growth and development of competing definitions of right and wrong. The high level of population turnover and community heterogeneity hindered the ability of the family and other primary groups to control the behavior of the children and local residents (Bursik & Grasmick, 1993). As argued by Sampson (1995), one of the major problems associated with socially disorganized areas is the inability to control the behavior of teenage peer groups, especially gangs.

This is where the importance of informal social control comes into play. Informal social control is derived from neighbors watching out for the wellbeing of each other. While formal social control mechanisms can impact behavior, informal social control can be a very powerful force in controlling crime and deviance. In fact, some have argued that the impact of informal social control is much stronger than formal control mechanisms, such as the police (Cohen & Felson, 1979; Felson, 1998).

Informal social control goes hand-in-hand with collective efficacy, a concept that Sampson and a number of co-authors have been actively developing. Collective efficacy is defined as "social cohesion among neighbors combined with their willingness to intervene on behalf of the common good" (Sampson et al., 1997, p. 918). Collective efficacy may be thought of as the opposite of social disorganization (Vold et al., 2002). Neighborhoods with high levels of collective efficacy are marked by residents who know and trust each other well—well enough to intervene if they see children misbehaving or when acts of vandalism or other problems occur. High levels of social cohesion and trust leads to the development of shared expectations for behavior. People know the rules of the neighborhood, they respect the rules, and they pass along these expectations for behavior to the youths of the area, reinforcing a shared definition of right and wrong. As a result, the levels of crime, disorder, and other social ills are much lower in areas that have high levels of collective efficacy (Morenoff et al., 2001; Reisig & Cancino, 2004; Sampson & Raudenbush, 1999).

Conversely, in socially disorganized environments marked by high residential turnover, norms and values that support criminal and delinquent behaviors tend to develop. Left unchecked, these alternative norms and values may come to support a subculture of delinquency. As the local residents come and go, the subcultural values remain in neighborhoods and are passed along to new residents in a process called cultural transmission (Einstadter & Henry, 1995; Kornhauser, 1978). Whatever social organization exists in inner city areas has the tendency to be supportive of delinquent and criminal norms and values (Gold, 1987). Generally speaking, one is more likely to find high levels of social disorganization in inner city neighborhoods, while the suburbs are marked by collective efficacy among the local residents.

The Thoughts of Scholars Past and Present: Policing Urban Spaces

How do the police function in socially disorganized urban spaces? Interestingly, there has been relatively little research that explores whether or not police function differently in various neighborhoods (Klinger, 1997; Slovak, 1986; Terrill & Reisig, 2003). The turbulent period of the 1960s spawned a few researchers to examine the issue, especially with respect to police behavior in minority communities.

One such study was conducted by Carl Werthman and Irving Piliavin (1967), who spent about 18 months interviewing and observing interactions between gang members and police officers in Oakland and San Francisco. The researchers found that police officers look for certain clues to assist them in categorizing neighborhoods and individuals as suspicious or dangerous. As phrased by the authors:

> Policemen develop indicators of suspicion by a method of pragmatic induction. Past experience leads them to conclude that more crimes are committed in the poorer sections of town than in the wealthier areas, that Negroes are more likely to cause public disturbances than whites, and that adolescents in certain areas are a greater source of trouble than other categories of the citizenry. On the basis of these conclusions, the police divide the population and physical territory under surveillance into a variety of categories, make some initial assumptions about the moral character of the people and places in these categories, and then focus attention on those categories of persons and places felt to have the shadiest moral characteristics. (1967, p. 75)

Werthman and Piliavin noted that the neighborhood in which a person lives is the most general indicator of criminality. In fact, many officers they spoke with felt that *all* residents of certain neighborhoods had a weak commitment to the traditional moral order, and some expressed the belief that certain neighborhoods were morally inferior to others. The gang members noted that officers were particularly harsh when they attempted to travel into neighborhoods of different socioeconomic or racial status than their "home" territory. Furthermore, if an African American or Hispanic youth was found in a predominately White neighborhood, the youth was viewed as "out of place" and was labeled as particularly suspicious.

The authors concluded that the actions and beliefs of the police were a function of how patrol was organized. Patrol officers are disproportionately assigned to "lower class neighborhoods" and as a result these areas are patrolled with greater awareness and intensity than suburban neighborhoods. Therefore, the nature of the interactions the officers are exposed to can be skewed. Werthman and Piliavin found that many of the officers admitted to being prejudiced against the local minority youths, but stated that these beliefs had resulted from their work as officers. The researchers noted that the officers' perceptions of the youths were often jaded by the perceived negative characteristics of the neighborhoods in which they lived, a process that was labeled "ecological contamination." In effect, all youths living in a "bad" neighborhood are labeled as bad simply because of the characteristics of the area in which they lived.

Why is it that the police are disproportionately assigned to certain neighborhoods? There are differing opinions on the answer to this question. One view is summarized by Walker, Spohn, and DeLone (2007) who argue that the disparate assignment of police in minority and/or lower income areas occurs for a number of reasons. Officers are assigned to neighborhoods based on the number of reported crimes and calls for service that occur in a particular area. Crimes tend to be concentrated among minority group members and the very poor. Additionally, minority group members and members of lower socioeconomic classes tend to call the police with greater frequency to resolve both criminal and non-crime-related problems. As a result, more officers are assigned to handle the large volume of calls for assistance. This view is sometimes called the "social service explanation," in which the police are called upon to resolve family quarrels, maintain peace and quiet, and even assist in transportation to medical facilities (Sever, 2003).

A second view falls under what is known as the "threat hypothesis." Proponents of this view argue that the presence of economically disadvantaged strata creates a threat to dominant groups, to which the police must respond. The general notion is that certain structural variables, such as the proportion of non-White residents in a community and rate of poverty, may be used to predict the level of social control used by the police (see, generally, Chamlin, 1989; Liska, 1992; Liska, Chamlin, & Reed, 1985; Smith & Holmes, 2003). The power of the police is used to control members of "dangerous classes" in our society and to maintain existing social stratification (Blalock, 1967; Jackson,

1989). As a result, areas with higher numbers of poor and/or minority neighborhoods experience heightened levels of patrol. Interestingly, prior research suggests that the relationship between police strength and minority communities varies based on the race/ethnicity of the community. Areas with high concentrations of poor Hispanics do not have the same level of police involvement as areas with high numbers of Black residents (Sever, 2003), although this relationship appears to be changing over time as the population of Hispanics continues to grow (Kent & Carmichael, 2014).

More recently, researchers have moved beyond the issue of police patrol strength and the size of poor, minority populations overall to the geographic concentration of minorities across a city (Capers, 2009). Basically, the question focuses on how police behavior is different in areas where there is a high level of racial desegregation versus neighborhoods where minorities are residentially isolated. When Whites and minorities live in close proximity to each other, the "contact hypothesis" argues that prejudice and racial stereotypes are reduced. The result is a reduced need for increased levels of police as minorities are no longer perceived as a threat to the majority population. Kent and Carmichael (2014) found that the most integrated urban areas have smaller police departments. However, consistent with the threat hypothesis, once areas become more segregated the number of police officers per resident increases. Interestingly, there appears to be a "tipping point" in communities with extreme levels of segregation; the number of police per resident declines in neighborhoods with predominantly Black populations.

It should be noted that just because more police officers may be assigned to certain neighborhoods, this does not automatically mean that the officers are aggressively enforcing the letter of the law through apprehension and formal arrest. Rodney Stark (1987) argued that poor, urban areas tend to suffer from more *lenient* enforcement of the law. Stark stated a number of reasons for this more relaxed level of patrol, including his observation that residents of stigmatized neighborhoods are less likely to assist the police throughout the prosecution of a case. This lack of cooperation reduces the motivation of the officers to seek out crime and criminals. Furthermore, since many of the incidents involve vice-related crimes such as prostitution, there are few complaints from citizens and little pressure for the police to react. This leniency impacts the community in a number of ways, including reduced respect for the law and heightened levels of crime and deviance. Other criminals will see these neighborhoods as attractive and come to these areas, which ultimately increases the level of social disorganization even further.

Similarly, Joseph Goldstein (1960) found that nearly 90 percent of the serious felonious assaults that occurred in an urban precinct in a one month period were not prosecuted because the police discouraged victims from signing complaints. Many of these assaults involved stabbings and other serious injuries, which one officer described as "run of the mill" in the district. Goldstein described how the private value system of the officers impacted their enforcement of the law. This was especially true if the assault involved marginalized citizens in the poor neighborhoods for whom the police felt that assault was an acceptable means for settling arguments. In the view of the officers, investigating the assault was not worth their time and effort in this low-income, ghetto neighborhood. Donald Black (1971) also noted that officers in three major cities did not use their arrest powers as often as the law would allow; leniency was relatively commonplace.

In a more contemporary analysis, David Klinger (1997) theorized that police enforcement of the law is different in some neighborhoods due to a number of factors, including the perceived "deservedness" of the victim, the level of police cynicism, and the workload of the officers in the district. All of these factors were linked to the local level of crime and deviance. With respect to victims, Klinger raised two facts: First, many crime victims played a role in their own victimization and second, many crime victims were criminals themselves. In effect, there were few "innocent" victims and, as crime rises, more criminals may find themselves victimized. The police were less likely to aggressively pursue complaints involving victims who were not defined as deserving.

Klinger also noted that police cynicism increased as the level of crime and deviance escalated. Officers became hardened as they encountered more criminal incidents and grew increasingly frustrated at the perceived lack of sanctions for those arrested. Heightened levels of cynicism resulted in less aggressive enforcement.

Finally, as crime increased so did the workload, and in the face of limited resources the attention of officers was shifted from misdemeanor "quality of life" issues to more serious criminal offenses. As a result of these interwoven factors, Klinger concluded that officers working in higher crime neighborhoods did not enforce the law as aggressively as officers assigned to areas with lower levels of crime.

Other researchers have explored police behavior across diverse neighborhoods. Smith (1986) used data from the Police Services Study, which was based on 60 different neighborhoods. Smith found that the characteristics of the neighborhood did have an impact on the behavior of officers. Officers were more likely to use force when dealing with African American citizens, but this difference was driven more by the racial make-up of the neighborhood than by the race of the individual citizen. Smith also noted that citizens in lower income areas were more likely to be arrested than those in more affluent areas.

Terrill and Reisig (2003) noted that the level of use of force by police officers was influenced by neighborhood characteristics. Officers were more likely to use force in poorer socioeconomic areas characterized by higher levels of crime. In a study of 93 Canadian communities, Pare, Felson, and Ouimet (2007) found that the police were more likely to solve crimes in smaller, more rural communities than in large urban areas.

The issue of racial residential segregation and the level of law enforcement has also been examined. According to the "benign neglect" hypothesis, areas with highly segregated minority populations will have fewer police assigned and criminal activity will not be met with aggressive enforcement. Why? It has been argued that the police are more responsive to *inter*-racial crime (i.e., Black on White) than *intra*-racial crime (Black on Black). Following this argument, neither the police nor the majority population demands high levels of enforcement in highly segregated communities (Kent & Charmichael, 2014).

So where does all of this leave us? Since the behavior of the police may vary based on neighborhood characteristics, is it a good thing or a bad thing for the police to exercise some level of non-enforcement in high-crime areas? What is the best strategy for the police working in urban areas to reduce crime? As a point of review, if one buys into the arguments raised by the proponents of the Chicago School (and, it should be noted that not all do), there are certain aspects of urban life that may encourage heightened levels of crime and delinquency. The sheer size of the city, population density, residential turnover, and heterogeneity all contribute to a culture of mistrust and social disorganization. In order to reduce crime and improve social conditions, programs designed to build community ties and enhance social cohesion are needed. If urban residents had a real sense of community then the mechanisms of informal social control could be better utilized to keep peoples' behavior in check. Police in urban centers, therefore, should employ strategies to enhance collective efficacy and community ties among residents. Community policing, with its emphasis on shared efforts between the local residents and the police, seems like a great strategy to reduce crime and build communities.

Community Policing in Urban Areas: Can It Work?

We will first begin with a quick overview of community policing. The term "community policing" has become a buzzword used to describe a variety of programs and organizational philosophies. Trojanowicz and Bucqueroux (1990, p. 5) defined the philosophy of community policing in the following manner:

> Community Policing is a new philosophy of policing, based on the concept that police officers and private citizens working together in creative ways can help solve contemporary community problems related to crime, fear of crime, social and physical disorder, and neighborhood decay. The philosophy is predicated on the belief that achieving these goals requires that police departments develop a new relationship with the law-abiding people in the community, allowing them a greater voice in setting local police priorities and involving them in efforts to improve the overall quality of life in their neighborhoods. It shifts the focus of police work from handling random calls to solving community problems.

Others have translated the philosophy of community policing into a number of practical applications. Permanent assignment by both beat and shift is an essential element of community policing (Bracey, 1992; Goldstein, 1993). In order for the police to establish community partnerships with local citizens, the officers must be provided with the opportunity to develop close personal relationships with residents. One common measure of success of community policing is whether or not local residents know their locally assigned community police officer by name (Goldstein, 1987).

In addition to enhancing police-community relationships, permanent assignment also leads to the establishment of geographic responsibility and accountability (Weisel & Eck, 1994). If an officer has been assigned to a specific beat, then that officer should know what is going on in their area and be held responsible for the conditions in that area. If a rash of graffiti suddenly appears or a group of teenagers is hanging out at the local convenience store late at night, it is the duty of the locally assigned police officer to recognize that these conditions have surfaced and to work in conjunction with local residents and business owners to do something about it.

In order to enhance geographic responsibility, many agencies have also adopted a decentralized approach to the delivery of services. Instead of having one large, sometimes ominous, centralized command post for all police services, many police departments have turned to smaller district offices. These smaller offices may be located in strip malls, shopping malls, entertainment areas, or freestanding buildings. Regardless of their physical design, the decentralized system provides service centers that are viewed as less intimidating and more convenient for local residents to visit. Residents can stop by the station and meet one-on-one with their locally assigned regular officer, hopefully a familiar face to them.

Another essential element of community policing is the notion that the police must become more proactive in the prevention of crime and disorder (Goldstein, 1993). Instead of just responding from call to call, police (with the assistance of the community) should attempt to identify root causes of problems in the area. Crimes are viewed as symptoms of other underlying problems in the community (Lab, 2000). An arrest may take care of a specific incident, but will do nothing to solve the larger problem. The emphasis on solving community problems has been described as "the most important element of community policing" (Lab, 2000, p. 164). This approach, often called problem-oriented policing (POP), oftentimes goes hand-in-hand with community policing.

But can community policing work in areas plagued by high levels of social disorganization? Unfortunately, community policing efforts tend to be least successful in the neighborhoods that need them the most (Bursik & Grasmick, 1993; Peak & Glensor, 2002). In lower income areas plagued by high levels of crime, high residential turnover, and racial heterogeneity, these types of programs have had the lowest levels of success. Conversely, programs in middle class, relatively homogeneous neighborhoods where a "core" of a community already exists tend to report higher levels of success (Skogan, 1990).

Part of the problem has to do with participation in community events. The success or failure of a community policing effort rests on the involvement of the local residents, and some segments of the population are more likely to get involved in their community than are others. Bursik and Grasmick (1993) noted that involvement in various crime prevention and community programs is dependent upon social class, marital status, residential stability, and age. The most typical participants are middle aged, higher educated, upper to middle class, residentially stable homeowners who are married with children. Therefore, in areas with high numbers of elderly residents and/or poor, single parents renting their homes, participation is expected to be low. As many of these same characteristics go hand-in-hand with socially disorganized neighborhoods, the lack of success in economically challenged, residentially unstable neighborhoods should not come as a surprise.

In an analysis of participation at community policing meetings in Chicago, Skogan (2004) noted that certain segments of the community were much more likely to attend than others. While renters occupied about 60 percent of the beat dwellings, on average 75 percent of the meeting participants were homeowners. Latinos were seriously underrepresented, but older residents and those with higher levels of education were regular attendees. Long-time residents were the norm; individuals who attended the meetings lived in their homes nine years longer than the typical area resident. Only about 25 percent of the attendees were male. Skogan also noted that individuals who attended the meetings were much more concerned about neighborhood problems than were their non-attending neighbors.

Another part of the problem with community policing efforts in urban areas has to do with the negative attitudes that many hold towards the police. Johnson and Gregory (1971, p. 95) summarized the belief of many urban residents that the police were "soldiers of a White occupation army in a bitterly hostile country." Public opinion polls conducted over the past several decades have consistently reported that minority citizens, especially African Americans, rate the performance of the police lower than do White Americans. Further, individuals reporting lower incomes and educational levels report lower satisfaction with the police than do persons of higher socioeconomic status (Lersch, 1998; Walker, 1992). If citizens do not trust or respect the police, then they are less likely to participate in community policing activities.

A number of large cities, including Boston, MA, San Antonio, TX, Richmond, VA, Chicago, IL, San Diego CA, and Miami-Dade County, FL, have experimented with community policing strategies with mixed results (Stevens, 2003a; 2003b). For example, the City of Boston employed a number of initiatives, including a program called Same Cop Same Neighborhood (SC/SN), in which officers were required to spend no less than 60 percent of their shift in their assigned neighborhood. The goal was to provide opportunities for communication between officers and local residents and to encourage problem solving efforts. Other programs, such as neighborhood revitalization and partnerships with other city agencies, were employed as well. Unfortunately, a review of their activities noted that while the agency had successfully deployed a number of community policing initiatives, violent crime had not been significantly reduced and fear of crime was commonplace among local residents (Stevens, 2003a). Similarly, despite the deployment of several community policing efforts, residents of Miami-Dade County, Florida, reported that they were afraid to live in their own neighborhoods; the respondents were particularly fearful of home invasions. Residents further implied that any reductions in the level of crime reported by the police were a result of fewer citizen-initiated calls for service to the police and that community policing had not had a real impact on the level of crime.

Overall, results of research on the impact of community policing efforts on levels of violent crime have not been encouraging. Foot patrols, a common strategy employed in inner-city, downtown areas, have been shown to have little or no impact on violent crime and victimization. Similarly, neighborhood watch programs have demonstrated negligible results at best (McDonald, 2002;

Sherman et al., 1997). In a study of 164 cities with populations greater than 100,000, McDonald (2002) reported that community policing efforts were not effective at reducing violent crime in urban areas.

One point that should be noted is that inner city neighborhoods tend to experience a different type of community policing than middle class areas. While the suburban residents may experience "Officer Friendly" at neighborhood meetings and get-togethers, the experiences of inner city residents may be a bit grittier, as agencies struggle to curb violent crime, open air drug markets, and gangs. In higher crime, inner city neighborhoods, a more aggressive law enforcement tactic has been used that is packaged as an offshoot of community policing: Operation Weed and Seed.

Operation Weed and Seed (OWS) started in 1991 when the United States Department of Justice provided grant opportunities to law enforcement agencies to target high-crime neighborhoods. The goal of OWS is based on its name: First, violent offenders and drug dealers are "weeded out" through aggressive, pro-active law enforcement and dogged prosecution. The underlying philosophy is that the neighborhoods cannot be improved without removing the dangerous elements from circulation. After the criminal offenders have been removed, the area is "seeded" with various programs designed to improve the quality of life for the local residents, including economic opportunities, drug and alcohol treatment programs, juvenile intervention and diversion programs, community enrichment, and crime prevention strategies (Roehl et al., 1996; Simons, 2002). Unfortunately, the seeding portion of the program has taken a back seat to weeding; the emphasis of the Weed and Seed programs has been on aggressive, pro-active law enforcement (Bridenball & Jesilow, 2005; Miller, 2001). The weeding strategy, with its emphasis on arrest and incapacitation, is very similar in philosophy to another form of policing called zero-tolerance policing.

Zero-tolerance policing advocates the full use of the formal criminal justice process for any and all minor law violations. Arrests for even trivial offenses send the message that acts of disorder will not be tolerated under any circumstances. By tightening the formal control mechanisms, ultimately the "decent folk" may regain control of their neighborhoods, feel more comfortable walking the streets at night, and institute their own informal forms of social control.

Conversely, under the philosophy of community policing, an officer should use his or her arrest powers as the last resort to a problem. The idea is that while making an arrest may take care of an immediate concern, an arrest does nothing to address the underlying problem that caused the situation to arise in the first place. Furthermore, issuing citations and making arrests for minor offenses may ultimately erode the confidence and trust needed to make police-community partnerships effective.

While the goals of zero-tolerance policing and community policing are the same (i.e., fear reduction, reduced levels of crime), the means used to achieve these goals are very different. Changes in our urban centers stemming from the crack cocaine epidemic and chronic unemployment have made some police agencies question whether or not community policing efforts is the best strategy to fight crime.

A Note on Contemporary Views of Urban Life: Crack Cocaine and the New Urban Poor

It has been argued that the quality of urban life over the past 40 years or so has taken a sharp turn downward as the joblessness rate has climbed. William Wilson (1996, p. 19) defines the new urban poverty as "poor, segregated neighborhoods in which a substantial majority of individual adults are either unemployed or have dropped out of the labor force altogether." Wilson argues that neighborhoods with high levels of joblessness are also more likely to have high levels of social disorganization, which ultimately results in heightened levels of criminal activity, drug trafficking, and family disruption. The lack of legitimate opportunities to earn a living results in increased incentives for urban youths to sell drugs. This trend was especially evident during the crack cocaine epidemic of the 1980s. As argued by Wilson:

> Violent persons in the crack-cocaine marketplace have a powerful impact on the social organization of a neighborhood. Neighborhoods plagued by high levels of joblessness, insufficient economic opportunities, and high residential mobility are unable to control the volatile drug market and the violent crimes related to it. As informal controls weaken, the social processes that regulate behavior change ... Drug dealers cause the use and spread of guns in the neighborhood to escalate, which in turn raises the likelihood that others, particularly the youngsters, will come to view the possession of weapons as necessary or desirable for self-protection, settling disputes, and gaining respect from peers and other individuals. (1996, p. 21)

Others have echoed Wilson's thoughts, pointing to the growth of the global economy and deindustrialization as economic trends that have been devastating to our urban centers (Anderson, 1999; Websdale, 2001). Many unskilled and semi-skilled jobs formerly held by urban residents in factories and manufacturing centers have been moved overseas. Welfare reform efforts have significantly reduced the number of urban residents receiving various forms of public assistance. Between 1980 and 1993, the level of federal spending on employment and training opportunities was cut in half (Bassuk et al., 1996; Bowling, 1999). In an analysis of urban life in New York City, British researcher Benjamin Bowling described the infrastructure in the area where he conducted his fieldwork as being "on the verge of collapse." Sewer and water lines had ruptured due to neglect, subway stations were in deplorable condition, overcrowded schools were in disrepair, and it was not uncommon to find abandoned buildings and vacant lots (Bowling, 1999). Arguably, the level of social disorganization was at its peak.

The impact of the cocaine epidemic and its implications for urban policing cannot be understated. In New York City, there was a 62.5 percent increase in the number of homicides from 1985–1990; the largest increase in homicides was those occurring in public places where a firearm was used (Bowling, 1999). This increase roughly coincided with the arrival of crack cocaine in our urban centers. Crack quickly became the drug of choice for many urban residents due to its cheap price.

There were aspects of the drug and its potential customers that made the market quite unique and particularly devastating to urban neighborhoods. As Blumstein (1995) argued, purchasers of crack cocaine often did not have the monetary means to purchase multiple hits at one time, nor did they have safe places to store their stash. This lead to a demand for multiple points of sale that were scattered throughout neighborhoods, which in turn led to the demand for more and more individuals to sell the drugs at the various locations. Many of these new dealers had not been involved in the drug trade previously. Guns were necessary in order for the dealers to protect their goods and cash. Inexperienced personnel combined with weapons and high income earning potential lead to an extraordinary increase in the level of street violence.

The dual edged sword of the cocaine epidemic coupled with the impact of the poor economic conditions has been devastating, especially in minority communities. Neighborhoods became more and more violent as greater numbers of youths were drawn into the underworld economy. As a result, residents lost faith in the ability of the police and the criminal justice system as a whole to protect them and defend their rights. Urban residents became more likely to turn to self-help, and children were taught to defend themselves physically and meet violence with violence (Anderson, 1999). The War on Drugs was not just a catchy metaphor, but a reality in many large, urban agencies. As a result of the heightened levels of crime, many agencies have abandoned their community policing efforts in favor of a more assertive form of law enforcement, namely zero-tolerance policing.

A New Era in Urban Policing?

The crime fighting efforts of the New York City Police Department have emerged as a very interesting case study. In 1993, Rudolph Giuliani successfully ran for mayor of New York. Key to his platform was the idea that community policing was "soft" on crime and that the police needed to be more aggressive in enforcing the letter of the law even for minor, quality of life offenses such as panhandling, vandalism, drinking alcohol in public, etc. Zero-tolerance policing (or order-maintenance policing, as it is sometimes called) is based on the notion of the broken windows theory of policing developed by James Q. Wilson and George Kelling (1982). The general notion is that crime and disorder go hand in hand. If someone breaks a window and it goes unrepaired, a message is sent that no one cares. A spiral of degeneration begins. Informal social control deteriorates, and crime rates skyrocket. According to Wilson and Kelling, if the police focus on the "little things," such as minor disorders and low-level criminal acts, then more serious crime will be reduced and neighborhood stability will be restored (Greene, 1999; Hart & Lersch, 2015; Vitale, 2005)

Guiliani appointed William Bratton as his police commissioner. When Bratton was chief of the New York City Transit Police, he initiated an aggressive campaign against fare-jumpers and other petty criminals, a strategy which he credited for a dramatic decrease in more serious crime on the subway system. Bratton deployed this same strategy on a city-wide scale, incorporating crime mapping and other technologies that provided timely data to officers and supervisory personnel. The COMPSTAT model became synonymous with aggressive law enforcement and is based on the principles of timely and accurate intelligence, effective strategies and tactics, rapid deployment of personnel and resources, and relentless follow-up and assessment (Hart & Lersch, 2015; McDonald, 2002).

The reduction in violent crime levels in New York during the 1990s was dramatic. From 1993 to 1997, the city experienced a 44.3 percent decrease in the overall number of felony complaints, a 60.2 percent decrease in the number of murders and nonnegligent homicides, nearly a fifty percent decrease in robberies, and a 12 percent drop in forcible rape (Greene, 1999). While some have pointed to zero-tolerance policing as the key to the decline, others have argued that its impact has been exaggerated. Critics state that the crime rate was already declining when Guiliani "unleashed the cops," and that crime rates fell in other jurisdictions across the country even when such aggressive tactics were not put in place (Greene, 1999).

Others have argued that zero-tolerance policing (ZTP) has caused more harm than good, as the efforts tended to be concentrated in low-income, minority neighborhoods. In 2006, approximately 80% of Black youths ages 16–17 were stopped at least once by the NYPD compared to only 10 percent for White teens (Tyler, Fagan, & Geller, 2014). These aggressive tactics may lead to greater levels of hostility and violence not only towards the police, but other local residents. This effect is especially concentrated among minorities in our urban centers (Brunson & Miller, 2005; Fagan & Davies, 2000). When the police are perceived as acting in a biased, discriminatory manner, the legitimacy of the police is adversely impacted. The police are not viewed as a reliable source of protection for local residents, which may ultimately lead to greater levels of violence as people feel the need to turn to self help to protect themselves from crime and criminals (Gau & Brunson, 2015).

Described as "one of the most hotly debated issues in policing in the past 10 years" (Vitale, 2005, p. 99), aggressive, proactive policing has had some reported success. MacDonald (2002) argued that the research is "promising," noting that aggressive enforcement can result in significant reductions in violent crime when it is implemented successfully. A number of researchers have found that ZTP-style enforcement tactics have been effective in reducing violent crime (Sampson & Cohen, 1988; Wilson & Boland, 1978) while others have found no direct causal relationship (see Sousa, 2010). In an analysis of robbery and homicide rates in 164 large cities, MacDonald concluded that "proactive policing methods related to aggressive enforcement may be the most effective law enforcement resource on a national level to prevent violent crime" (2002, p. 612).

The Future of Urban Policing

We have taken a bit of a journey in this chapter, from looking at definitions of urban areas, theories of urban life, classical and contemporary policing practices in cities, and an examination of a contemporary debate between which are the most effective policing strategies. What will the future hold? Will crime rates continue to decline, or will the current economic crisis in our country cause an increase in criminal activity? How will the police respond? Or, possibly a better question, how *should* the police respond? Is it better to try to build collective efficacy through community policing strategies, or are aggressive, proactive arrest strategies the best way to curb social disorganization?

These are the questions that policing scholars have wrestled with for decades, and, more than likely, will continue to debate.

Recently, the President's Task Force on 21st Century Policing (2015) outlined a number of action items for law enforcement agencies, including building trust and legitimacy; policy and oversight; technology and social media; community policing and crime reduction; officer training and education; and officer safety and wellness. An overarching recommendation for these central reforms focused on the need for law enforcement agencies to join together and engage in a comprehensive examination of community-based initiatives that are directed at core social issues, including poverty, education, health, and safety. While immediate implementation of the action items was encouraged, the task force recognized the fact that law enforcement agencies cannot solve community ailments alone. As phrased by the task force (2015, p. 8), "It will be through partnerships across sectors and at every level of government that we will find the effective and legitimate long-term solutions to ensuring public safety."

References

Anderson, E. (1999). *The code of the street: Decency, violence, and the moral life of the inner city.* New York: W.W. Norton & Company.

Bassuk, E., Browne, A., & Buckner, J. (1996, October). Single mothers and welfare. *Scientific American,* 36–41.

Black, D. (1971). The social organization of arrest. *Stanford Law Review, 23,* 1087–1092.

Blalock, H. (1967). *Toward a theory of minority-group relations.* New York: John Wiley & Sons.

Blumstein, A. (1995). Youth violence, guns and the illicit drug industry. *Journal of Criminal Law and Criminology, 86*(1), 10–36.

Bowling, B. (1999). The rise and fall of New York murder: Zero tolerance or crack's decline? *British Journal of Criminology, 39*(4), 531–554.

Bracey, D. (1992). Police corruption and community relations: Community policing. *Police Studies, 15*(4), 179–183.

Bridenball, B., & Jesilow, P. (2005). Weeding criminals or planting fear: An evaluation of a Weed and Seed project. *Criminal Justice Review, 30*(1), 64–89.

Brittain, A. (2015, October 24). Police killed their son and saved their lives. *Washington Post.* Retrieved from http://www.washingtonpost.com/sf/investigative/2015/10/24/police-killed-their-son-and-saved-their-lives/.

Brunson, R. K., & Miller, J. (2006). Young black men and urban policing in the United States. *British Journal of Criminology, 46*(4), 613–640.

Bursik, R., Jr., & Grasmick, H. (1993). *Neighborhoods and crime: The dimensions of effective community control.* New York: Lexington Books.

Capers, B. (2009). Police, race, and place. *Harvard Civil Rights-Civil Liberties Law Review, 44,* 43–79.

Chamlin, M. (1989). Conflict theory and police killings. *Deviant Behavior, 10*(4), 353–368.

Cohen, L., & Felson, M. (1979). Social change and crime rate trends: A routine activity approach. *American Sociological Review, 44*(4), 588–608.

Coleman, J. S. (1988). Social capital in the creation of human capital. *American Journal of Sociology, 94,* 95–120.

Curran, D., & Renzetti, C. (2001). *Theories of crime* (2nd ed.). Boston: Allyn and Bacon.

Eck, J. E., & Maguire, E. R. (2000). Have changes in policing reduced violent crime? An assessment of the evidence. In A. Blumstein & J. Wallman (Eds.), *The crime drop in America* (pp. 207–265). New York: Cambridge University Press.

Einstadter, W., & Henry, S. (1995). *Criminological theory: An analysis of its underlying assumptions.* Fort Worth: Harcourt Brace College Publishers.

Fagan, J., & Davies, G. (2000). Street stops and broken windows: Terry, race and disorder in New York City. *Fordham Urban Law Journal, 28*(2), 457–505.

Felson, M. (1998). *Crime and everyday life* (2nd ed.). Thousand Oaks: Pine Forge Press.

Gau, J. M., & Brunson, R. K. (2015). Procedural injustice, lost legitimacy, and self-help: Young males' adaptations to perceived unfairness in urban policing tactics. *Journal of Contemporary Criminal Justice, 31*(2), 132–150.

Gold, M. (1987). Social ecology. In H. Quay (Ed.), *Handbook of juvenile delinquency* (pp. 62–105). New York: John Wiley & Sons.

Goldstein, H. (1987). Toward community-oriented policing: Potential, basic requirements, and threshold questions. *Crime and Delinquency, 33*(1), 6–30.

Goldstein, H. (1993). *The new policing: Confronting complexity.* National Institute of Justice, Research in Brief, Washington, DC: U.S. Department of Justice.

Goldstein, J. (1960). Police discretion not to invoke the criminal process: Low-visibility decisions in the administration of justice. *The Yale Law Journal, 69,* 543–594.

Gottdiener, M., & Hutchison, R. (2006). *The new urban sociology* (3rd ed.). Boulder, CO: Westview Press.

Greek, C. (1992). *Religious roots of American sociology.* New York: Garland.

Green, J. A. (1999). Zero tolerance: A case study of police policies and practices in New York City. *Crime & Delinquency, 45*(2), 171–187.

Hart, T., & Lersch, K. M. (2015). *Space, time, and crime* (4th ed.). Durham: Carolina Academic Press.

Jackson, P. (1989). *Minority group threat, crime, and policing: Social context and social control.* Westport, CT: Praeger Publishers.

Johnson, D., & Gregory, R. (1971). Police-community relations in the United States: A review of recent literature and projects. *Journal of Criminal Law, Criminology, and Police Science, 62*, 94–103.

Kent, S. L., & Carmichael, J. T. (2014). Racial residential segregation and social control: A panel study of the variation in police strength across U.S. cities, 1980–2010. *American Journal of Criminal Justice, 39*(2), 228–249.

Kindy, K. (2015, May 30). Fatal police shootings in 2015 approaching 400 nationwide. *The Washington Post.* Retrieved from https://www.washingtonpost.com/national/fatal-police-shootings-in-2015-approaching-400-nationwide/2015/05/30/d322256a-058e-11e5-a428-c984eb077d4e_story.html.

Klinger, D. (1997). Negotiating order in patrol work: An ecological theory of police response to deviance. *Criminology, 35*(2), 277–306.

Kornhauser, R. (1978). *Social sources of delinquency.* Chicago: University of Chicago Press.

Lab, S. (2000). *Crime prevention: Approaches, practices and evaluations* (4th ed.). Cincinnati: Anderson Publishing Co.

Lersch, K. M. (1998). Police misconduct and malpractice: A critical analysis of citizen complaints. *Policing: An International Journal of Police Strategies & Management, 21*(1), 80–96.

Liederbach, J., & Frank J. (2006). Policing the big beat: An observational study of county level patrol and comparisons to local small town and rural officers. *Journal of Crime and Justice, 29*(1), 21–44.

Liska, A. E. (1992). *Social threat and social control.* Albany, NY: State University of New York.

Liska, A. E., Chamlin, M. B., & Reed, M. D. (1985). Testing the economic production and conflict models of crime control. *Social Forces, 64*(1), 119–138.

MacDonald, J. M. (2002). The effectiveness of community policing in reducing urban violence. *Crime and Delinquency, 48*(4), 592–618.

Macionis, J. J., & Parrillo, V. N. (2007). *Cities and urban life* (4th ed.). Upper Saddle River, NJ: Prentice Hall.

Martin, R., Mutchnick, R., & Austin, W. (1990). *Criminological thought: Pioneers past and present.* New York: Macmillan Publishing Company.

McDonald, P. (2002). *Managing police operations: Implementing the New York crime control model-COMPSTAT.* Belmont: Wadsworth.

Merriam-Webster. (2007). *Merriam-Webster's Collegiate Dictionary* (11th ed.). New York: Merriam-Webster.

Miller, L. (2001). *The politics of community crime prevention: Implementing Operation Weed and Seed in Seattle.* Burlington: Ashgate.

Mirowsky, J., & Ross, C. E. (1983). Paranoia and the structure of powerlessness. *American Sociological Review, 48*(2), 228–239.

Morenoff, J., Sampson, R., & Raudenbush, S. (2001). Neighborhood inequality, collective efficacy, and the spatial dynamics of urban violence. *Criminology, 39*(3), 517–560.

Office of Management and Budget. (2000, December). *Standards for defining metropolitan and micropolitan statistical areas; notice.* Washington, DC: Office of Information and Regulatory Affairs.

Office of Management and Budget. (2013, February). *Revised delineations of metropolitan statistical areas, micropolitan statistical areas, and combined statistical areas, and guidance on uses of the delineations of these areas.* Washington, DC: Office of Information and Regulatory Affairs.

Pare, P., Felson, R. B., & Ouimet, M. (2007). Community variation in crime clearance: A multilevel analysis with comments on assessing police performance. *Journal of Quantitative Criminology, 23*(3), 243–258.

Peak, K., & Glensor, R. (2002). *Community policing and problem solving: Strategies and practices* (3rd ed.). Upper Saddle River: Prentice Hall.

President's Task Force on 21st Century Policing. (2015). *Final report of the President's Task Force on 21st Century Policing.* Washington, DC: Office of Community Oriented Policing Services.

Reaves, B. A. (2015, May). *Local police departments, 2013: Personnel, policies and practices.* Washington, DC: U.S. Department of Justice.

Reisig, M. D., & Cancino, J. M. (2004). Incivilities in nonmetropolitan communities: The effects of structural constraints, social conditions, and crime. *Journal of Criminal Justice, 32*(1), 15–29.

Roehl, J., Huitt, R., Wycoff, M., Pate, A., Robich, D., & Coyle, K. (1996). National process evaluation of Operation Weed and Seed. *National Institute of Justice Research in Brief.* Washington, DC: U.S. Department of Justice.

Ross, C. E., Mirowsky, J., & Pribesh, S. (2002). Disadvantage, disorder, and urban mistrust. *City & Community, 1*, 59–82.

Sampson, R. (1995). The community. In J. Wilson & J. Petersilia (Eds.), *Crime* (pp. 193–216). San Francisco: Institute for Contemporary Studies Press.

Sampson, R., & Cohen, J. (1988). Deterrent effects of the police on crime: A replication and theoretical extension. *Law and Society Review, 22*(1), 163–189.

Sampson, R., & Groves, W. (1989). Community structure and crime: Testing social-disorganization theory. *American Journal of Sociology, 94*, 774–802.

Sampson, R., & Raudenbush, S. (1999). Systematic social observation of public spaces. *American Journal of Sociology, 105*, 603–651.

Sampson, R., Raudenbush, S., & Earls, F. (1997). Neighborhoods and violent crime: A multilevel study of collective efficacy. *Science, 277*(5328), 918–924.

Sever, B. (2003). The minority population / police strength relationship: Exploring past research. *Criminal Justice Studies, 16*(2), 153–171.

Shaw, C., & McKay, H. (1969). *Juvenile delinquency and urban areas* (rev. ed.). Chicago: The University of Chicago Press.

Sherman, L., Gottfredson, D., MacKenzie, D., Eck, J., Reuter, P., & Bushway, S. (1997). *Preventing crime: What works, what doesn't, what's promising.* Washington, DC: U.S. Department of Justice.

Simons, C. (2002). The evolution of crime prevention. In D. Robinson (Ed.), *Policing and crime prevention* (pp. 1–18). Upper Saddle River: Prentice Hall.

Skogan, W. (1990). *Disorder and decline: Crime and the spiral of decay in American neighborhoods.* New York: Free Press.

Skogan, W. (2004). Representing the community in community policing. In W. Skogan (Ed.), *Community policing: Can it work?* (pp. 57–76). Belmont: Wadsworth/Thomson Learning.

Slovak, J. (1986). *Styles of urban policing.* New York: New York University Press.

Smith, B. W., & Holmes, M. D. (2003). Community accountability, minority threat, and police brutality: An examination of civil rights criminal complaints. *Criminology, 41*(4), 1035–1069.

Smith, D. (1986). The neighborhood context of police behavior. In A. J. Reiss, Jr., & M. Tonry (Eds.), *Communities and crime.* Chicago: University of Chicago Press.

Sousa, W. H. (2010). Paying attention to minor offenses: Order maintenance policing in practice. *Police Practice and Research, 11*(1), 45–59.

Stark, R. (1987). Deviant places: A theory of the ecology of crime. *Criminology, 25*(4), 893–909.

Stevens, D. J. (2003a). *Case studies in applied community policing.* Boston: Pearson Education.

Stevens, D. J. (2003b). *Applied community policing in the 21st Century.* Boston: Pearson Education.

Taylor, I., Walton, P., & Young, J. (1973). *The new criminology: For a social theory of deviance.* New York: Harper Torchbooks.

Terrill, W., & Reisig, M. D. (2003). Neighborhood context and police use of force. *Journal of Research in Crime and Delinquency, 40*(3), 291–321.

Trojanowicz, R., & Bucqueroux, B. (1990). *Community policing: A contemporary perspective.* Cincinnati: Anderson Publishing Co.

Tyler, T. R., Fagan, J., & Geller, A. (2014). Street stops and police legitimacy: Teachable moments in young urban men's legal socialization. *Journal of Empirical Legal Studies, 11*(4), 751–785.

United States Census Bureau. (2007, April). *Table 9. Cumulative estimates of the components of population change for metropolitan and micropolitan statistical areas: April 1, 2000 to July 1, 2006.* Washington, DC: Population Division, U.S. Census Bureau.

Vitale, A. S. (2005). Innovation and institutionalization: Factors in the development of "quality of life" policing in New York City. *Policing & Society, 15*(2), 99–124.

Vold, G., Bernard, T., & Snipes, J. (2002). *Theoretical criminology* (5th ed.). New York: Oxford University Press.

Walker, S. (1992). *The police in America: An introduction.* New York: McGraw Hill.

Walker, S., Spohn, C., & DeLone, M. (2007). *The color of justice: Race, ethnicity and crime in America* (2nd ed.). Belmont: Thomson Higher Education.

Websdale, N. (2001). *Policing the poor: From slave plantation to public housing.* Boston: Northeastern University Press.

Weisel, D., & Eck, J. (1994). Toward a practical approach to organizational change: Community policing initiatives in six cities. In D. P. Rosenbaum (Ed.), *The challenge of community policing: Testing the promises* (pp. 110–126). Thousand Oaks: Sage Publishing.

Werthman, C., & Piliavin, I. (1967). Gang members and the police. In D. Bordua (Ed.), *The police: Six sociological essays* (pp. 56–98). New York: John Wiley.

Wilson, J. Q., & Boland, B. (1978). The effect of the police on crime. *Law and Society Review, 12*, 367–390.

Wilson, J. Q., & Kelling, G. (1982, March). Broken windows. *Atlantic Monthly, 249*, 29–38.

Wilson, W. J. (1996). *When work disappears: The world of the new urban poor.* New York: Vintage.

Wirth, L. (1938). Urbanism as a way of life. *American Journal of Sociology, 44*, 3–24.

8

Policing Educational Spaces: Status, Practices, and Challenges

Emmanuel P. Barthe

Introduction

Today's elementary, secondary, and postsecondary educational (PSE) institutions' campuses were once bucolic, carefree places (notwithstanding the rigors of academic life), where one could generally feel very safe while frequenting those environs, if nowhere else. Such is not the case today, however. Consider, for example, the deadliest mass campus shooting in U.S. history: a senior English major killed 33 and wounded 15 students at Virginia Polytechnic Institute and State University (Virginia Tech) in April 2007 (Hauser & O'Connor, 2008). Following this tragedy, PSE institutions were compelled to reconsider their approaches to campus safety and urged to engage in better monitoring and treatment of students with emotional problems. Also in the wake of Virginia Tech, many colleges and universities (including Rhode Island's Brown University, three Iowa state universities, and several institutions in Massachusetts) initiated discussions concerning whether their campus police officers should be armed (see, for example, Associated Press, 2007; Kocian, 2008; *U.S. News and World Report*, 2012; Associated Press, 2016).

There were other repercussions as well as a flurry of legislation to lift gun bans on campus based on the premise that armed faculty or students could stop or deter an active shooter. As of 2016, 9 states have affirmative policies that allow guns on campus while 21 states have banned them. Although a bill was submitted to lift the campus gun ban in Virginia in the wake of the shooting at Virginia Tech, it did not pass (Morse et al., 2016). Other institutions, such as Southern Illinois University-Edwardsville (SIUE), began giving students tips on how to survive if a gunman were to begin shooting on campus. SIUE also issued an online training video that the administrators hope will make the students better prepared if bullets start flying (SIUE Police, 2017)).

Unfortunately, Virginia Tech was not an anomaly; other such attacks, although less massive in their loss of life but still very traumatic in nature, occurred early in this millennium at postsecondary institutions in the U.S.:

- A 49-year-old man killed himself and his two sons during a visit to the campus of Shepherd University (in West Virginia) in September 2006.
- In January 2002, a student who had been dismissed from Virginia's Appalachian School of Law went to campus and killed the dean, a professor, and a student, and wounded three others. Later that year, in October, a failing nursing student and Gulf War veteran fatally killed an instructor in her office at the University of Arizona; then, while armed with five guns, he entered a nursing classroom and killed two more instructors.
- A University of Arkansas student murdered his English professor after being dropped from a doctoral program in August 2000 (CBS News, 2000).
- In 2012, twenty children and six adults were killed at Sandy Hook Elementary school in Newtown, Connecticut, and since then, there have been 186 shootings on school grounds across the United States (*Los Angeles Times*, 2016).

In short, the last few years have seen numerous school-related incidents, prompting the discussion surrounding school safety, protocols, and proper police responses.

Of course, high school campuses have not been spared this mayhem; from 1992 to 1999, there were 238 school-associated violent deaths, including the April 1999 massacre of 13 people at Columbine High School in Littleton, Colorado (Marlin & Vogt, 1999). K-12 school safety continues to be a major concern, and several initiatives have been developed. For example, in addition to having their own dedicated police organizations, many schools now have school resource officers (SROs) for safety planning efforts, to assess the schools' structure, and to determine where potential problems exist. The K-12 police presence can now even include gang officers, and many school police agencies have developed a plan of action in the event of an active shooter situation. Recent analyses of school resource officers, however, have demonstrated that there may be some inequality in the distribution of these officers across the nation's schools. A report by *The New York Times* in 2009 on campus policing found that schools where at least half of the children are non-White, as well as high-poverty schools, are home to the highest percentages in the country of K-12 campus law enforcement (Anderson, 2015).

Unfortunately, all of this violence on U.S. campuses has also led Americans to now accept campus shootings as inevitable; a recent Gallup poll (2007) found that only 17 percent of all Americans believe campus shootings can be prevented, but that postsecondary institutions should engage in better monitoring and treatment of students with emotional problems.

This chapter concerns crime and policing on educational spaces, now consisting of 75.5 million people (17.6 million in colleges and universities) ages three and older, who are enrolled in school at 125,000 public and private elementary and secondary schools, and 4,200 institutions of higher learning (post-secondary, or PSE) that confer degrees (U.S. Census Bureau, 2008). We will focus on how academic environs affect law enforcement practices, what the police are doing to deal with campus crimes such as those described above, and how campus policing is different from and similar to their county and municipal counterparts—all within the context of the contemporary era of community-oriented policing and problem solving.

First we look at how policing developed in educational settings, from their humble beginnings in the early 1900s, through the social and campus unrest of the 1960s and 1970s, and until today. Included in this contemporary view are the characteristics of campus organizations, their role definition, agency jurisdiction, and authority, and the attributes of chief executives.

Next we look at how campuses are unique in their clientele, infrastructure, and, therefore, policing. Then we consider how campus crime is reported under recent legislation, as well as other legal considerations (e.g., the duty of care and special relationship that exist today between campus police and their clientele). The chapter concludes with an overview of challenges that are posed by the specter of terrorism as well as computer crime.

In sum, this chapter brings to the fore the development—and highly challenging nature—of the organizations that are charged with providing safety and order for those people and property forming the educational space of America.

Development of Campus Policing

Humble Beginnings

As noted above, with respect to crime, U.S. elementary, secondary, and PSE campuses were once idyllic in nature, and until the mid-1900s there was actually little need for campus law enforcement organizations. Educational institutions handled most campus disciplinary problems internally and depended on local police agencies' assistance only in serious criminal violations. During this period there was a heavy reliance on a "watchman" system, primarily using men who were retired from other jobs to protect university property from fire, water, or other damage. However, in 1894, Yale University became the first to send forth a campus patrol; this development was prompted by a rumor circulating through the City of New Haven that Yale medical students were removing buried bodies from local cemeteries for use as cadavers; a mass riot ensued, many students and townspeople were injured, and two New Haven officers were assigned to the Yale campus (Yale University Police Department, 2008).

To be sure, early police at PSE institutions were not intended to function as they do today. Campuses did not have high crime rates, nor were there concerns with duty owed to students for safety and security, crimes in residence halls, mass demonstrations, gang influences, drug or alcohol abuse problems, or other social problems that visit campuses today. Eventually, however, the nation's campuses became a microcosm of the larger society, and these once pastoral places and were beset with behaviors, events, and problems that required a stronger hand of authority. University administrators recognized these issues and, coupled with the need to provide a safer environment for campus clientele, opted to provide this presence.

Therefore, during the 1950s, with the unprecedented growth in student enrollment and in physical size, PSE institutions began hiring people—often retired municipal police officers—to serve as "campus security" officers. The officers' duties during this decade were primarily custodial in nature; indeed, these officers typically had no more power to control the behavior of people than did ordinary citizens, and the doctrine of *in loco parentis* (the state to act in the place of the parent guided the actions of campus security organizations (Sloan, 1992).

The 1960s and 1970s

Legal, social, and international events in the 1960s and early 1970s dramatically changed the need for security and policing at PSE campuses in the

U.S. As social and campus unrest grew, universities relied on public police forces to handle campus crime and disorder. But in case after case, the consequences of calling in city police to deal with campus disorder were disastrous; the presence of the city police often exacerbated conflict and polarized the campus (Skolnick, 1969). Soon a growing number of PSE administrators were realizing that unless they took measures to keep order on campus, outside police agencies would be forced to do so for them. The idea of campus security forces, which better represented college norms and values, naturally appealed to university administrators (Powell, 1971). Therefore, it was during this period of social upheaval that many campuses developed their own police departments, and by the early 1970s officers at state institutions were beginning to possess full arrest powers granted by statute or through local deputization (Brubacher & Willis, 1968; Gelber, 1972; Esposito & Stormer, 1989).

Concomitantly, it was deemed important that the image of campus officers as being old, overweight, and only interested in fire prevention, door-shaking, and the issuance of parking tickets had to change (Webb, 1975), and that sworn, trained law enforcers were needed (Sloan, 1992). Continuing into the 1980s and early 1990s, therefore, the campus officers became increasingly autonomous. They developed a greater similarity to urban police departments in their administration, structure, and operations; continued to elevate educational and training standards for their personnel; fomented more of a dedicated career path for employees; and generally became an increasingly integral part of the fabric of American PSE campuses (cf. Peak, 1988; Sloan, 1992).

Furthermore, during the past few decades there has been further professionalization in the characteristics of the campus organizations and the officers, both of which will be addressed in greater detail below. It should be noted that certainly the past 20 years have witnessed significant changes in public expectations and the practices of *all* forms of police work. Policing today is now in the community policing era, where the police focus on working collaboratively with the community to address crime and disorder (Peak & Glensor, 2008; Oliver, 2004; Clarke, 2004; Goldstein, 1990). The attacks of September 11, 2001, also changed forever the way the police must view domestic security and plan for the specter of terrorism, while greatly heightened drug problems have forced police agencies to develop new methods to increase interdiction efforts (Goldstein, 1990). Also, gangs have nearly blanketed the nation and require different methods and tactics. And on some campuses, major incidents—including murders of sworn officers and students—have compelled the police to take a more hardline perspective with regard to their role and function. Finally, emphases on police organizational diversity and hiring practices have also changed the face of the modern police organization.

Campus Policing Today

In 2008, Peak, Barthe, and Garcia reported their findings of a national survey of campus police organizations that compared the findings of a study by Peak two decades earlier (Peak, 1987). Their study demonstrates the extent to which campus policing has grown and developed over those intervening 20 years. Next we discuss some of their findings concerning organizational characteristics, role definition, jurisdiction and authority, and attributes of chief executives and other personnel.

Organizational Characteristics

Perhaps one interesting finding of the study by Peak et al. (2008) concerns the titles of campus law enforcement agencies. From 1986 to 2006 there was a 62 percent increase in the use of the formal title of "Police Department," with a marked decrease (65 percent) in designations like "security office" or "security department." The title "Department of Public Safety" is also heavily used, at 29 percent of the organizations; some agencies use this term to describe what they perceive to be a broader mission that includes law enforcement, security, safety, crime prevention, emergency medical, and other services and functions. The dramatic increase in the adoption of the Police Department designation also supports the idea that there has been a movement towards professionalization in campus law enforcement agencies.

Over the past 20 years, it appears that more PSE campuses have evolved in their role, moving away from the more mundane and basic security tasks to more formal police activities, with uniformed patrols and full arrest and investigative powers. Indeed, in 1986 the most commonly reported campus-policing activities involved parking issues; by 2006, the top activity involved investigations.

Like local police forces, campus police agencies are organized hierarchically with paramilitary ranks. Peak et al. (2008, p. 251) found these organizations to be similar to municipal or county police in their rank structure. While the 1986 survey reported supervisory positions were present in campus law enforcement agencies, the 2006 study shows a definite increase in the usage of *all* ranks, indicating a greater emphasis on specialized assignments. Specifically, there was a 16 percent increase in the use of assistant chief ranks, a 29 percent increase in detective ranks, a 22 percent increase in lieutenant ranks, and a 71 percent increase in the rank of corporal.

With respect to personnel hiring and training, today many current agencies rely heavily on psychological and polygraph examinations (71 percent and 69 percent, respectively). Similarly, while only 19 percent of agencies used physical agility tests in 1986, in 2006, 42 percent of agencies used these tests for selection purposes. Required annual in-service training of personnel also increased dramatically: the mean number of required annual in-service training hours was 14.5 in 1986; by 2006 this number had spiked to 47 hours.

Another related consideration is that of image. While many campus police departments enjoy a large measure of respect from their county and municipal counterparts, others may still be attempting to shed the "door-shaker" stereotype. Owing to the movement to professionalize, however, today most campus police departments are not perceived in that light. Jacobs and O'Meara (1980) argued that professional campus police forces increasingly resemble other American police departments and that three decades of steady growth and professionalization have enabled these campus units to evolve into the very kind of law enforcement they were originally intended to replace.

The aforementioned changes in campus law enforcement agencies appear to have had a positive effect on organizational image. When asking respondents about their reputation with local police departments, Peak et al. (2008) found a 9 percent increase in the number of campus police agencies that reported a satisfactory reputation, when compared with 1986; there was also a 19 percent increase in positive relations with campus faculty and staff, a 12 percent increase with the student body, and a 9 percent increase with the university administration.

While the 1986 survey determined that three-fourths of the responding organizations had full (i.e., arrest and investigatory) police powers, the 2006 survey found that over 82 percent of respondents reported that their staff had such authority. It is probably safe to assume that the higher rate of agencies having full police powers is linked to greater use of the formal title of "police department," as discussed above.

Campus law enforcement agencies also appear to be moving toward greater use of full-time sworn personnel, with an average number of 21 officers in 1986 and 29 officers in 2006 (a 38 percent increase). Part-time sworn officers were less common in 2006, with an average of 3.1 officers compared to 6 in 1986 (a 48 percent decrease).

Role Definition

Notwithstanding the above areas of improvement in the professionalization of campus police agencies, some agencies still struggle with their role definition. In the eyes of many, the exact role of campus police officers is still not clear. Consider, for example, the aforementioned debate that ensued on many campuses following the Virginia Tech shootings in 2007 concerning whether or not the officers should be armed. It is clear that some PSE institutions are still grappling with the issue of armed sworn officers patrolling campuses.

In a perfect world, campus officers could remain true to their roots, having primarily a *service* orientation and "walking softly" among their highly educated and generally very law-abiding clientele, while eschewing the harder image and specialization (e.g., special weapons and tactics teams) of their municipal and county cousins. Once again, however, today's reality is that these officers must be trained, equipped, and prepared to deal with many crime- or disaster-related exigency that humans or nature may wrought. Their role has indeed changed, and it must continue to evolve so as to conform to the complex milieu in which they function.

Another area where the local and the campus police may have role differences concerns how offenders should be handled. Notwithstanding their political roots, and perhaps occasional pressure to not arrest the "wrong" politically influential person, the local police normally have no problem with decisions concerning whom they will and will not arrest. But on campuses, historically the range of treatment of offenders has been less defined; certainly these institutions have always had the latitude of referring a criminal matter involving a student to the civil authorities for prosecution; historically, however, it is probably fair to say that many campuses had unofficial policies of handling most criminal matters in-house, through the campus disciplinary process. To be sure, many misdemeanors committed on campus can be of the relatively harmless "prank" variety and can and have been dealt with in-house, while felonies are typically viewed as another matter altogether. Although there have not been any comprehensive studies concerning how campus police deal with their offenders, Bordner and Petersen (1983, p. 209) found that 94 percent of campus police officers felt that all students and others "should suffer the consequences of their actions."

Certainly, differential treatment of campus offenders could cause a role dilemma for the officer, who may not know "when to be aggressive and when not to" (Bordner & Petersen 1983, p. 215). However, many campus police administrators apparently tend to agree that students should not escape legal responsibility for committing felony offenses simply by virtue of their having paid the price of tuition. One midwestern campus police director put it thusly:

> [M]ore and more universities have come to treat crime on campus more like crime in the surrounding community and less like in-house "incidents." The doctrine of the university acting "in loco parentis" has all but disappeared. As a result, students are coming more and more to expect to be treated the same as any other member of society. A 19-year-old student who shoplifts from the campus bookstore should ex-

> pect the same treatment as a 19-year-old auto mechanic who shoplifts from that same bookstore. It is ... fundamentally wrong for the student to be taken to the dean's office and receive a one-year academic probation while the auto mechanic goes to jail. (Denney, 1992, p. 6)

Some postsecondary institutions may still prefer to keep their crime problems in-house; being concerned with their public image, some observers (Seng & Koehler 1993; Seng, 1994) feel these institutions may attempt to look for loopholes in the Campus Security Act of 1990 when publishing their crime information; of course, it would be unlawful and very unwise and imprudent to adopt such a strategy.

Agency Jurisdiction and Authority

What is the proper jurisdiction of the campus police? Should it extend to any state property, or only to campus properties? Should it be included within a specified radius of the campus proper? If so, what is the proper radius—one mile? Ten miles? Or, rather, should their jurisdiction only extend to the middle of the streets bordering the campus? And should the campus police be allowed to respond to an incident in an area that is "adjacent to campus" if a student is involved? What about outlying campus properties (e.g., farms, other administrative or instructional buildings)? And should a campus officer be allowed to take official action if he or she detects criminal behavior while en route to patrol at those off-campus sites (e.g., an intoxicated driver is observed on a public street or highway)? How should a campus police officer react if another police agency requests backup to deal with a problem located a few blocks away from their normal jurisdiction?

Some or all of these questions and situations have been, and probably still are problematic for some PSE institutions, particularly in the aftermath of 9/11 and given the recent increase in school shootings and other forms of crime and violence. Many states grant campus police officers full sworn status while on campus, but limit the officers' authority if off campus. Such officers generally are often allowed to exercise police powers, however, if they leave their campuses in a valid chase, under the so-called "hot pursuit" doctrine (Smith, 1988). Again, the public's perception of the campus police is implicated here, as that may dictate in large measure how the state legislature views and allows officers to have extended jurisdiction. The shooting of a Black motorist by a University of Cincinnati campus police officer for a minor traffic stop in July 2015 has once again raised the question of school police jurisdiction. Since the shooting, the mayor has requested that campus police officers not conduct off-campus traffic stops.

Recent reports show, however, that several stops have been made since the mayoral order, upsetting the political climate even further (*USA Today*, 2016).

Peak et al. (2008) found that campus agencies have experienced an increase in their jurisdictional responsibilities. In 1986, only 10 percent of agencies had statewide jurisdiction, with that number climbing to 18 percent in 2006. While the boundaries of the campus are the first priority of any campus law enforcement agency, a small increase has occurred in their being granted jurisdiction beyond their immediate campus borders: in 1986, 46 percent of agencies reported having jurisdiction only on their campuses, as compared to 42 percent in 2006. Similarly, while 13 percent of the agencies in 1986 reported having jurisdiction only within 10 miles of their campus, that percentage dropped to 7 percent in 2006. It seems clear that with increased police powers, these agencies also have greater jurisdictional control over the areas surrounding their campuses. This could also be due to the realization that some campus problems can be addressed by solving other problems off-campus. For example, campus police can more likely curb drug use in a dormitory if nearby off-campus drug areas are addressed. This is especially important since other research has shown that alcohol and drugs were implicated in 95% of all campus offenses (Sloan, 1994).

Similarly, traffic enforcement on major roadways leading to the campus can reduce student speeding and accidents. Finally, increasing personnel jurisdiction recognizes that campus law enforcement agencies can be most efficient when they are free to investigate and intervene on and off campus alike.

Chief Executive Attributes

While Peak (1987) found in the 1986 survey that 87 percent of campus police directors were Caucasian, the 2006 survey found a slightly lower rate of 84 percent (a 3 percent decrease). More significantly, there was a 10 percent decrease in the number of males in this position, going from 97 percent in 1986 to 87 percent in 2006. These two findings reflect a slight trend in hiring diversity when it comes to campus police agencies. There is, however, a definite trend toward older administrators, indicating that such positions are reserved for those with experience and proper supervisory training. Peak et al. (2008) found a 60 percent decrease in administrators between the ages of 31–40 years over the last twenty years.

Regarding the levels of experience of campus police chief executive officers, today most campus police administrators have previously held some sort of supervisory role in a law enforcement agency. Specifically, Peak et al. (2008) found that 23 percent (compared to 18 percent in 1986) of these administrators had been supervisors in another campus law enforcement agency, and 28 percent (23 percent in 1986) had been supervisors in their current agency; this indicates a slight increase in "external hires." And with respect to the administrators' educational levels, in 1986, 24 percent of the respondents stated they held a master's degree and only 2 percent had a doctorate degree; in 2006, 43 percent held a master's (a 78 percent increase) and 4 percent held a doctorate.

Campus Policing as Work: Philosophical and Operational Considerations

Anyone who has ever visited a postsecondary or K-12 campus knows that the clientele and infrastructure of those educational spaces are vastly different from non-campus venues. For example, college and university clientele (i.e., students and faculty) are highly educated and seek the social and cultural opportunities and lifestyle that are unique to this environment. Therefore, they expect the campus to be a place of peace and safety, and may take a more dispassionate view of crime prevention, especially in terms of protecting their persons and their property.

The populations of these settings—particularly during major events, which can number in tens of thousands of people—are often quite dense, as are the buildings that compose these campuses, and facilities exist for the gathering of large numbers of people at social, athletic, and cultural events. Campus environs are often abuzz with such activities, while Greek and other organizations may regularly conduct parties on or near campus property. The students, faculty, and staff of these institutions, moreover, traverse the campuses and are in their offices at all hours of the day and night, attending classes and special events, engaging in research, working in laboratories, and so on. In addition, there will be thousands of vehicles parked on campus that require security and a system of enforcement.

That the educational setting is densely populated, has many remote and/or secluded locations (e.g., in parking garages, libraries, and other buildings), and contains valuable property (both personal and technological, particularly computers) will not be lost on those who would encroach on this peaceful environment to rob, plunder, rape, or worse.

How must such a unique space be policed? Certainly, the philosophy and methods of those who protect such environs, like the clientele and their activities, must also be unique. To begin, there must be a *service*, rather than *law enforcement*, orientation, including a commitment to crime prevention rather than reactively investigating them. Instead of working myriad traffic collisions and addressing domestic disputes and bar fights, these officers are more often performing such activities as escorting people to their vehicles after late-night classes, giving directions to visitors, checking buildings for intruders and other problems, and unlocking faculty and staff offices and classrooms. But the potential for human emergency or a natural disaster is always present. Therefore, while "walking softly," campus police must also be prepared to deal with all manner of emergencies and criminal behaviors.

Given that campuses can be magnets for persons with criminal intent, crime prevention should obviously be accorded a high priority. Means must be developed for making these settings less conducive to unwanted or illegal activities, while making criminal activity less attractive to offenders. Crime prevention through environmental design (CPTED) is an important concept on campuses and includes using proper design and the environment to reduce the fear and incidence of crime. This goal is accomplished by such approaches as: natural access control (doors, shrubs, fences, and gates to deny admission to a crime target); natural surveillance (e.g., the proper placement of windows, lighting, and landscaping to increase the ability to observe intruders); territorial reinforcement (using such elements as sidewalks, landscaping, and porches to distinguish between public and private areas and helps users exhibit signs of "ownership" that send "hands off" messages to would-be offenders).

Much of the above crime prevention effort requires crime analysis information, which can be accomplished by using another process that is rapidly spreading across the U.S.: CompStat, for "computer statistics." CompStat is used to collect, analyze, and map crime data on a regular basis, and hold police managers accountable for their performance. Introduced by the New York City Police Department in 1994, CompStat's key elements are: accurate and timely intelligence, effective tactics, rapid deployment of personnel and resources, and relentless follow-up and assessment (Grant & Terry, 2005). Officers stop simply responding to crime and begin proactively thinking about ways to deal with it in terms of suppression, intervention, and prevention.

Campus Crime and the Cleary Act

Another significant change in the responsibilities of campus law enforcement agencies involved the 1998 Jeanne Clery Disclosure of Campus Security Policy and Campus Crime Statistics Act, codified at 20 USC 1092 (f). The law, originally enacted in 1990 by Congress as the Campus Security Act, was later amended and renamed the Clery Act for Jeanne Clery—a 19-year-old Lehigh University freshman in Bethlehem, Pennsylvania, who was raped and murdered in her campus residence hall in 1986. This federal law requires colleges and universities to disclose certain timely and annual information about campus crime and security policies. All public and private post-secondary educational institutions participating in federal student aid programs are subject to this law. We discuss Clery more below.

The aforementioned Clery Act has also modified, professionalized, and made more transparent today's campus policing operations as well. Prior to 1990, statistics were informally kept and due to the insular nature of many campus law enforcement agencies, parents, students, faculty, and staff were unaware of potential crime problems occurring on campuses. Because of its federal reporting requirement, the Clery Act improved the recordkeeping practices of many campus police agencies, and directed administrators to address crime problems quickly and efficiently. Some researchers, however, point out that the reporting system has certain flaws. For example, while thefts are the most common campus crimes, these do not have to be reported, and off-campus crimes involving students are exempt from the reporting requirement (Seng, 1995). Obviously, the 1986 survey provided no data concerning this not-yet-existing reporting requirement, but the 2006 sample demonstrated the impact this legislation had on their agencies. Some agencies relied on sworn personnel for required data collection, while others utilized civilian personnel. Of those relying on sworn staff, approximately 88 percent of respondents stated that they had at least two *sworn* staff members assigned to the maintenance of the crime statistics log; conversely, 75 percent of respondents relied on *civilian* personnel and stated that they also had at least two employees devoted to that function. While the act mandates an annual reporting requirement, it also states that potential students, parents, and members of the community are allowed to request crime-related information at any time. When queried about the number of requests the agencies received on a monthly basis, 75 percent of the respondents indicated that they had to fulfill between 1–3 requests per month, and 10 percent reported having to fulfill 4–6 requests.

(Note that the Federal Bureau of Investigation's Uniform Crime Reporting Program's "Crime in the United States" includes annual crime statistics for about 400 colleges and universities, at http://www.fbi.gov/ucr/05cius/data/table_09.html; also, Security on Campus, Inc., reports Clery Act campus crime data for 4,000 institutions, at http://www.securityoncampus.org/crimestats/index.html.)

Other Legal Considerations

Certainly the nation's campuses have not been spared from possessing legal duties regarding the safety of their clientele, and from being sued when their responsibilities have not been met. Next we consider the legal responsibilities that attach to educational spaces. First we briefly review what is meant by such relevant legal terms as "duty of care" and "special relationship," and then discuss some related court cases that serve as precedent for other states to follow.

Duty of Care

The "public duty doctrine" is derived from Common Law and holds that police have no duty to protect the general public from harm, absent a "special relationship (discussed below)." Generally, police legal duties can arise from many sources, including laws, customs, court decisions, and agency policies. Today the law imputes to colleges and universities a duty to provide reasonably adequate security and protection. This duty may arise in two ways: either under a "negligence" theory based on tort law, or on a breach of contract theory based on some assurance that the institution has given as to protection or safety. Security protection can take many forms, of course, such as: police officers, locks, fences, security guards, the lighting of campus and parking garages, trimming or elimination of shrubbery, providing of monitoring devices and emergency telephones, and use of campus escort services (e.g., for persons getting out of classes late at night). But of equal importance is ensuring that classes, residence halls, libraries, cafeterias, and parking lots are not offered in remote or lonely places and are safely accessible and constantly watched.

Once a campus is on notice of the "foreseeability" of criminal harm because of a history of criminal incidents at a location, the institution has not only a duty to warn but also a duty to use due care to provide reasonably adequate security protection. How much is reasonably adequate? The answer must be determined by the facts and circumstances of each individual case, given the history and location of the place, and other pertinent risk data.

An early and leading case illustrating the need for adequate security measures is *Miller v. State of New York* (467 N.E.2d 493, 1984), by New York's highest court. There, a university was held liable for personal injuries sustained by a rape victim in a dormitory that was not properly secured. Because of the special relationship between the university and a resident student, the state institution was not exempt from the charge of negligence (Marschall & Peak, 1994).

Foreseeability need not be based on a history of campus crimes, however. Other sorts of danger may suffice. For example, in *Mullins v. Pine Manor College* (389 Mass. 47, 1983), Massachusetts' highest court addressed a crime much like that in Miller, but took a different posture as to the foreseeability issue. Lisa Mullins was awakened in her dormitory room by a male intruder who raped her; although prior known offenses on the campus were negligible, the jury found foreseeability based on, among other things, the proximity of campus to transportation lines leading to downtown, and on college policies allowing men to stay overnight in women's dorms. The court noted that the college had itself acknowledged the danger of crime in its orientation program for new students, dorm rooms could be unlocked with credit cards or knives, that fences around the campus were inadequate, and that no assurances were provided that two security guards were actually patrolling.

Special Relationship

Special relationships are where the police know or have reason to know the likelihood of harm to someone if they fail to do their duty, and are thus defined by the circumstances surrounding an injury or damage. A special relationship can be based on:

1. whether the officer could have foreseen that he/she was expected to take action in a given situation to prevent injury (e.g., a campus officer observes a male trying to enter a female's dorm room with a credit card; the male states (falsely) that he resides there, the officer fails to check out his story and leaves, and the female resident is then attacked and raped).
2. departmental policy or guidelines that prescribe or prohibit a certain course of action (e.g., officers are to frequently patrol women's dormitories, but fail to do so).
3. the spatial and temporal proximity of the defendant-officer behavior to the injury damage (e.g., a student is observed walking on campus who appears to be extremely intoxicated, is stopped by an officer and questioned, released, and soon thereafter is fatally struck by a car when walking into a nearby street).

Current Challenges: Terrorism and Technology

Due to threats to national security stemming from September 11, 2001, police departments nationwide have had to implement new information sharing systems and to develop protocols for improving responses to terrorist attacks. In 2003, the Department of Homeland Security developed the National Incident Management System (NIMS) (see, for example, Peak, Gaines, & Glensor, 2004; Peak, 2007), designed to standardize information sharing protocols and to improve responses to large-scale domestic incidents. Because the population of many university campuses can range from 5,000 to over 40,000 students and staff, many campus law enforcement agencies have followed suit and undertaken steps to improve their ability to handle emergencies. According to Peak et al. (2008), 71 percent of campus police departments have some sort of policy regarding NIMS protocols, and 77 percent reported that they are in fact using NIMS. In terms of readiness against threats of weapons of mass destruction, 7 percent of agencies reported having received some federal funding for assisting in that effort, 4 percent had purchased emergency response equipment, and 11 percent had instituted some policies or guidelines concerning response procedures. "Training and education" was the most common response (71 percent) concerning preparations for dealing with the potential threat of a serious terrorist attack.

With the advent of computers and technology, campus police administrators have an added responsibility to become "cyber-cops." While incidents of theft and assault may be the traditional and prevalent crime problems on college campuses, campus police are now faced with the growing problem of computer-related crimes. Wright (2000) highlighted some incidents that occurred on college campuses using computers, showing the new challenges faced by campus law enforcement agencies:

- A student sent threatening emails to numerous minority students
- A graduate student extorted money from an online company using school computers and sent threatening emails when he was not paid
- A student was charged with felony communications fraud after he rigged his online election to student body president
- Students illegally downloaded music and shared pornographic materials
- Pedophiles used the university's library computers to compile information about underage boys in the area

Other potential problems involving technology include identity theft, mainframe hacking, online stalking, and sexual harassment, to name a few. With their high concentration of computers and scores of skilled users, college campuses have become fertile grounds for computer and other technology-related crimes, creating unique and particular challenges for campus law enforcement officials.

Utilizing Technology to Manage Crime and Inform Campuses

With the advent of mobile technology and wireless services, police agencies can now be more proactive when it comes to gathering and disseminating crime-related information. In terms of data collection, law enforcement officers can receive text or email alerts from concerned students or faculty apprising them of problems on or around campus. For example, this approach is commonly used during athletic events at the University of Nevada, Reno, where fans are asked to text police and give seat locations of intoxicated or unruly people at the event. This allows campus police to quickly identify and handle problems. When it comes to sharing information, many agencies now rely on "crime alerts" that are sent to students and faculty on their smartphones, social media outlets, or streamed across computer terminals. This immediate alert system ensures that all of the campus is notified at once with instructions from the police department concerning a serious event occurring on campus. The Higher Education Opportunity Act (Public Law 110-315) requires institutions to inform their respective campuses of conditions posing a threat to life, safety, and security so that members of the community can take necessary precautions to protect themselves.

In terms of analyzing crime data, many campus police agencies have adopted CompStat or similar approaches to examining local crime problems. CompStat is a management tool that involves data collection and analysis of crime and related quality of life issues to improve tailored police responses. CompStat has been summarized as follows: "Collect, analyze, and map crime data and other essential police performance measures on a regular basis, and hold police managers accountable for their performance as measured by these data" (DeLorenzi, Shane, & Amendola, 2006, p. 34).

Since the CompStat process was introduced by the New York City Police Department in 1994, it has been widely adopted: a national survey found that 58 percent of large agencies (those with 100 or more sworn officers) had either adopted or were planning to implement a CompStat-like program (CompStat is partly responsible for contributing to significant improvements in the way many organizations control crime and conduct daily business).

The key elements of CompStat are as follows:

- Specific objectives
- Accurate and timely intelligence
- Effective tactics

- Rapid deployment of personnel and resources
- Relentless follow-up and assessment. (Grant & Terry, 2005)

The role of commanders has changed under CompStat, and they have stopped simply responding to crime, and begun proactively thinking about ways to deal with it in terms of suppression, intervention, and prevention. Commanders must explain what tactics they have employed to address crime patterns, what resources they have and need, and with whom they have collaborated. Brainstorming problem solving sessions ensue about proactively responding to the crime problems, and suggestions for strategies are made at subsequent meetings, with relentless follow-up by top brass to further ensure accountability (Grant & Terry, 2005).

Operational and Practical Considerations

The Militarization of Campus Police Departments

The last few years have seen an increase in the militarization of police departments in order to address crime and disorder problems (Kraska, 2001). This growing reliance on military-grade arsenals has raised some concerns from the public. While some municipal agencies can point to larger crime problems to justify such an arsenal, the question of whether or not educational spaces warrant such armamentaria is still being debated in the public sphere. The summer 2014 protests in Ferguson, Missouri, against police brutality have led to a renewed discussion concerning the acquisition and use of SWAT-like equipment on college campuses. Some changes in federal legislation now limit the amount of battle surplus local agencies can purchase, but according to some reports, there are other programs from the Department of Homeland Security that facilitate such transactions, albeit in a different manner (*The Washington Post*, 2015). A recent exposé on the militarizing of American police departments revealed that since 2005, at least 100 campus police agencies across the country have received military-grade equipment as part of the federal give-away programs (*Rolling Stone*, 2015). This move toward arming college campus police officers can lead to a cooling effect when it comes to community-police relations as the efforts of community policing are harder to see when the officers are hidden behind military-like equipment. In 2011, an incident at the UC Davis campus involving a campus officer who doused several protesters on the university quad with orange pepper spray made national headlines and resulted in the officer being fired. UC Davis eventually settled a federal lawsuit by paying $1 million to three dozen protesters who were pepper-sprayed (Garofoli, 2016).

Training for Officers Working in Educational Arenas

A widely circulated video recorded in a classroom at Spring Valley High School in Columbia, South Carolina, showed a White officer assigned to the school, Ben Fields, grabbing a Black female student seated at a desk, flipping her backward, then dragging and throwing her across the floor. The incident brought up several issues: the issue of proper school police responses, the adequate levels of force to be used against uncooperative students, and finally, training for school resource officers. Some school districts have acknowledged the need for specialized training, and in 2015, Texas passed HB2684, mandating training for police in Texas public schools. Specifically, "HB2684 requires school districts with an enrollment of 30,000 or more students to adopt a youth-focused education and training program for school resource officers and school district police officers. HB2684 requires the Texas Commission on Law Enforcement (TCOLE) to create, adopt, and distribute training materials to school district police departments, law enforcement agencies that place officers in schools, and any entity that provides training to school district police" (Texas Legislature, HB2684).

In the above described training, programs must cover the following learning objectives:

- Child and adolescent development and psychology;
- Positive behavioral interventions and supports, conflict resolution techniques, and restorative justice techniques;
- De-escalation techniques and techniques for limiting the use of force, including limiting the use of physical, mechanical, and chemical restraints;
- The mental and behavioral health needs of children with disabilities or special needs; and
- Mental health crisis intervention.

It is therefore evident that special attention must be given to school resource officers (and university campus police officers) when it comes to recruitment, hiring, and training practices. While some cases may call for traditional law enforcement responses, many instances encountered by school police officers will require more communication skills than tasers or pepper sprays.

Crime Mapping on College Campuses

A large part of the CompStat process is the visual depiction of the spatial distribution of crimes or incidents using desktop GIS packages (i.e., ArcView and ArcGIS). Crime mapping relies on a simple process called geocoding that allows a user to plot geographic addresses on a street map to determine if there are patterns or "hot spots," Once these are identified, administrators can develop strategies to reduce the number of events at particular locations. Traditionally, police departments map crimes on a citywide level, although crimes can also be mapped at the neighborhood or census tract level.

Campus police administrators seeking to adopt crime mapping technologies are faced with distinct challenges. One of these challenges involves attempting to map crimes at the campus level, many of which remain relatively small geographic entities. For the crime mapping process to lend fruitful results, incident locations need to be very discrete and well defined, so that spatial analyses can distinguish between different areas of the campus. For example, if campus police incident reports only list the university's main address as the crime location, little will be gained from crime mapping because all of the incidents will be geocoded to a single point on the street layer.

Campus police must therefore adopt crime reporting practices that identify very specific locations on their campuses when reporting incidents. The more specificity when recording crime locations across campuses, the more information will be produced by the crime mapping process. For example, car break-ins should not just be attributed to a parking deck, but to locations *within* the parking structure (floor, area, space number, etc.). In short, crime mapping practices on college campuses must be based on specific locations across campus and must not simply rely on the traditional practice of geocoding to street addresses. Interested readers should consult the Police Foundation's *Crime Mapping News* (2005), which is dedicated to crime mapping and geographic information system applications for college campuses.

Situational Crime Prevention on College Campuses

Unlike municipal police departments that patrol city streets and respond to calls for service across all hours and days of the week, campus police departments face specific policing challenges based on the layout and the "rhythm" of campus life. For example, there are greater chances that alcohol-related events would occur in or near the dormitories during weekend nights than in the cafeteria during Tuesday's lunch period. Campus police departments should therefore be very familiar with the ebb and flow of their campus communities, analyzing the times at which people circulate on campus, which are the most popular or heavily visited venues, and the dynamics behind special events such as football games, pep rallies, or other similar school functions.

Are some events more prone to attract problems? Are there problem-prone areas on campus that facilitate rowdy student behaviors (i.e., proximity to bars or public streets) that routinely pose safety problems for students and residents alike? Using the popular S.A.R.A problem solving model, campus police agencies need to identify the source and location of most problems on campus to eventually develop and adopt effective crime prevention strategies to reduce future events. For example, long walkways or desolate parts of campus can be made less frightening and crime conducive by installing "Code Blue Phone Kiosks" that allow instant communication with emergency personnel. Closed circuit televisions are also important crime fighting tools, as they provide more "eyes on the street" and increase the campus' guardianship levels. In sum, college campuses present a special population with particular spatial and temporal characteristics and police departments need to adopt responses that are tailored to these unique needs.

Summary and Conclusions

This analysis of campus policing has shown the development and professionalization of the organizations that police on educational environs, particularly during the past three decades. Campus policing clearly is becoming more like its municipal and county counterparts, probably most appreciably since September 11, 2001. Clearly, these police agencies "have become an integral part of the fabric of America's postsecondary educational institutions" and have "carved a niche following the genesis of many such units during the turbulent 1960s" (Peak, 1988, pp. 34–35). History has shown that these organizations also must be prepared for the entire gamut of human and natural disorder.

Campus police organizations have thus grown both in number and in popularity; they are in an excellent position to take advantage of, and are able to participate fully in the rapidly developing era of community policing and problem solving because of the inherent community cohesiveness that campuses enjoy. They will hopefully continue to emphasize service over law en*force*ment for many millennia to come.

However, although campuses represent an area of policing that has progressed immeasurably in the past half century, these police organizations and their operations must also be rigorously evaluated and continuously revised to address changing problems on their campuses. As importantly, since the enactment of the Clery Act there is the need for a national forum at which campus-based community policing practices can be shared and comprehensive research programs developed and instituted. Ongoing attention must also be directed toward hiring personnel with a community policing orientation as well as with an eye toward greater diversification of campus police forces.

References

Anderson, M. (2015). When schooling meets policing. *The Atlantic.* Retrieved from http://www.theatlantic.com/education/archive/2015/09/when-schooling-meets-policing/406348/.

Associated Press. (2007, September 13). Universities arming statewide. Retrieved from http://www.iowastatedaily.com/news/article_86792ed0-64d3-513f-880d-646312b184bd.html.

Associated Press. (2016, April 19). Colorado school district arms security guards with rifles. NBC News. Retrieved from http://www.nbcnews.com/news/us-news/colorado-school-district-arms-security-guards-rifles-n558776.

Balko, R. (2015, May 18). Obama moves to demilitarize America's police. *The Washington Post.* Retrieved from https://www.washingtonpost.com/news/the-watch/wp/2015/05/18/obama-moves-to-demilitarize-americas-police/.

Buerger, M. E. (2005). COMPSTAT: A strategic vision. *The Associate,* (January–February), pp. 18–23.

Bordner, D. C., & Petersen, D. M. (1983). *Campus policing: The nature of university police work.* Lanham, MD: University Press of America.

Brantingham, P., Brantingham, P., & Seagrave, J. (1995). Crime and fear of crime at a Canadian university. In J. J. Sloan & B. Fisher (Eds.), *Campus crime: Legal, social, and policy perspectives* (pp. 123–155). Springfield, IL: Charles C Thomas.

CBS News. (2000). U. Arkansas deaths murder-suicide. Retrieved from http://www.cbsnews.com/news/u-arkansas-deaths-murder-suicide/.

Clarke, R. V. (2004). Defining police strategies: Problem solving, problem-oriented policing and community-oriented policing. In Q. C. Thurman & J. Zhao (Eds.), *Contemporary policing: Controversies, challenges, and solutions* (pp. 18–25). Los Angeles: Roxbury.

DeLorenzi, D., Shane, J. M., & Amendola, K. L. (2006). The compstat process: Managing performance on the pathway to leadership. *The Police Chief.* Retrieved from http://policechiefmagazine.org/magazine/index.cfm?fuseaction=display_arch&article_id=998&issue_id=92006.

Denney, J. R. (1992, August). Policing a college campus. Paper presented at the annual conference, Society for Campus and University Planners, Minneapolis, Minnesota, p. 6.

Esposito, D., & Stormer, D. (1989). The multiple roles of campus law enforcement. *Campus Law Enforcement Journal, 19*(3), 26–30.

Garofoli, Joe. (2016, April 15). UC Davis pepper-spray officer awarded $38,000. *San Francisco Chronicle.* Retrieved from http://www.sfgate.com/politics/joegarofoli/article/UC-Davis-pepper-spray-officer-awarded-38-000-4920773.php.

Gelber, S. (1972). *The role of campus security in the college setting.* Washington, DC: U.S. GPO.

Gold, H. K. (2015, June 24). 6 ways campus cops are becoming more like regular police. *Rolling Stone.* Retrieved from http://www.rollingstone.com/politics/news/6-ways-campus-cops-are-becoming-more-like-regular-police-20150624.

Goldstein, H. (1990). *Problem-oriented policing.* New York: McGraw-Hill.

Grant, H. J., & Terry, K. J. (2005). *Law enforcement in the 21st century.* Boston: Allyn & Bacon), pp. 329–330.

Hauser, C., & O'Conner, A. (2007). Virginia shooting leaves 33 dead. *The New York Times.* Retrieved from http://www.nytimes.com/2007/04/16/us/16cnd-shooting.html.

Kocian, L. (2008, May 1). Arming police on campus. *The Boston Globe.* Retrieved from http://www.boston.com/news/local/articles/2008/05/01/arming_police_on_campus/.

Kraska, P. (2001). *Militarizing the American criminal justice system: The changing roles of the armed forces and the police.* Boston, MA: Northeastern University Press.

Krishnakumar, P. & Degroot, L. (2015, October 1). Since Sandy Hook, a gun has been fired on school grounds nearly once a week. *Los Angeles Times.* Retrieved from http://graphics.latimes.com/school-shootings-since-newtown/.

Marlin, G., & Vogt, B. (1999, April). Violence in the schools. *The Police Chief,* 169.

Marschall, J. P., & Peak, K. J. (1986, June). The high cost of public safety. *American School and University, 58*(10), 26–36.

McDonald, P. (2002). *Managing police operations: Implementing the New York crime control model-Compstat.* Belmont, CA: Wadsworth, p. 1.

Morse, A., Sisneros, L., Perez, Z., & Sponsler, B. A. (2016). *Guns on campus: The architecture and momentum of state policy action.* Retrieved from NASPA website: https://www. naspa. org/rpi/reports/guns-on-campus-the-architecture-andmomentum-of-state-policy-action.

Murphy, K. (2016, June 6). UC police made traffic stops against city orders. Cincinnati.com. Retrieved from http://www.cincinnati.com/story/news/2016/06/06/ucpd-made-traffic-stops-against-city-orders/85257874/.

Oliver, W. (2004). The third generation of community policing: Moving through innovation, diffusion, and institutionalization. In Q. C. Thurman & J. Zhao, *Contemporary policing: Controversies, challenges, and solutions* (pp. 39–53). Los Angeles: Roxbury.

Peak, K. (1987, June). Campus policing in America: The state of the art. *The Police Chief, 54*(6), 22–24.

Peak, K. (1995). The professionalization of campus policing: Comparing campus and municipal law enforcement agencies. In J. J. Sloan & B. Fisher (Eds.), *Campus crime: Legal, social, and policy perspectives* (pp. 228–245). Springfield, IL: Charles C Thomas.

Peak, K., Barthe, E. P., & Garcia, A. (2008). Campus policing in America: A twenty-year perspective. *Police Quarterly, 11*(2), 239–260.

Peak, K. J., Gaines, L. K., & Glensor, R. W. (2004). *Police supervision and management: In an era of community policing* (2nd ed.). Upper Saddle River, NJ: Prentice Hall.

Peak, K. J., & Glensor, R. W. (2008). *Community policing and problem solving: Strategies and practices* (5th ed.). Upper Saddle River, NJ: Pearson.

Police Foundation. (2005). *Crime Mapping News, 7*(1).

Powell, J. W. (1971). The history and proper role of campus security. *Security World, 8*, 21.

Powell, J. (1981). *Campus security and law enforcement*. Woburn, MA: Butterworth.

Saad, L. (2007, May 2). Americans skeptical about preventing Virginia Tech-like incidents. Gallup. Retrieved from http://www.gallup.com/poll/27430/Americans-Skeptical-About-Preventing-Virginia-TechLike-Incidents.aspx.

Seng, M. J. (1994). The crime awareness and campus security act: Some observations, critical comments, and recommendations. In J. J. Sloan & B. S. Fisher (Eds.), *Campus crime: Legal, social, and policy issues*. Springfield, IL: Charles C Thomas.

Seng, M. J., & Koehler, N. S. (1993). The crime awareness and campus security act: A critical analysis. *Journal of Crime and Justice, 16*, 97–110.

SIUE. (2017). Campus safety services & crime-prevention tips. Retrieved from https://www.siue.edu/police/safety/tips-active-shooter.shtml.

Skolnick, J. (1969). *Politics of protest*. Washington, DC: U.S. Government Printing Office.

Sloan, J. (1992). Modern campus police: An analysis of their evolution, structure, and function. *American Journal of Police, 11*, 85–104.

Snow, R. L. (1996). *SWAT teams: Explosive face-offs with America's deadliest criminals*. New York: Plenum Press.

Texas Legislative Session. (2015). Update from Texas' 84th Legislative Session, HB2684: Training for Police in Texas Public Schools.

U.S. Census Bureau. (2008). Back to school, 2006–2007. Retrieved from http://www.census.gov/Press-release/www/releases/archives/facts_for_features_special_editions/007108.html.

U.S. News and World Report. (2012, December 24). Should there be more armed guards in schools? Retrieved from http://www.usnews.com/debate-club/should-there-be-more-armed-guards-in-schools.

Wright, S. (2000). Campus cops try to fill roles as cyber heroes. *Black Issues in Higher Education, 17*(13), 64–66.

Yale University Police Department. (n.d.). History. Retrieved from http://www.yale.edu/police/overview.html.

9

The Meaning of Surveillance in Public Space

Gregory J. Howard and Elizabeth A. Bradshaw

Public spaces are increasingly subject to intensive and extensive forms of surveillance that have significant implications for policing and society. While "new surveillance" techniques emerge with rapidity in an age of disruptive digital technology (Marx, 2002), these innovative ways of observing and being seen are difficult to evaluate outside of their situational deployment in a specific surveillance regimen. Surveillance is a systematic practice by which information is collected with sophisticated instruments and processed in various ways to achieve some purpose through targeted interventions by agents who may encounter resistance from those who become aware of being watched. This chapter uses three case studies to demonstrate how the meaning of surveillance and its potential for rousting resistance grows from the way it is organized toward particular visions of order and propriety and how essential features of the surveillance regimen are concealed or promoted. To achieve a richer appreciation of the social significance of surveillance, we propose that surveillance studies might accept the invitation of cultural criminology and attend to the "immediacy" of surveillance in the lives of the observed and observer (Ferrell, 1997, p. 3).

On Surveillance

Many people have at least a passing appreciation of surveillance, generally associating it with closed circuit television (CCTV) or video surveillance. As Zurawski (2007) has observed, "CCTV cameras and their adjunctive system have become the icons of modern surveillance technologies" (p. 269). The centrality of CCTV as a form of surveillance is no doubt pushed by the wide use of CCTV footage as source material for television news and other "reality" programming. Regular contact with video surveillance systems in everyday interactions at the grocery store and the mall, residences and schools, gas stations, entertainment venues, and banks has also made this form of surveillance an obvious artifact of our age. Video observation plays an important role in the surveillance of public spaces, but surveillance involves much more than CCTV. Walby (2005b) has observed that, among other things, surveillance refers to "face-to-face supervision, camera monitoring, TV watching, paparazzi stalking, GPS tailing, cardiac telemonitoring, the tracking of commercial/Internet transactions, [and] the tracing of tagged plants and animals" (p. 158). Before we can fully appreciate the meaning of surveillance in public space, we need to develop a fuller understanding of the characteristics of surveillance.

Surveillance is an important feature of all societies. According to Norris and Armstrong (1999), "Surveillance is recognized as an elementary building block of all human societies since the act of socialization would be unthinkable without the surveillance of adults" (p. 5). Lyon (2007) wrote "surveillance practices are probably basic to human society and start with any elementary watching of some by another in order to create an effect of looking *after* or looking *over* the latter" (p. 3, italics in original). The lion's share of surveillance studies, like this chapter, radically truncates the field of study and focuses on what Marx (1985, 2002, 2003) has called "the new surveillance." This makes sense since new surveillance technologies are becoming widely dispersed in all societies and they effect just about everybody's daily life. Still, we should be mindful that surveillance has a long history in human societies; it is not a new social phenomenon, although its contemporary technologies are powerful and revolutionary. Based on a study of a Roman quarry and a Bronze Age road near the southwestern edge of the Dead Sea, for instance, Yekutieli (2006) demonstrated that "various ancient policing arrangements drew on hidden surveillance in order to induce particular behavior in people" (p. 66). Not only does surveillance stretch deep into human history, it is also an element in the social lives of all animal species (Wilson, 1975), and Shoemaker (1996) has even asserted that the surveillance function in animal societies might be fruitfully understood from an evolutionary perspective.

In the inaugural issue of the research journal titled *Surveillance and Society*, Marx (2002), one of the more persistent and thoughtful students of surveillance in a rapidly expanding field of study, maintained that the pursuit of information is an essential characteristic of all surveillance, but he also contended that important varieties of surveillance can be identified based on the means by which this information is acquired and the purpose/content of the information gathering exercise. Fixing on the means by which surveillance is accomplished, Marx (2002) further specified multiple dimensions that distinguish between what he calls "traditional surveillance" and the "new surveillance." According to Marx (2002), the new surveillance involves:

> Technologies for collecting personal information which transcend the physical, liberty enhancing limitations of the old means.... These probe more deeply, widely, and softly than traditional methods, transcending natural (distance, darkness, skin, time, and microscopic size) and constructed (walls, sealed envelopes) barriers that historically protected personal information. (p. 9)

A central feature of the means by which the new surveillance is accomplished is its ability to move through borders that previously had made information gathering difficult or impossible. For instance, the new surveillance can "transcend time" since the collected information can be "socially freeze-dried" in deep computer storage and activated instantly when necessary, perhaps years or decades after the initial observation (Marx, 1985, p. 30). Moreover, the new surveillance can overcome the difficulties posed by distance, lighting, and physical enclosures. As Marx (1985) has explained, "technical impossibility and, to some extent, inefficiency have lost their roles as unplanned protectors of liberty. Sound and video can be transmitted over vast distances, infrared and light-amplifying technologies pierce the dark, intrusive technologies can 'see' through doors, suitcases, fog" (p. 30). Capital intensive, largely invisible, decentralized to the point that self monitoring is promoted, and obsessed with prevention, the new surveillance probes ever more deeply and widely into our lives and traffics in a "categorical suspicion" that leaves everyone guilty until proven innocent (Marx, 1985).

But surveillance is more than the means by which information is gathered. Marx (2002) also described how "the content and predominant forms of surveillance have significantly changed over the last five centuries" (p. 17). While religious surveillance was commanding in the fifteenth century, political surveillance by fledgling nation-states became ascendant from the sixteenth through the seventeenth centuries. As nation-states became more established, surveillance was directed toward the administration of "various welfare and intervention programs" (Marx, 2002, p. 18). Government-centered surveillance has subsequently been complemented by systematic information gathering on the job, in commerce, in schools, and in medicine (Marx, 2002). As mobile communication devices have proliferated with their image and audio recording abilities, observational capacity has become widely distributed such that most anyone can now act as a surveillance agent. In short, the new surveillance is a means for producing control and discipline, but this means can be employed toward a variety of ends.

Alongside Gary Marx stands David Lyon as the most often referenced student of surveillance. For his part, Lyon (1994) defined surveillance as the "garnering of personal information to be stored, matched, retrieved, marketed, and circulated using powerful computer databases" (p. ix). Furthermore, he declared that surveillance is "a shorthand term to cover the many, and expanding, range of contexts within which personal data is collected by employment, commercial, and administrative agencies, as well as in policing and security" (Lyon, 1994, p. ix). In the main, Lyon agrees with Marx in his conceptualization of surveillance. Both recognize surveillance as especially concerned with information collection. They also agree on the importance of the means by which the information is gathered and distributed, with Lyon addressing computer enhanced surveillance and Marx highlighting the boundary busting capacities of the new surveillance. Finally, they share the view that surveillance is conducted by a range of public and private agents for myriad reasons. As Lyon (2006, p. 403) put it: "Surveillance is a routine and focused attention to personal details for the purposes of influence, management, care, and control." In other words, while surveillance can be deployed in a repressive fashion, it also has benevolent applications, such as when public health authorities keep track of the spread of disease or welfare authorities determine one's eligibility to receive benefits.

The conceptualization of surveillance extracted from the work of Marx and Lyon is reflected widely in the surveillance studies literature. Consider these examples which can be taken as representative of the field:

> Plugged into the information circuitry and organizational interests of the mall, the CCTV operators use the camera technology, as well as their practical knowledge and familiarity with the store, to collect and collate televisual data which they use to manage the flow of shoppers. (Walby, 2005a, p. 194)
>
> Surveillance involves the collection of information about populations for institutional and personal purposes. (Haggerty & Gaszo, 2005, p. 170)
>
> Surveillance, defined simply as the production of knowledge about populations useful in their administration, serves not only the negative purposes of control, but also the positive purposes of the security and prosperity of populations. (Ericson, 2007, p. 28)
>
> Surveillance ... refers not to the cloak-and-dagger stuff of hidden microphones, but to the increasingly routine use of personal data and

> systematic information in the administration of institutions, agencies, and businesses. (Gilliom, 2001, p. 2)

Defined in the most general of terms, surveillance involves the collection of information by specific means for particular purposes. Of course, this overarching definition neglects some important details. To produce a more nuanced understanding of surveillance, we would like to stress seven of its defining features, including its concern with information management, its dependence on instruments for recording observations, its need for an orientation or purpose, its use of data processing mechanisms, its tendency to produce a response on the part of the surveillance agent, its capacity to influence the awareness and experience of those subject to observation, and its ability to produce a counter-response or resistance amongst the observed.

Information Management

First, as we have already indicated, a core feature of surveillance is its concern with the *management of information*. This involves the gathering of sensory input or other data about the environment with which to answer questions or to resolve practical problems. All surveillance seeks to establish knowledge of the world. Where have cases of anthrax been detected? Who has opened that door? When did a worker log on to her computer terminal? What are the contents of this suitcase? Who is a threat? Where should pesticide be applied in a field? Surveillance exists to provide data-driven answers to questions like these and more.

In the surveillance literature, three competing visions of surveillance are often used to guide discussion and research. Two visions, one building on Orwell's (1949/1961) rendering of the totalitarian state of Oceana and the other drawing on a panoptic metaphor refined by Foucault (1977), depict surveillance as a hierarchical form of information management. Another vision, building on a rhizomatic metaphor, conceives of surveillance as a networked form of information management. Here is how Haggerty and Ericson (2000) described the difference:

> For both Orwell and Foucault, surveillance is part of a regime where relatively few powerful individuals or groups watch the many, in a form of top-down scrutiny. Contemporary studies of surveillance continue to emphasize this hierarchical aspect of observation.... [Yet, s]urveillance has become rhizomatic, it has transformed hierarchies of observation, and allows for the scrutiny of the powerful by both institutions and the general population. (p. 617)

The models of surveillance depicted by Orwell, Foucault, and Haggerty and Ericson agree on the importance of information to surveillance—each recognizes that surveillance is built on facts and empirical senses of the world—but they differ on the way surveillance is organized to handle this information.

The dystopia imagined by Orwell (1949/1961) in *1984* is widely known. Winston Smith, the protagonist in the novel, is a member of the outer party in Oceania and employed in the Ministry of Truth as a record keeper. His job is to modify back issues of the *Times*, the party newspaper, to bring stories from the past into alignment with the needs of the present. We can see from the nature of Winston's job that control of information is important to the rule of Big Brother and the INGSOC party that he represents. Aiming to "arrest progress and freeze history at a chosen moment," INGSOC is an extremely conservative force that seeks social stability through the manipulation of human consciousness. As the party's slogan puts it: "Who controls the past controls the future; who controls the present controls the past." Consciousness is shaped through music, movies, news, and education, all centrally directed by the Ministry of Truth. For "every citizen important enough to be worth watching" (i.e., members of the inner and outer party), consciousness is also shaped by the Ministry of Love, the government apparatus concerned with law and order. Through a surveillance operation that makes use of undercover "thought police," hidden microphones, citizen informants, and telescreens capable of simultaneous reception and transmission of information, the Ministry of Love is able to make good on the promise that "Big Brother is Watching":

> A Party member lives from birth to death under the eye of the Thought Police. Even when he is alone he can never be sure that he is alone. Wherever he may be, asleep or awake, working or resting, in his bath or in bed, he can be inspected without warning and without knowing that he is being inspected. Nothing that he does is indifferent. His friendships, his relaxations, his behavior toward his wife and children, the expression of his face when he is alone, the words he mutters in sleep, even the characteristic movements of his body, are all jealously scrutinized. Not only any actual misdemeanor, but any eccentricity, however small, any change of habits, any nervous mannerism that could possibly be the symptom of an inner struggle, is certain to be detected. (pp. 173–174)

The surveillance of *1984*, at least for members of the party, is total and unyielding. Information flows from the bottom to the top as agents of the state seek out deviations from party discipline and wavering devotion to Big Brother. Obedience must be absolute in a grim world of fear and suffering. As Winston's interrogator, O'Brien, suggested to Winston prior to his experience with the infamous Room 101: "Imagine a boot stamping on a human face—forever."

The other vision of surveillance based on a hierarchical arrangement of information management employs Bentham's idea for a panopticon, which has been analyzed at length by Foucault (1977). Bentham's design called for a building shaped like a ring with a tower situated in the center of the ring. The ring was to be divided into cells on multiple floors in which individuals in need of observation and training would be placed. Owing to backlighting produced by windows on the outside and inside walls of the cells, an inspector in the central tower could gather information about the behavior of the inmate in each cell. Because the central observation tower would be constructed with a series of impenetrable sensory barriers, inmates in their respective cells could not tell whether there was anyone in the tower let alone whether the inspector was looking in their direction. Moreover, solid walls between the cells would prevent any lateral communication between the individuals in the cells. As Foucault (1977) summarized: "The Panopticon is a machine for dissociating the see/being seen dyad: in the peripheric ring, one is totally seen, without ever seeing; in the central tower, one sees everything without ever being seen" (p. 202). Information in the panopticon flows only in one direction—from the individuals cloistered in their cells toward the central observation post. In principle the panopticon produces "in the inmate a state of conscious and permanent visibility that produces the automatic functioning of power" with the inmate "caught up in a power situation of which they are themselves the bearer" (p. 201). No jackboot on the face here, even for a moment, just self-produced compliance under a constant threat of exposure.

In a widely cited article in the *British Journal of Sociology*, Haggerty and Ericson (2000) acknowledged that the Big Brother and panoptic models highlight important features of surveillance and its management of information, but they maintained that recent developments in surveillance demand a fresh perspective. According to Haggerty and Ericson (2000):

> ... [W]e are witnessing a convergence of what were once discrete surveillance systems to the point that we can now speak of an emerging "surveillant assemblage." This assemblage works by abstracting human bodies from their territorial settings and separating them into discrete data flows. These flows are then reassembled into distinct "data doubles" which can be scrutinized and targeted for intervention. In the process, we are witnessing a rhizomatic leveling of the hierarchy of surveillance, such that groups which were previously exempted from routine surveillance are now increasingly monitored. (p. 606)

The surveillant assemblage is made possible by the development of computer networks that distribute information in a lateral as well as a hierarchical fashion. Previously, the information managed by surveillance systems was contained within the records of distinct organizations and bureaucracies. Often, this meant that the records were kept in a central depository, typically in paper form. With the rise of digital surveillance and its reduction of information to binary code, information became much more manageable in terms of storage, transmission, and computation (Graham & Wood, 2003). More information can now be gathered and it can be shared and analyzed with increasing ease and economy. As Ericson (2007) explained:

> A single surveillance technology such as a CCTV camera is usually a mile wide but only an inch deep because it does not in itself provide detailed knowledge about the person whose behavior is being momentarily captured and made visible. However, when combined with other technologies—for example, combining digitized CCTV systems with computer databases—depth and intensity of surveillance are achieved. (p. 52)

With a capacity to capture and make sense of "the trails of information which have become the detritus of contemporary life," such as credit card purchases, airline travel, telecommunications, and educational records, "the surveillant assemblage is a visualizing device that brings into the visual register a host of heretofore opaque flows of auditory, scent, chemical, visual, ultraviolet, and informational stimuli" (Haggerty & Ericson, 2000, p. 611). As the informational shards of our transactions and interactions with institutions are combined and recombined according to the designs of unknown observers, "a new type of individual, one comprised of pure information" is produced, a "data double" that signals "access to resources, services, and power in ways which are often unknown to its referent" (Haggerty & Ericson, 2000, pp. 613–614). The surveillant assemblage makes the notion of anonymity a historical curiosity as monitoring by social institutions becomes more intensive and extensive. In this sense, it does not much deviate from the basic principle of the panopticon announced by Foucault (1977): "Visibility is a trap" (p. 2000). As Haggerty and Ericson (2000) stressed, however, the surveillant assemblage flattens the hierarchy of observation that has previously characterized surveillance regimens in that "it allows for the scrutiny of the powerful by both institutions and the general population" (p. 617). In this sense the surveillant assemblage is like a rhizome: relatively low to the ground, growing horizontally and very little vertically, with shoots emerging unpredictably all over the place that feed on an interconnected root system.

Instruments for Observing

A second important feature of surveillance is its dependence on *instruments for recording observations*. Historically, sensory organs such as eyes, ears, fingers, and noses have combined with brains to organize the information gleaned from surveillance operations into records and files. This reliance on human observation is highlighted in the panoptic model analyzed by Foucault (1977). Surveillance based on human observation can be very effective, as studies of bureaucratic surveillance (Dandeker, 1990) and undercover policing (Marx, 1988) evidence, but human observation is necessarily limited by subjective frailties (e.g., our powers of discernment decline with sleep deprivation) and physiological design (e.g., our eyes are not so keen in the dark nor can we hear sounds of certain frequencies). The history of technology is filled with ingenious inventions that have enhanced and extended the limited powers of human observation, including telescopes and microscopes, cameras, and tape recorders. The emergence of the information technology revolution and the rise of computer networks, however, have dramatically refined the instruments by which information can be generated and exchanged (Castells, 2009). Remote sensors can now adjust lights and climate control when a person walks into a room, and they are also used on the U.S.-Mexico border to detect the footsteps of illicit border crossers (Andreas, 2000). As the cell-site simulator and drone cases considered later in this chapter show, techniques of observation that can extract more observations of the world from increasingly sensitive recording instruments are no longer just around the corner.

Purpose of Surveillance

A third basic requirement of surveillance is an *orientation* toward the world. It is impossible to take in everything at once. As Katti (2002) explained:

> In order for something to be observable at all, other things—certain fields that are ambiguously linked to observation and organize it in a certain way—drop out of the same observation. In brief, the paradox emerges that by means of producing something (an observation), we unwillingly also produce its opposite (concealing). (p. 53)

A decision must be made about what the object of observation will be within a particular surveillance regimen. Some common objects of surveillance include deer, terrorists, viruses, suspicious behavior, tainted foods, and employees' performance. "It is crucial to remember that surveillance is always hinged to some specific purpose," wrote Lyon (2007), "[t]he marketer wishes to influence the consumer, the high school seeks efficient ways of managing diverse students and the security company wishes to insert certain control mechanisms—such as PIN entry into buildings or sectors" (p. 15). With an orientation toward the world, the operator of a surveillance regimen has some criteria with which to evaluate the relevance of the overwhelming information about the world that is potentially at one's fingertips. The orientation or purpose for deploying surveillance acts as a filter; some information about the world is left outside of the surveillance regimen while other data are allowed to flow in.

Processing the Information

A fourth chief characteristic of surveillance is its capacity for data *processing*. Information about the objects of observation that has been collected by surveillance instruments must be analyzed to detect associations along the lines dictated by the orientation. Is this person authorized to enter this area? Is that person wanted by the police? Is this person a risk to air transportation? Is that person violating behavioral norms or local ordinances? The brain has been the primary mechanism for processing the information collected through surveillance practices to answer questions such as these, but computers are now crucial to the enterprise. Marx (1985) described the importance of matching (i.e., comparing information from two or more distinct data sources) and profiling (i.e., correlation of data to evaluate how closely an event or person approximates a previously specified model of violations and violators) to contemporary surveillance practices. Lyon (2007) has stressed the role of data mining, which involves working through information collected by surveillance systems to locate patterns and reveal relationships. Central to data mining is Lyon's concept of social sorting: "To consider surveillance as social sorting is to focus on the social and economic categories and the computer codes by which personal data is organized with a view to influencing and managing people and populations" (Lyon, 2003, p. 2). This process of social sorting, with its dependence on categories based on the ideological predispositions of human beings, raises serious questions of social justice in Lyon's view, since "such classification is both an outcome not only of social differences but of advantage and disadvantage, and often serves to reinforce inequalities of life-chances" (Lyon, 1994, p. 19). Importantly, a surveillance regimen that does not have a specified process for analyzing the information that is gathered will not amount to much since no targeted interventions will be forthcoming and resistance from an alert body of observed people will be unlikely to materialize. Automated systems of enforcement made possible by algorithms, however, make this possibility of leaving information unscrutinized less likely (Kerr, De Paoli, & Keatinge, 2014).

Targeted Intervention

A fifth distinguishing feature of surveillance is that it can ultimately lead to some sort of *targeted intervention* on the part of the surveillance agent (Hörnqvist, 2010). This response is generally concerned with imposing the will of the agent on the object of scrutiny. That imposition can be conceived as a form of judgment aimed at the control, discipline, and care of the observed. Of course, contemporary surveillance practices operate with a precautionary principle in which prevention of violations or trouble is the ideal (Ericson, 2007). As Marx (1985) explained: "Rather than simply reacting to what is served up around us, anticipatory strategies seek to reduce risk and uncertainty. Publicity about omnipresent and omnipowerful surveillance is to deter violations" (p. 30). This expectation for surveillance to serve its purpose without formal intervention by public or private authorities is central to the panoptic model:

> Hence the major effect of the Panopticon: to induce in the inmate a state of conscious and permanent visibility that assures the automatic functioning of power. So to arrange things that the surveillance is permanent in its effects, even if it is discontinuous in its action; that the perfection of power should tend to render its actual exercise unnecessary; that this architectural apparatus should be a machine for creating and sustaining a power relation independent of the person who exercises it; in short, that the inmates should be caught up in a power situation of which they are themselves the bearers. (Foucault, 1977, p. 201)

When this "automatic functioning of power" fails and a violation occurs, surveillance regimens provide an opportunity to catch the deviant in action and, short of that, yield evidence with which to hold the violator to account at some later date. Still, as the field research into the operation of CCTV systems in the United Kingdom by Norris and Armstrong (1999) made clear, the detection of violations by system operators rarely translated into the deployment of police or private security guards.

Awareness among the Watched

Although surveillance can remain surreptitious as even a response, when it occurs, can be unknown to the object of surveillance (e.g., consider the subtle efforts to influence the consumer practices of visitors to online shopping sites with advertisements, specials, and suggestions based on previous webpage visits), a sixth important feature of surveillance is that often some degree of *awareness* is precipitated in the scrutinized. This awareness of being the object of surveillance can alter one's identity and transform the fabric of experience. Of course, as described above, this is the dream of the "automatic functioning of power" envisioned by Bentham and his panopticon. But surveillance is also an emotional experience for human beings (Koskela, 2000, p. 257). Surveillance is a relationship with other human beings that produces a variety of feelings, including paranoia, fear, and self-consciousness. As McGrath (2004) has argued, "Surveillance has proliferated not least because we desire it—we enjoy it, play with it, use it for comfort" but also because "at root, all of our experiences of surveillance are structured by the expectation of death" (p. vii). As these observations attest, the awareness sometimes provoked in those subject to surveillance arrangements has existential implications.

Resistance

The seventh and last important feature of surveillance is the possibility of *counter-response and resistance* on the part of those who are subjected to surveillance. Given the widespread use of surveillance regimens in our ordinary lives, it is increasingly difficult to avoid them. Faced with increased contact with surveillance, individuals must cope in one manner or another. Lyon (2007) has identified compliance, negotiation, and resistance as typical coping mechanisms. In fact, compliance is the most common response to surveillance. We willingly use passwords to enter secure websites, punch in PIN numbers at the ATM, walk past CCTV installations without hesitation, and travel on the airlines after being inspected. The conveniences and necessities to which we gain access through surveillance, such as medical care, education, and pension benefits, make anything other than compliance seem impossible (Haggerty & Ericson, 2000). Indeed, McGrath (2004) has even argued that "we are not necessarily conceding defeat or loss of self when we admit to loving Big Brother" (p. ix). Unfortunately, there has been relatively little study of compliance or adulation in the surveillance studies literature.

More commonly, essays and research in surveillance studies examine resistance to surveillance, including the kind of critical questioning that characterizes Lyon's (2007) negotiation. As Gilliom (2001) learned from his study of low-income mothers in Appalachia: "Subjects of surveillance frequently challenge and resist these acts of observation, depiction, and control, and these struggles between the watchers and the watched mark important political battles" (p. xiii). Marx (2003) catalogued eleven techniques for neutralizing and resisting surveillance, ranging from "discovery moves" (i.e., finding out if surveillance is being practiced), "avoidance moves" (i.e., withdrawing from the surveillance), and "piggybacking moves" (i.e., evading surveillance by becoming attached to a legitimate object or person, such as driving in behind a car that has activated a security gate) to "breaking moves" (i.e., rendering surveillance devices inoperable through sabotage), "refusal moves" (i.e., declining to provide information requested or demanded by surveillance agents), and "cooperation moves" (i.e., convincing a surveillance agent to aid in the subversion of the surveillance system). Notwithstanding these resistance tactics, Haggerty and Ericson (2000) expressed reservations about the utility of confronting single surveillance systems one at a time:

> In the face of multiple connections across myriad technologies and practices, struggles against particular manifestations of surveillance, as important as they may be, are akin to efforts to keep the ocean's tide back with a broom—a frantic focus on a particular unpalatable technology or practice while the general tide of surveillance washes over us all. (p. 609)

The fluid and networked nature of the surveillant assemblage, like the Internet designed by scientists funded by the Department of Defense, makes for a robust system relatively impervious to attack. On Haggerty and Ericson's view, acts of resistance against surveillance are likely to be little more than symbolic gestures.

Ultimately, surveillance is about power. As Foucault (1977) wrote: "But the panopticon must not be understood as a dream building: it is the diagram of a mechanism of power reduced to its ideal form" (p. 205). Applicable on occasions when one has a number of individuals in a limited space who are supposed to be engaged in a particular behavior, the panopticon perfects the exercise of power by reducing the number who exercise power and increasing the number who are subject to it, making intervention possible at any moment, producing disciplined individuals without direct intervention, and using architecture and geometry to achieves its objectives (Foucault, 1977). Gilliom (2001) contended "the American conversation about surveillance would be a better, more engaging, and more vital one if we worked to move questions about power and domination to the forefront" (p. 9). Lyon (2007) has agreed, declaring "whether it is the massive Department of Homeland Security in the USA or some rural school board with cameras in buses, power is generated and expressed by surveillance" (p. 23).

Surveillance and Public Space

Our discussion so far has centered on the principle features of surveillance. We have established that surveillance regimens involve the collection and processing of information according to particular orientations, allowing agents to make targeted interventions against those who are watched and potentially resistant owing to an awareness of the scrutiny directed at them. Although it is tempting to examine exclusively new surveillance technologies, raising a hue and cry or promising Panglossian futures based on an assessment of a new mode of observing, the full import and meaning of a surveillance practice is better discerned through attention to all seven of the defining features of surveillance regimens, although the "situated logic and emotion" of surveillance agents and the observed lead to embellishment on some of these dimensions of surveillance and silence or manipulation on still others. To advance this thesis we turn now to a consideration of three cases of surveillance in public space. Cell-site simulators and drones are two new surveillance techniques whose meaning is in flux because so little is known about the kinds of surveillance regimens in which they have or will be activated. On the other hand, a surveillance installation in Chicago, while criticized by some, has enjoyed relatively little serious resistance from members of the community. We suggest that the relatively frictionless incorporation of this surveillance practice into public space, affirmed by the dramatic growth of the apparatus over the years, has been accomplished by the careful linkage of observational techniques to a purposive scheme with cultural resonance. Taken together, these case studies show how informed assessments of surveillance regimens are difficult to produce because one or more of the essential dimensions of the surveillance practice is concealed from scrutiny or otherwise manipulated to recast the reality of surveillance.

Cell-Site Simulators

Cell-site simulators (also known as Stingrays, Triggerfish, International Mobile Subscriber Identity [IMSI] Catchers, Wolfpack, Gossamer, and Swamp Box) are an electronic device the size of a suitcase that mimics a cellular phone tower and tricks all phones within a given area to register location data and personal information with the simulator (Owsley, 2014). Law enforcement agencies have publicly admitted that the devices can collect locational information and are capable of identifying, tracking, and locating cellular phones. Furthermore, the devices can record numbers from a phone's incoming and outgoing calls register and intercept the content of voice and text communications as well. Another controversial feature of Stingrays is the ability to block mobile cellular communications, for example, in war zones to prevent detonation of an explosive with a cell phone or during political protests to inhibit activists from organizing with their mobile phones (Zetter, 2015). As these examples show, the meaning of cell-site simulators can vary dramatically from life preserver to crusher of dissent and freedom of assembly.

During the 1990s and early 2000s, only federal government intelligence agencies had access to cell-site simulators. After the September 11th attacks, however, the federal government began to facilitate state and local law enforcement use of the devices through homeland security grants (Handley, 2014). Providing a conservative estimate, the American Civil Liberties Union (2016) has identified 61 agencies in 23 states and the District of Columbia that own the technology. Although often justified on the basis of national security or counter-terrorism, the devices are more frequently used for ordinary criminal investigations and the majority of cases that have been made public involved suspected fraud or drug trafficking (Electronic Freedom Foundation, 2016). A great deal of secrecy surrounds the use of cell-site simulators, making it difficult to assess the scope of their use by state and local law enforcement. One report concludes that New York City police have used the technology more than 1,000 times between 2008 and May 2015 (New York Civil Liberties Union, 2016). Further, Baltimore City Police have been at the center of controversy when it was revealed that the department used the technology 4,300 times between 2007 and 2015, often without a search warrant (Glenza & Woolf, 2015). These figures suggest that the cell-site simulator is seeing significant action, but the cover of secrecy makes it challenging to know toward what ends this observational technique is being directed.

Extremely protective about its product information, the Harris Corporation is one of the major producers of cell-site simulators sold to law enforcement and intelligence agencies in the United States (U.S.). As the Electronic Freedom Foundation (2016) argues, the Department of Justice (DOJ), and specifically the Federal Bureau of Investigation (FBI), appears to have colluded with the Harris Corporation to keep the technology and its capabilities secret by signing nondisclosure agreements with state and local law enforcement and withholding important information about the technology from judges and criminal defendants. Non-disclosure agreements in Florida, New York, and Maryland revealed that the FBI effectively prohibited local law enforcement agencies from disclosing information about the capabilities or even the existence of Stingrays. Under the agreements, police must contact the FBI in cases where they think the prosecutor is even considering using information about the technology in trial so that the FBI may intervene to protect information about the technology from being publicly disclosed (Glenza & Woolf, 2015). For example, one agreement made between the FBI, the Baltimore City Police, and the State Attorney's Office in Maryland required local authorities never to disclose the use of the Stingray device, even requiring prosecutors to drop cases if the technology could be revealed (Fenton, 2016).

At the state level, there are various provisions that might be used to regulate the use of cell-site simulators, but much of this legislation does not specifically mention the technology as such. Rather, statutory language targets tracking or real-time location information and addresses obtaining location information from cell phone providers directly (Electronic Freedom Foundation, 2016). In September 2015, the DOJ issued policy guidelines for the use of cell-site simulators, calling for increased privacy protections and higher legal standards for their use in the field. The policy requires law enforcement agencies under the DOJ (including the FBI, U.S. Marshals, Drug Enforcement Agency, and Alcohol, Tobacco, and Firearms) to obtain a warrant before using Stingrays. Similarly, the Department of Homeland Security (DHS) and the Internal Revenue Service have agreed to comply with the regulations as well. These policies also require DOJ and DHS agents to make clear before the courts that they are using cell-site simulators in their investigations and to implement requirements that data be deleted quickly after the target of surveillance is located. However, these policies apply only within criminal investigations and warrants are not required for national security purposes and "exceptional circumstances." Furthermore, the policy guidelines are currently self-imposed, meaning they do not have the force of law and could be altered at any time (Electronic Freedom Foundation, 2016), although a finding by a federal district court judge in Manhattan that cell-site simulators are Fourth Amendment searches requiring warrants suggests that the judicial branch may come to regulate their use more stringently across the country (Weiser, 2016). Evading scrutiny from Congress for nearly two decades, "… the StingRay has significantly expanded the government's surveillance capabilities in criminal investigations while it has, nevertheless, gone largely unnoticed and unregulated" (Pell & Soghoian, 2014, p. 165). In the absence of information about the place of Stingray observational technology in a surveillance regimen, it is difficult to establish the full meaning of the practice.

Drones

Unmanned aerial vehicles or drones have been a part of U.S. military adventures as offensive weapons since the Balkans war; their reconnaissance and killing applications have been expanded lately by the U.S. Air Force in

Afghanistan and Iraq as well as by the Central Intelligence Agency (CIA) in covert actions in places like Pakistan and Yemen (Cole & Wright, 2010). As drones become more nimble and user friendly, and an industry looks for domestic markets to augment sales in military circles, increasing attention is being paid to their domestication. In this process, the ends toward which drones might be applied, and the orientations that guide these applications, is being actively contested (Associated Press, 2015).

Of course, drones have already been at work policing space in the U.S. with Customs and Border Protection (CBP) deploying a fleet of Predator-B drones out of bases along the southwest border with Mexico in 2005 and the northern border with Canada in 2009 (Sengupta, 2013; Office of Public Affairs, 2015). With a variant called the "Guardian," which can operate in a maritime environment, CBP envisions deployment of Predator-B drones "throughout the border regions" (a space that extends 100 miles to the interior from the territorial border) under the guidance of a command and control system that is dispersed at fixed and mobile locations across the country (Office of Public Affairs, 2015). Touting its "high quality streaming video," CBP positions its observational capacity as a key tool in its "priority mission of anti-terrorism by helping to identify and intercept potential terrorists and illegal cross-border activity" (Office of Public Affairs, 2015). In addition to this anti-terrorism orientation, CBP also establishes its drones as an important instrument for "first responders" who might seek "aid in emergency preparations and recovery operations." Similarly, CBP claims that the drones have been used in the "disaster relief and emergency response efforts of its Department of Homeland Security partners" (Office of Public Affairs, 2015). The polished presentation of CBP drones offered by the Office of Public Affairs politely ignores other ways CBP has considered using its fleet, such as launching non-lethal rounds to "immobilize" the targets of surveillance or eavesdropping "to monitor phone calls and other communications on the ground below" (Gallagher, 2013; Sengupta, 2013).

Outfitted with a variety of "electro-optical/infrared sensors" and "surface search radar" capable of identifying targets on the ground, CBP has groomed their drones as a valuable surveillance regimen centered on policing the borders of sovereignty (Office of Public Affairs, 2015). Small drones being acquired by local police departments promise similar spatial control in urban locations. State legislatures are working to develop frameworks within which law enforcement agencies may use drones (Price, 2014). There has been a strong reaction against the deployment of armed drones by police departments, with many bills in the states banning such lethality, although North Dakota has determined that lethal police drones have a role to play in producing public order

(Wagner, 2015). Further, the demonstration by an engineering student in the northeast that a commercially available drone could carry and discharge a handgun suggests that targeted killings by private drone users might be an additional threat (Haigh, 2016). Bills introduced into state legislatures include provisions that demand judicially issued search warrants for police to gather evidence of crimes; some bills limit how long data gathered by police drones can be stored and otherwise restrict the way the data can be analyzed. Concerned that the full range of threats and challenges posed by police drones was still not adequately understood, Virginia imposed a two-year moratorium on their use in 2013 (National Conference of State Legislators, 2016). In the main, the state bills work to position drones as technical advancements on conventional police goals of crime fighting and providing rescue services. In this respect, efforts to domesticate drones at the state level follow the lead of CBP.

A drone is a platform on which sensors and payload can be airlifted by remote control or preprogrammed instructions. Its role in a surveillance regimen is twofold in that it necessarily works to collect observations while also facilitating targeted interventions. Sometimes these targeted interventions can be controversial, like when the CIA purposely killed without judicial review an American citizen with a drone strike in Yemen (Mazzetti, 2015). Other times these targeted interventions can be seen as rather humane; for instance, some groups are testing drones for their ability to operate in disaster zones to deliver payloads of food, water, and medicine (Shaw, 2012). As the public relations documents of CBP reveal, the deployment of the Predator-B has been cast as a weaponless defense against terrorist and other threats to sovereignty as well as a tool for humanitarian intervention in times of natural disaster. This careful pitch for the use of domestic drones is now accompanied by an abundance of others as commercial ventures using drone technology are rapidly emerging. Some want farmers to use drones in the reconnaissance of their fields and in targeted interventions on their rows with herbicides and pesticides (Associated Press, 2013). Others envision environmental quality officers enforcing regulations, pipeline operators inspecting for cracks or spills, real estate agents producing stunning sales materials, news organizations getting another angle on a pressing story, individuals taking self-surveillance while on the move to entirely new heights, and peeping toms advancing in their aim to look in on others' private worlds (Associated Press, 2015). Many eagerly await drones from Amazon and Google with their payload of consumer goods while others are impatient for the global connectivity promised by Facebook's forthcoming high-altitude fleet of drones bearing communications gear (Dougherty, 2014; Garside, 2014). Of course, the Federal Aviation Administration takes domestic drones as a direct if not manageable threat to commercial aviation, and there are certainly national security officers who can see little else in drones other than devices by which terrorist organizations might deliver a targeted intervention (Kang, 2015). The meaning of drones becomes difficult to pin down in this turbulence because there are wildly divergent purposes toward which they might be directed.

Chicago's CCTV Installation

Following the lead of the United Kingdom and many other countries, cities throughout the U.S. have adopted surveillance systems like CCTV. Consider "Operation Disruption" in Chicago, which has been characterized as "one of the nation's most aggressive uses of surveillance to curb violent crime" (Colias, 2004, p. 1). Initiated in the summer of 2003, its aim is to suppress drug sales, gang activity, and violence.

A central feature of Operation Disruption is the deployment of a large number of "police observation devices" (PODs). These PODs, about the size of a filing cabinet and distinguished by a Chicago Police Department (CPD) logo and its widely recognized checkerboard markings, are mounted on light or utility poles at intersections and along public streets. They are mobile so they can be placed at locations determined by intelligence and data analyzed by the CPD's Deployment Operations Center (Daley & Weis, 2008). Each POD contains a video camera that can pan 360 degrees and zoom tight enough to read a license plate. The cameras are capable of performing day or night and can record in all weather conditions. Topped with a blue strobe light, areas where the PODs are stationed have been called "blue light districts" (Colias, 2004, p. 1).

Operation Disruption began with 30 cameras and saw the number of cameras in operation climb to 80 by the end of the first year of deployment (Daley & Weis, 2008). The cameras were initially monitored in the field by police officers. Using a monitor and joystick neatly packed into a rugged case, officers could pan and zoom the cameras and monitor the video feed inside or outside of the cruiser. In the second phase of the project, the cameras were provided with wireless capabilities that permit more widespread transmission to control devices in the field, at police stations, and at the city's Office of Emergency Management and Communications Center. A later phase has seen smaller camera units installed on rooftops and on high-rise buildings. PODs were also placed around some 20 Chicago high schools in 2006 to create "safe zones." By summer in 2007, over 100 PODs were installed at the schools, which were monitored by officers inside each facility and can also be watched from all of the locations to which the PODs transmit wirelessly. Video produced by the cameras can be preserved for investigations if it is requested within 72 hours. Funds to procure the cameras come from drug asset forfeitures (Daley & Weis, 2008).

While the PODs serve as a platform for CCTV cameras, acoustic sensors have also been included on some PODs. These acoustic sensors, which are marketed by a number of companies, are designed to locate the sound of gunfire. For instance, the "ShotSpotter" gunshot location system is a technology used by the U.S. military to identify the location of snipers on battlefields in Iraq and Afghanistan. It has been adopted by 29 cities in the U.S., including Chicago (Rajan, 2008). The device can identify the location of gunfire or an explosion within 80 feet in less than seven seconds. It uses triangulation to pinpoint the spot:

> The ShotSpotter GLS uses a network of weatherproof acoustic sensors to locate and record gunshots and other loud noises. When a gun is fired, spherical sound waves radiate up to two miles. The sensors detect the sound and identify it as a possible gunshot, then transmit the recording to a server at police headquarters, along with the direction from which the sound came, the time it was detected, the sensor's location, and the current temperature. When at least three sensors have detected the sound, the server triangulates the exact location based on time-of-arrival readings from the sensors. (Siuru, 2007, p. 1)

Within a second of locating the gunshot or explosion, linked CCTV cameras can be automatically trained on the spot. Because the devices only pick up sound within a certain frequency range, this acoustic surveillance system cannot be used to eavesdrop on conversations (Rajan, 2008). Another gunshot location system called SENTRI has also been used in Chicago as a part of Operation Disruption. This system employed dynamic synapse neural network (DSNN) technology that processes information like the human brain. SENTRI was to learn and adapt like the human brain so that it could distinguish between different types of weapons based on their report. The DSNN technology also promised recognition of "security-breaching sounds, like the climbing of a chain-link fence, the sound of a vehicle engine approaching a perimeter, and the sound of footsteps in a location where access is restricted" (Siuru, 2007). As these acoustic surveillance possibilities indicate, a surveillance regimen may begin gathering one type of observation but later move into new fields of sensory input. As CBP points out about its drones, one of their advantages is that their assembly of sensors and observational equipment can be switched out as circumstances and technological developments warrant (Office of Public Affairs, 2015).

Plans in Chicago call for the installation of computer software that will analyze the video feeds from buildings and other structures considered terrorist targets. This software will alert police officials when someone "wanders aimlessly in circles, lingers outside a public building, pulls a car onto the shoulder of a highway, or leaves a package and walks away from it" (Kinzer, 2004, p. 1). Images of people detected in one of these scenarios will be highlighted in color to make it easier for those monitoring the CCTV screens to pick out the potential threat (Kinzer, 2004). As camera systems become more complex with more video feeds to monitor, the use of algorithms to detect visual patterns, including faces, will become important as a means to make the unrelenting flow of information more manageable (Graham & Wood, 2003; Norris & Armstrong, 1999).

Under "Operation Virtual Shield," all of Chicago's various cameras as well as cameras owned by numerous other public and private entities are united under a single system. Operated by the Office of Management and Communications as part of its disaster prevention and management function, the agency maintains a command center where all cameras in the Operation Virtual Shield network can be monitored. Moreover, CPD officers are also able to view and operate the cameras at the CPD's Crime Prevention Information Center in addition to local precinct houses and even on computers in equipped squad cars (American Civil Liberties Union of Illinois, 2011, p. 10). Dramatically increasing the power of the government to watch people, newer cameras possess "pan-tilt-zoom" capacities that can increase the size of images, facial recognition software that can search crowds for a person's face, and an automatic tracking function that can follow a person or vehicle across multiple cameras as the target moves through the city (American Civil Liberties Union of Illinois, 2011, p. 3).

Though secretive about the number of cameras, undisputed public reports estimate that the City of Chicago has access to 10,000 publicly and privately owned cameras (American Civil Liberties Union of Illinois, 2011, p.1). Cameras are also operated by other agencies, including the Chicago Public Schools (with over 4,500 cameras inside and around buildings), the Chicago Transit Authority (1,800 cameras on buses and at train stations), O'Hare Airport (at least 1,000 cameras), and the McCormick Place Convention Center and Navy Pier (each with hundreds of cameras). Cameras are also owned and operated by the Chicago Park District, Chicago Housing Authority, Millennium Park, and Midway Airport (American Civil Liberties Union of Illinois, 2011, p. 10). The cost for such an extensive surveillance network is estimated to be over $60 million (American Civil Liberties Union of Illinois, 2011, p. 17). Taken together, the developments in Chicago suggest the growth of a surveillant assemblage. As former DHS Secretary Michal Chertoff stated, "I don't think there is another city in the U.S. that has as an extensive and integrated camera network as Chicago has" (American Civil Liberties Union of Illinois, 2011, p. 3).

Chicago is not alone in its use of surveillance in public space as a means to address crime and public order. Indeed, DHS has made available millions of dollars to local governments in the U.S. so that they can purchase surveillance cameras (Savage, 2007). With the help of these funds, surveillance regimens have been established in New York, Boston, Baltimore, San Francisco, Los Angeles, and Charleston (Abate, 2007; Klein, 2006; Savage, 2007). Savage (2007) reported that a *Boston Globe* study "of local newspapers and congressional press releases shows that a large number of new surveillance systems, costing at least tens and probably hundreds of millions of dollars, are being simultaneously installed around the country as part of homeland security grants" (p. A1). Citing the role that CCTV cameras played in the timely arrest of individuals associated with attempted car bombings in London and Glasgow in 2007, the chairman of the Senate Homeland Security Committee, Joseph Lieberman, concluded: "That is, they have cameras all over London and other of their major cities ... I think it's just common sense to do that here much more widely and of course we can do it without compromising anybody's real privacy" (Biesecker, 2007, p. 1).

Critics of the expansion of video surveillance systems in city centers, like the Electronic Privacy Information Center (2016), say there is reason to be cautious about the extravagant funding for urban surveillance systems in the U.S., as evaluations of existing surveillance systems have not been consistently positive. While federal and local government documents often tout surveillance systems like CCTV as effective crime fighting tools, more rigorous studies have typically been more qualified in their conclusions. Welsh and Farrington (2004), for example, reported that CCTV works best in reducing property crime, especially auto theft, but it does not work so well in reducing levels of violence, which is one of the chief aims toward which CCTV was publicly directed in Chicago. They also reported that evaluation studies show CCTV to be ineffective in the U.S. while the evidence is more favorable for systems deployed in the United Kingdom. Critics have also voiced concerns that expanded surveillance systems have civil liberty implications, but civil liberty arguments against surveillance practices in cities are generally discounted in the U.S., as Senator Lieberman's comment evidences. If one ventures into public space, the response goes, one has certainly forfeited a reasonable expectation of privacy.

Conclusion

We have sought in this chapter to use three case studies to show how a lack of transparency often makes a frank evaluation of surveillance regimens difficult. When surveillance schemes are launched in opaqueness, the public is left susceptible to slick presentations that resonate with favored cultural schemes like public safety, sovereignty and border control, and emergency interventions by first responders. Shrouded in mystery, surveillance regimens and the full import of their powers do not always come to the awareness of those who are observed or might otherwise care about the practices. In short, the meaning of surveillance and its potential for producing resistance grows from the way it is organized toward particular visions of order and propriety and how it is rendered before the public eye.

Our first and most substantial task in this chapter was to work out a conceptualization of surveillance. In that effort, we defined surveillance most simply as the collection of information by some specific means for a particular purpose. In elaborating upon that definition, we stressed a number of salient features of surveillance, including its management of information, its dependence on instruments to record observations, its requirement of an orientation or purpose to guide data collection and analysis, its use of data processing techniques like data mining and social sorting, its relationship to a potential response by surveillance agents, its capacity to produce awareness and emotional experiences in those subjected to surveillance, and its proclivity to provoke responses and perhaps resistance from those who are observed. Unpacking contemporary surveillance practices in this way provides a means for developing a fuller sense of its meaning for social life.

Surveillance in public space will undoubtedly expand in the coming years, as it will in other facets of our lives. Norris and Armstrong have claimed that "... with the integration of existing systems and the increasing automation of surveillance through the linking of cameras, computers, and databases, the architecture of the maximum surveillance society is now in place" (p. 12). We are confronted by an inexorable surge in surveillance techniques to be sure, but how that expansion in surveillance is to be judged can become complicated by the multiple purposes to which it can be applied. Drones can be deployed with the fierce firepower that permits the extrajudicial killing of targeted threats, as they do currently in the borderlands of Pakistan and in Yemen, but they will not likely fly in such a capacity over the skies of the U.S. any time soon, notwithstanding the protests of rabid crime control advocates. Instead, the capacity of drones to observe will probably be hitched to ends with far more cultural resonance; all the better to realize their full market value. Real estate will be moved, moving pictures will be produced, wildfires will be extinguished, pipelines and power lines will be inspected, and agricultural pursuits will be made more efficient and greener. Eventually, they will probably be used by police in the U.S. to neutralize active shooters and other folk devils, as the legislative move in North Dakota indicates. First the surveillance technique needs to be made familiar and comfortable to a population, then its mission can creep in ways never before anticipated. The basic problem with cell-site simulators is their opaqueness and outright denial; the Big Brother doublespeak used by government authorities to avoid commenting on their existence and use does little to earn a warm public embrace. Surveillance techniques that are fun to use and otherwise attend to popular efforts to circumvent secrecy are better poised to succeed. Meyrowitz (2009) has argued that the "public's typical equanimity in the face of increasingly pervasive surveillance" has been greased by the uptake of television in which "neither the watching of others nor the act of offering oneself up for watching by others can be perceived of as an odd or perverse activity" (p. 47). "We liked to watch," argues Meyrowitz (2009), and "an unwatched life—and a life without watching many others—now seems less worthy of living" (p. 47). Whether drones and cell-site simulators fare as well in the surveillance of public space as CCTV will depend on their ability to produce a cultural resonance for this technique of watching.

The meaning of surveillance cannot be established in the abstract. As counseled by advocates of cultural criminology, we can appreciate fully the social significance of surveillance only when we attend to "a bedrock question for cultural criminologists: What is the 'reality' of [surveillance] and who determines it?" (Ferrell, Hayward, & Young, 2008, p. 21). We have contended in this chapter that the "reality" of surveillance can be understood along several dimensions, but ultimately the meaning of surveillance regimens emerges from "the tangle of lived situations" in which these features of surveillance are experienced by the observed and the observers alike (Ferrell, 1997, p. 21). In some situations surveillance will be experienced as dark and menacing, as when cell-site simulators are used to gather evidence surreptitiously or to stifle political protest, while in other situations surveillance will be experienced as a source of empowerment, like when a citizen streams live on Facebook a violent and unlawful encounter with a police officer. Cultural criminology lobbies for "partial immersion in the situated logic and emotion that define criminal experiences" (Ferrell, 1997, p. 3), and this strategy seems promising for extracting a richer sense of the meaning of surveillance in our daily affairs. In attending to the "immediacy" of surveillance and the ways in which facets of a surveillance regimen are promoted or concealed, a better handle might be achieved on the reality of surveillance and on those who seek to massage that reality.

References

Abate, T. (2007, August 19). Airport makes most of surveillance tech. *San Francisco Chronicle*, p. B1.

American Civil Liberties Union of Illinois. (2011, February). *Chicago's video surveillance cameras: A pervasive and unregulated threat to our privacy.* Retrieved from http://www.aclu-il.org/wp-content/uploads/2012/06/Surveillance-Camera-Report1.pdf.

American Civil Liberties Union. (2016). Stingray tracking devices: Who's got them? Retrieved from https://www.aclu.org/map/stingray-tracking-devices-whos-got-them.

Andreas, P. (2000). *Border games: Policing the U.S.-Mexico divide.* Ithaca, NY: Cornell University Press.

Associated Press. (2013, December 14). Agriculture the most promising market for drones. *USA Today*. Retrieved from http://www.usatoday.com/story/news/nation/2013/12/14/agriculture-market-for-drones/4025559/.

Associated Press. (2015, January 6). Arrival of the drones: 20 uses for unmanned aircraft. *Omaha World-Herald*. Retrieved from http://www.omaha.com/money/arrival-of-the-drones-uses-for-unmanned-aircraft/article_4730b6a1-6d29-5673-a159-7847e23d8431.html.

Biesecker, C. (2007, July 3). Lieberman wants more use of surveillance cameras in U.S. cities. *Defense Daily*. Retrieved from http://www.defensedaily.com/publications/dd/.

Castells, M. (2009). *Communication power*. Oxford: Oxford University Press.

Cole, C., & Wright, J. (2010). What are drones? *Drone Wars UK*. Retrieved from https://dronewars.net/aboutdrone/.

Colias, M. (2004, April 30). Neighbors divided over Chicago's crime-busting cameras. *USA Today*. Retrieved from http://www.usatoday.com/tech/news/techpolicy/2004-04-30-chicago-police-cams_x.htm.

Daley, R. M., & Weis, J. P. (2008). Crime surveillance innovations in Chicago: The history of police observation devices (PODS). Chicago: Chicago Police Department. Retrieve from https://portal.chicagopolice.org/portal/page/portal/ClearPath/About%20CPD/POD%20Program/POD-History.pdf.

Dandeker, C. (1990). *Surveillance, power, and modernity*. Cambridge, UK: Polity.

Department of Justice. (2015, September 3). Department of Justice policy guidance: Use of cell-site simulator technology. Retrieved from https://www.justice.gov/opa/file/767321/download.

Dougherty, C. (2014, August 28). Google joins Amazon in dreams of drone delivery. *New York Times*. Retrieved from http://bits.blogs.nytimes.com/2014/08/28/google-joins-amazon-in-dreams-of-drone-delivery/.

Electronic Freedom Foundation. (2016). Cell-site simulators: Frequently asked questions. Retrieved from https://www.eff.org/sls/tech/cell-site-simulators/faq.

Electronic Privacy Information Center. (2016). EPIC domestic surveillance project. Retrieved from https://epic.org/privacy/surveillance/.

Ericson, R. V. (2007). *Crime in an insecure world*. Cambridge, UK: Polity.

Fenton, J. (2016, March 31). Maryland appellate court warrant required. *The Baltimore Sun*. Retrieved from http://www.baltimoresun.com/news/maryland/crime/bs-md-ci-stingray-court-decision-20160331-story.html.

Ferrell, J. (1997). Criminological verstehen: Inside the immediacy of crime. *Justice Quarterly*, *14*(1), 3–23.

Ferrell, J., Hayward, K., & Young, J. (2008). *Cultural criminology: An invitation*. Los Angeles: Sage.

Foucault, M. (1977). *Discipline and punish: The birth of the prison*. (A. Sheridan, Trans.). New York: Vintage Books.

Gallagher, R. (2013, July 3). U.S. border agency has considered weaponizing domestic drones to "immobilize" people. *Slate*. Retrieved from http://www.slate.com/blogs/future_tense/2013/07/03/documents_show_customs_and_border_protection_considered_weaponized_domestic.html.

Garside, J. (2014, March 28). Facebook buys UK maker of solar-powered drones to expand internet. *The Guardian*. Retrieved from https://www.theguardian.com/technology/2014/mar/28/facebook-buys-uk-maker-solar-powered-drones-internet.

Gilliom, J. (2001). *Overseers of the poor: Surveillance, resistance, and the limits of privacy*. Chicago: University of Chicago Press.

Glenza, J., & Woolf, N. (2015, April 10). Stingray spying: FBI's secret deal with police hides phone dragnet from courts. *The Guardian*. Retrieved from http://www.theguardian.com/us-news/2015/apr/10/stingray-spying-fbi-phone-dragnet-police.

Graham, S., & Wood, D. (2003). Digitizing surveillance: Categorization, space, inequality. *Critical Social Policy, 23*(2), 227–248.

Haggerty, K. D., & Ericson, R. V. (2000). The surveillant assemblage. *British Journal of Sociology, 51*(4), 605–622.

Haigh, S. (2016, February 28). Drone-mounted handgun, flamethrower reignite lawmaker debate. *Hartford Courant.* Retrieved from http://www.courant.com/breaking-news/hc-ap-weaponized-drones-20160228-story.html.

Handley, J. (2014, December 19). Slip of an officer's tongue suggests police monitoring #BlackLivesMatter protesters' cell phones. *In These Times.* Retrieved from http://inthesetimes.com/article/17476/a_slip_of_an_officers_tongue_suggests_police_are_monitoring_ferguson_protes.

Hörnqvist, M. (2010). *Risk, power, and the state: After Foucault.* Oxfordshire, UK: Routledge.

Kang, C. (2015, December 27). F.A.A. drone laws start to clash with stricter local rules. *New York Times.* Retrieved from http://www.nytimes.com/2015/12/28/technology/faa-drone-laws-start-to-clash-with-stricter-local-rules.html.

Katti, C. (2002). "Systematically" observing surveillance: Paradoxes of observation according to Niklas Luhmann's systems theory. In T. Y. Levin, U. Frohne, & P. Weibel (Eds.), *Ctrl [Space]: Rhetorics of surveillance from Bentham to Big Brother* (pp. 50–63). Cambridge, MA: MIT Press.

Kerr, A., De Paoli, S., & Keatinge, M. (2014). Surveillant assemblages of governance in massively multiplayer online games: A comparative analysis. *Surveillance and Society, 12,* 320–336.

Kinzer, S. (2004, September 21). Chicago moving to "smart" surveillance cameras. *New York Times.* Retrieved from http://www.nytimes.com/2004/09/21/national/21cameras.html.

Klein, A. (2006, October 22). Gunshot sensors are giving D.C. police jump on suspects; System can determine location of crime. *The Washington Post,* p. A1.

Koskela, H. (2000). "The gaze without eyes": Video-surveillance and the changing nature of urban space. *Progress in Human Geography, 24,* 243–265.

Lyon, D. (1994). *The electronic eye: The rise of surveillance society.* Minneapolis, MN: University of Minnesota Press.

Lyon, D. (Ed.). (2003). *Surveillance as social sorting: Privacy, risk, and discrimination.* London: Routledge.

Lyon, D. (2006). Airport screening, surveillance, and social sorting: Canadian responses to 9/11 in context. *Canadian Journal of Criminology and Criminal Justice, 48*(3), 397–411.

Lyon, D. (2007). *Surveillance studies: An overview.* Cambridge, UK: Polity Press.

Marx, G. T. (1985). I'll be watching you: Reflections on the new surveillance. *Dissent, 32,* 26–34.

Marx, G. T. (1988). *Undercover: Police surveillance in America.* Berkeley, CA: University of California Press.

Marx, G. T. (2002). What's new about the 'new surveillance'? Classifying for change and continuity. *Surveillance and Society, 1*, 9–29.

Marx, G. T. (2003). A tack in the shoe: Neutralizing and resisting the new surveillance. *Journal of Social Issues, 59*, 369–390.

Mazzetti, M. (2015, April 23). Killing of Americans deepens debate over use of drone strikes. *New York Times*. Retrieved from http://www.nytimes.com/2015/04/24/world/asia/killing-of-americans-deepens-debate-over-proper-use-of-drone-strikes.html.

McGrath, J. E. (2004). *Loving big brother: Performance, privacy, and surveillance space*. London: Routledge.

Meyrowitz, J. (2009). We liked to watch: Television as a progenitor of the surveillance society. *The Annals of the American Academy of Political and Social Science, 625*, 32–48.

National Conference of State Legislators. (2016, July 7). Current unmanned aircraft state law landscape. Retrieved from http://www.ncsl.org/research/transportation/current-unmanned-aircraft-state-law-landscape.aspx.

New York Civil Liberties Union. (2016, February 11). NYPD has used Stingrays more than 1000 times since 2008. Retrieved from http://www.nyclu.org/news/nypd-has-used-stingrays-more-1000-times-2008.

Norris, C., & Armstrong, G. (1999). *The maximum surveillance society: The rise of CCTV*. Oxford, UK: Berg.

Office of Public Affairs. (2015). Unmanned aircraft system MQ-9 Predator B. Washington, DC: United States Customs and Border Protection. Retrieved from https://www.cbp.gov/sites/default/files/documents/FS_2015_UAS_FINAL_0.pdf.

Orwell, G. (1949/1961). *1984*. New York: Signet Classics.

Owsley, B. (2014). TriggerFish, StingRays, and Fourth Amendment fishing expeditions. *Hastings Law Journal, 66*, 183–233.

Pell, S., & Soghoian, C. (2014). A lot more than a pen register, and less than a wiretap: What the StingRay teaches us about how Congress should approach the reform of law enforcement surveillance authorities. *Yale Journal of Law and Technology, 16*, 134–171.

Price, M. L. (2014, March 11). States wrestle with developing, restricting drones. *The Seattle Times*. Retrieved from http://old.seattletimes.com/html/businesstechnology/2023099316_apxdronerestrictions.html.

Rajan, A. (2008, August 4). US device that finds gunman in seconds to be tested by police. *The Independent*, p. 6.

Savage, C. (2007, August 12). US doles out millions for street cameras: Local efforts raise privacy alarms. *The Boston Globe*, p. A1.

Sengupta, S. (2013, July 3). U.S. border agency allows others to use its drones. *New York Times*. Retrieved from http://www.nytimes.com/2013/07/04/business/us-border-agency-is-a-frequent-lender-of-its-drones.html.

Shaw, D. (2012, July 23). Disaster drones: How robot teams can help in a crisis. *BBC News*. Retrieved from http://www.bbc.com/news/technology-18581883.

Shoemaker, P. J. (1996). Hardwired for news: Using biological and cultural evolution to explain the surveillance function. *Journal of Communication, 46*(3), 32–47.

Siuru, B. (2007). Gunshot location systems. *Law and Order Magazine, 55*, 10, 12, 15–17.

Wagner, L. (2015, August 27). North Dakota legalizes armed police drones. *NPR*. Retrieved from http://www.npr.org/sections/thetwo-way/2015/08/27/435301160/north-dakota-legalizes-armed-police-drones.

Walby, K. (2005a). How closed-circuit television surveillance organizes the social: An institutional ethnography. *Canadian Journal of Sociology, 30*(2), 189–214.

Walby, K. (2005b). Institutional ethnography and surveillance: An outline for inquiry. *Surveillance and Society, 3*, 158–172.

Weiser, B. (2016, July 12). D.E.A. needed warrant to track suspect's phone, judge says. *New York Times*. Retrieved from http://www.nytimes.com/2016/07/13/nyregion/dea-needed-warrant-to-track-suspects-phone-judge-says.html?_r=0.

Welsh, B. C., & Farrington, D. P. (2004). Surveillance for crime prevention in public space: Results and policy choices in Britain and America. *Criminology and Public Policy, 3*, 497–526.

Wilson, E. O. (1975). *Sociobiology: The new synthesis*. Cambridge, MA: Harvard University Press.

Yekutieli, Y. (2006). Is somebody watching you? Ancient surveillance systems in the southern Judean Desert. *Journal of Mediterranean Archaeology, 19*, 65–89.

Zetter, K. (2015, October 28). Turns out police Stingray spy tools can indeed record calls. *Wired*. Retrieved from http://www.wired.com/2015/10/stingray-government-spy-tools-can-record-calls-new-documents-confirm/.

Zurawski, N. (2007). Video surveillance and everyday life: Assessments of closed-circuit television and the cartography of socio-spatial imaginations. *International Criminal Justice Review, 17*, 269–288.

10

Spatial Crime Prevention: Traditional and Non-Traditional Perspectives

Ronald G. Burns and Brie Diamond

Spatial crime prevention is one of the many transformative strategies in modern policing. Policing in the United States has undergone a series of changes over time. For instance, organizationally, departments were historically decentralized in structure and would later evolve into more centralized units. Many departments later shifted back to decentralized structures as community policing gained prominence. Organizational design, however, is not the only area in which departments have changed. Functionally, the focus of police departments has shifted as society, department goals, and agency objectives changed.

A notable shift in focus among police agencies involves a greater emphasis on crime prevention. Proactive policing, a primary component of community policing, emphasizes the prevention of crime through addressing any underlying problems contributing to criminal behavior. To be sure, policing remains largely reactive in nature, however, recent philosophical shifts within police departments incorporate greater emphasis on actively preventing crime through consideration of—and changes to—the physical environment.

The following chapter addresses both traditional and non-traditional aspects of spatial crime prevention. Particularly, the chapter examines the traditional aspects of spatial crime prevention with a specific focus on ecological, or environmental factors, as evidenced in many community policing crime prevention efforts. The discussion of traditional aspects of spatial crime prevention centers on defensible space theories, crime prevention through environmental design (CPTED) efforts, situational crime prevention approaches, and routine activity theory. These traditional spatial crime prevention approaches share many similar traits and approaches and are well documented in the research literature. They are, however, not comprehensive in both their ability to prevent all forms of crime, and as representatives of spatial crime prevention efforts. Accordingly, this chapter also addresses several non-traditional aspects of spatial crime prevention with the goal of demonstrating to readers the far-reaching nature of activities encompassed in spatial crime prevention. The non-traditional aspects of spatial crime prevention discussed in this chapter include: (1) crime prevention efforts in relation to cultural space; (2) geospatial crime prevention efforts; (3) crime prevention efforts with regard to cyberspace; and (4) examination of the developing study of police practices with regard to spatial and temporal factors. These topics are termed "non-traditional" primarily because they do not immediately elicit images of spatial crime prevention. Nevertheless, each is certainly worthy of discussion with regard to spatial crime prevention and will likely prove to be increasingly significant as research attention is further directed their way.

An overview of crime prevention efforts in general (with a particular focus on spatial crime prevention) and a focus on community policing with regard to spatial crime prevention precedes the discussion of traditional and non-traditional approaches to spatial crime prevention. These sections facilitate understanding of how spatial crime prevention fits within the context of current crime prevention approaches, and more generally, police practices.

Crime Prevention: An Overview

The term "crime prevention" encompasses a wide array of proactive practices taken to inhibit criminal behavior. Given the varied nature of the term "crime," which ranges from murder to simple theft, crime prevention exists in many places and forms. To facilitate understanding of the varied nature of crime prevention, researchers categorized crime prevention approaches into three areas: Primary prevention, secondary prevention, and tertiary prevention (see Brantingham & Faust, 1976). Primary prevention is concerned with addressing the conditions in the physical and social environments that provide opportunities for criminal behavior. Primary crime prevention incorporates alteration of the physical environment for public safety purposes, neighborhood surveillance, general deterrence as primarily provided by the criminal justice system, social crime prevention efforts (e.g., job training programs and addressing issues such as poverty and unemployment), and private security.

Secondary crime prevention includes efforts designed to identify potential criminals and intervene prior to one's involvement in crime (Brantingham & Faust, 1976). Secondary prevention includes attempts directed toward the early identification of problem individuals, crime area analyses, situational crime prevention efforts, community policing, substance abuse prevention and treatment programs, and crime prevention efforts implemented in schools. Tertiary crime prevention efforts, on the other hand, directly deal with known offenders in attempt to restrict them from further engaging in crime (Brantingham & Faust, 1976). Such efforts mostly involve actions taken by criminal justice authorities, including sanctions designed to meet the goals of deterrence, incapacitation, treatment, and/or rehabilitation.

Spatial crime prevention efforts appear in all three levels of crime prevention approaches. For instance, primary prevention incorporates use of environmental design to prevent crime. Examples of altering the environment for the sake of crime prevention include architects increasing visibility for residents through building design, residents adding and using lights and locks, and marking one's property for identification purposes. Architectural design is also used for access control in relation to pedestrian and motor vehicle traffic.

Spatial crime prevention is also evident in secondary crime prevention efforts, for instance with regard to crime area analyses and situational crime prevention. Mapping crime to assess the extent and nature of criminal behavior in specific locations is becoming increasingly common in law enforcement agencies across the United States. Situational crime prevention "attempts to identify existing problems at the micro level and institute interventions that are developed specifically for the given problem." Such interventions include changes to the physical environment, for instance, to improve surveillance (Lab, 2000, p. 21).

Spatial crime prevention is found within tertiary crime prevention approaches as well. Perhaps the most obvious example of a spatial, tertiary-level crime prevention approach is criminal sentences with incapacitation as the primary goal. Physically restricting individuals from committing additional crimes against society, for instance by putting them in prison for an extensive period of time, is a relatively common crime prevention effort found throughout the U.S.

Community Policing and Spatial Crime Prevention

The roots of police work are grounded in crime prevention. Policing in the United States is largely based on the model developed by Sir Robert Peel in England. Peel's police, often recognized as the first formal police department, were largely tasked with maintaining order and preventing crime. Early U.S. police departments modeled Peel's approach and initially focused their efforts on order maintenance and crime prevention. Policing in the U.S. would adopt more of a crime fighting approach around the 1960s, when turbulent times and volatile social issues generated a call for such an approach.

The adoption of community-oriented policing by most police departments beginning in the 1980s prompted less of a focus on crime fighting and greater emphasis on crime prevention. Among other benefits, community policing requires that police departments become increasingly proactive in their efforts to stop crime prior to its occurrence. The increasingly proactive approach taken by police departments is multifaceted and incorporates a wide array of crime fighting and crime prevention efforts. To be sure, community policing is not solely restricted to crime prevention, as crime fighting remains central to law enforcement objectives.

Community policing efforts can be deconstructed into three primary components: strategic-oriented policing, problem-oriented policing, and neighborhood-oriented policing (Oliver, 2001). Strategic-oriented policing consists of various patrol strategies, including aggressive patrol, directed patrol, and saturation patrol. With regard to spatial crime prevention, a particularly significant aspect of strategic-oriented policing concerns directed patrols. These types of patrol involve an emphasis on identifying hot spots where a disproportionate amount of crime occurs. Research suggests that a relatively small percentage of households are responsible for a disproportionate percentage of police calls for service (Sherman, Gartin, & Buerger, 1989). In basic terms, strategic-oriented policing incorporates a more tactical approach to policing and encompasses proactive policing, for instance, through enhanced patrol efforts.

Problem-oriented policing also encompasses crime prevention, although it does so by directly confronting problematic situations. Problem-oriented policing is recognized as a four-step process, which begins with the identification of a particular problem, followed by analysis of the extent and nature of the problem, response(s) to the problem, and assessment of the extent to which the problem was addressed. Successfully completing these four steps ensures that police efforts directly responded to the situation and hopefully addressed the root causes of the problem. Such efforts may or may not involve spatial crime prevention.

Neighborhood-oriented policing, the third component of community policing, encompasses a wide array of programs, actions, and efforts that many individuals in society directly relate to community policing efforts. Neighborhood-oriented policing can be divided into four programs: community social control programs, communications programs, community crime prevention, and community patrols (Oliver, 2001). The community crime prevention aspect of neighborhood-oriented policing is most relevant to the present discussion of spatial crime prevention. Basically, community crime prevention efforts include programs such as Neighborhood Watch and home security surveys. Each of these and related programs incorporate notable concerns for spatial components. For instance, Neighborhood Watch programs are designed to encourage neighborhood residents to provide surveillance and provide various forms of assistance with regard to preventing crime in their respective neighborhood.

Another community crime prevention effort concerns home security surveys, which typically include law enforcement assessments of residential homes and commercial businesses with concern for ecological factors such as the height of shrubbery, lighting, access control, and other considerations. Home security surveys are perhaps one of the most identifiable spatial crime prevention efforts taken by police departments. As part of their community policing mandates, many police departments will survey existing or proposed sites of homes or business with regard to personal safety, security, and environmental design. For instance, the Crime Prevention Unit of the Springfield (Missouri) Police Department (SPD) offers, free of charge to Springfield residents, a crime prevention through environmental design (CPTED) security survey for homes and businesses. The survey is designed to protect homes and businesses by reducing opportunities for crime to occur through addressing physical design features that discourage crime and encourage legitimate use of the property. The survey includes an evaluation of the location (or future location) of the property, the advantages and disadvantages of the facility with regard to CPTED strategies, precautions that might hamper CPTED strategies for the facility, and recommendations for the facility to employ CPTED strategies. The surveys include consideration of numerous factors, including lighting, landscaping, windows, doors, communication systems, indoor and outdoor activities, access, security systems, walls, fences, signs, safe paths, common areas, boundaries, and public spaces (CPTED Security Survey, 2008). The SPD is certainly not the only police department that provides security surveys for its residents, and is among the many departments that strongly consider spatial characteristics with regard to crime prevention efforts.

In sum, policing-based, spatial crime prevention efforts exist in a variety of forms and are implemented in a variety of ways, including several other efforts not discussed in this work. The present discussion, nevertheless, highlights the more prominent approaches and sheds light on what many believe to be an effective means of preventing crime.

Traditional Spatial Crime Prevention

Spatial crime prevention owes its roots to the study of social ecology, or how the social environment breeds behavioral responses. During the early part of the twentieth century, researchers from the University of Chicago's Department of Sociology proposed that ecological conditions and variables in Chicago contributed to variations in crime rates throughout the city (e.g., Burgess, 1925; Shaw & McKay, 1929). Jane Jacobs, in her 1961 book *The Death and Life of Great American Cities*, further noted a relationship between crime and the physical environment. In response to the relationship, Jacobs argued that improving opportunities for surveillance would contribute to greater crime prevention (Jacobs, 1961). Related to Jacobs' work are the contributions offered by Elizabeth Wood, who also proposed a relationship between crime and the physical environment. Focusing on public housing developments, Wood identified how the physical characteristics of public housing facilities restricted interaction and contact among residents, which subsequently hampered informal social control efforts (Wood, 1981). These and other earlier works (e.g., Angel, 1968) set the stage for more theoretically sound approaches to spatial crime prevention, including those offered by defensible space theorists, proponents of CPTED, Lawrence Cohen and Marcus Felson as part of their routine activity theory, and supporters of situational crime prevention efforts.

Defensible Space

Similar to other, early researchers who focused on spatial crime prevention, Oscar Newman examined the environmental aspects of public housing buildings in his introduction of "defensible space." Newman cited the importance of four key components in his discussion of defensible space: territoriality, natural surveillance, image, and milieu. Territoriality emphasizes the sense of ownership residents maintain over an area that encourages them to react when problems appear. Natural surveillance refers to the ability to view the activity, both inside and outside of structures, without the aid of particular devices (e.g., video cameras). Newman recognized the importance of image with regard to neighborhoods or areas having an appearance of being isolated and uncared for, which generates the impression that residents are not concerned about what occurs. Milieu, as discussed by Newman, refers to the belief that locating a community within a low-crime area will reduce the presence of criminal activity (Newman, 1972).

Newman's work is credited with being the seminal work with regard to the first-generation defensible space theorists, yet it has also been the subject of criticism (Taylor, Gottfredson, & Brower, 1980; Rosenbaum, Lurigio, & Davis, 1998). Some called Newman's work "deterministic" and "overly restrictive" (Taylor, Gottfredson, & Brower, 1980), suggesting that first-generation defensible space theories ignored the impacts of the social characteristics of residents and surrounding areas on crime rates (e.g., Wilson, 1990). It is also argued that first-generation defensible space theorists failed to define key concepts such as territoriality, neglected to empirically assess assumptions regarding residents' behaviors, focused on modifications to the external environment while neglecting internal considerations, and lacked concern for intervening variables (Taylor, Gottfredson, & Brower, 1980; Paulsen & Robinson, 2004).

CPTED

The shortcomings of the first-generation defensible space theorists encouraged some researchers to consider and include social and cultural values in their crime prevention models. They also gave more consideration to residents' thought processes and behaviors with regard to territoriality (Taylor, Gottfredson, & Brower, 1980; Rosenbaum, Lurigio, & Davis, 1998). In 1971, C. Ray Jeffery championed his notion of CPTED, an extension of defensible space, which "attempts to apply physical design, citizen participation and law enforcement strategies in a comprehensive, planned way to entire neighborhoods and even major urban districts." CPTED can also apply to urban subsystems, including schools and transportation systems (National Crime Prevention Institute, 1986). Among the goals of CPTED are access control, surveillance, activity support, and motivation reinforcement. Access control refers to the ability to regulate who enters or exits a building or territory, with the primary goal of limiting access to legitimate users. Surveillance includes actions that contribute to the ability of legitimate users to monitor the presence of others, either through active (e.g., closed-circuit television) or passive (e.g., unobstructed views through windows) means. Activity support refers to the functions and activities that promote interaction between residents and other legitimate users in the area. Finally, motivation reinforcement pertains to promoting feelings of territoriality and social cohesion through particular construction of the physical design and promoting pride in the area (Kushmuk & Whittemore, 1981).

Research on crimes such as burglary provides meaningful insight into the policy relevance of CPTED. Analyses of burglary data indicate that land use diversity, the presence of garages, rear-facing neighboring houses, and cul-de-sacs are associated with a reduced likelihood of victimization (Armitage,

Monchuk, & Rogerson, 2011; Sohn, 2016). The latter finding has become so common as to influence modern community development designs. Armitage and colleagues (2011) advocate for collaborations between land use developers and law enforcement to design public and private spaces that reduce the likelihood of crime.

Put simply, CPTED was designed to reduce crime, minimize the fear of crime, and ultimately improve quality of life issues (Crowe, 1991). The 1971 edition of Jeffery's *Crime Prevention Through Environmental Design*, which includes his original version of CPTED, heavily emphasized the impact of the environment upon human behavior. The revised edition of his work, however, included an expanded version of CPTED that stressed an integrated systems model which suggested that factors in addition to the environment (e.g., biological factors, including genetics and brain functioning) contribute to human behavior (Jeffery, 1977). CPTED advanced the aforementioned defensible space theories, however, CPTED was also the subject of criticism (Rosenbaum, Lurigio, & Davis, 1998). For instance, it was argued that CPTED strategies had not been empirically evaluated across socioeconomic strata (Westinghouse Electric Corporation, 1976), although researchers would eventually find that CPTED strategies could effectively apply in both luxury apartment buildings and public housing developments (Feins & Epstein, 1996).

Situational Crime Prevention

Similar to the approaches of both CPTED and defensible space, situational crime prevention seeks to reduce opportunities for crime to occur, for instance, through target hardening and/or changes to the physical environment. Situational crime prevention may also involve broader strategies than those associated with CPTED and defensible space (Lersch, 2007). In his book *Situational Crime Prevention*, Ronald Clarke suggested that situational crime prevention "refers to a preventive approach that relies, not upon improving society or its institutions, but simply upon reducing opportunities for crime" (Clarke, 1992, p. 3). Clarke noted that situational prevention encompasses opportunity-reducing efforts that are directed toward specific types of crime, involve managing or altering the immediate environment in a systematic and permanent manner, and seek to increase the risks and efforts associated with crime while concurrently reducing the rewards associated with the criminal act.

Clarke and colleagues continuously refined their work on situational crime prevention in response to particular criticisms. Following several revisions, a third version of Clarke's original typology was introduced and includes twenty-five techniques of situational crime prevention under five primary headings.

These techniques range from strengthening formal surveillance (e.g., red light cameras and security guards) to preventing disputes (e.g., reduced crowding in pubs). The major categories within this effort are increasing the offender's effort, increasing the risks associated with crime, reducing the rewards associated with crime, reducing provocations, and removing excuses (Cornish & Clarke, 2003).

In accord with all theoretical explanations of crime, situational crime prevention has been the subject of critique. Among the notable limitations of situational crime prevention is the assumption of rationality on behalf of offenders (Hayward, 2007). Some view the underlying rational choice theory inherent in situational crime prevention as lacking applicability to many crimes, especially expressive forms of violent crime. Proponents, however, argue that *all* criminal behavior is rational; for instance, even mass murders or offenders clearly caught on camera contain lucid assumptions and actions (Farrell, 2010). All offenders operate under *bounded rationality* (Simon, 1957; Brezina, 2001), meaning that they make decisions—albeit many impulsive and ill conceived—within the framework of their capabilities, experiences, and situational inducements. Therefore, while many crimes may appear irrational in the traditional sense, situational crime prevention efforts must understand the rational decision-making that does take place in context.

Situational crime prevention primarily focuses on altering the environment to reduce or eliminate the opportunity to commit crime. Accordingly, another critique of this approach is that it offers very little with regard to changing criminal inclinations. Situational crime prevention circumvents motivation in favor of finding environmental strategies that fail to ignite these inclinations. Situational crime prevention has also been accused of merely displacing criminal behavior, although research suggests that situational crime prevention efforts do not merely shift crime to other, non-protected areas and often produce a diffusion of benefits to surrounding communities (Guerette & Bowers, 2009; Paulsen & Robinson, 2004).

Routine Activity Theory

Routine activity theory, as proposed by Cohen and Felson, holds that criminal behavior occurs when a motivated offender, the presence of suitable targets, and an absence of capable guardians to prevent crime converge in time and space (Cohen & Felson, 1979). Removal of one of these elements is, according to routine activity theory, justification for the prevention of a crime. Accordingly, individuals seek to protect themselves through providing guardianship to prevent crime (e.g., by installing locks on their doors); demotivating criminals, or removing motivated offenders from society (e.g., through counseling or prison), and/or; removing the presence of suitable targets (e.g., by refusing to wear expensive jewelry or drive an expensive car). Routine activity theory proposes that the likelihood of an individual being victimized by an offender is influenced by their daily routines.

Among the criticisms of routine activity theory are the difficulties associated with measuring the three primary components. Operationalization is particularly problematic, for instance, as it can be difficult to measure *ex post facto* an offender's motivation at the time of their actions. Routine activity theory has also been criticized on the grounds that it assumes that criminals (and others) are consistently acting in a rational manner. This theory more or less assumes that offenders are constantly motivated to commit crime without elaborating upon the reasons for (or population variance of) such inclinations.

Routine activity theory, defensible space, CPTED, and situational crime prevention are much alike in their considerations of the physical environment in attempt to reduce opportunities for criminal behavior. An identifiable difference among the approaches concerns the extent to which they recognize both the external environment and the internal composition of individuals who wish to engage in crime. Both routine activity theory and CPTED give notable consideration to internal factors, with Jeffery's later version of CPTED acknowledging numerous internal and external factors and moving beyond the assumption that all potential offenders think and behave in a rational manner. Despite any differences, these crime prevention approaches have contributed much to our understanding of how spatial factors affect criminal behavior and how environmental influences can be altered to deter, or prevent crime. They provide guidance for police departments to better prevent and control crime, for instance through working with home and business owners, developers, policy makers, and others to consider the influences of spatiality on crime.

Non-Traditional Spatial Crime Prevention

The non-traditional aspects of spatial crime prevention discussed in this chapter include crime prevention efforts in relation to cultural space, geospatial crime prevention efforts, crime prevention efforts with regard to cyberspace, and spatial and temporal policing. By non-traditional it is meant that these aspects generally differ from the ecological studies and theoretical bodies primarily associated with spatial crime prevention (e.g., defensible space,

CPTED, situational crime prevention, and routine activity theory). The following discussion centers on topics that are non-traditional, yet certainly worthy of consideration with regard to spatial crime prevention, as they each maintain unique characteristics and implications for the study of how spatiality influences crime prevention.

Crime Prevention Efforts in Relation to Cultural Space

Examinations of the traditional methods through which physical space can be altered to prevent crime are well represented in the research literature. Another consideration of spatial crime prevention requires recognition of the cultural aspects of preventing crime, or how crime prevention efforts impact various cultures. Relevant to this discussion is the study of cultural criminology, which "interweaves particular intellectual threads to explore the convergence of cultural and criminal processes in contemporary social life" (Ferrell, 1999, p. 395). A key concept within cultural criminology is cultural space, including efforts by cultural groups to establish, and various authorities to remove, cultural space.

Cultural space is considered "a place of contested perception and negotiated understanding, a place where people of all sorts encode their sense of self, neighborhood, and community." Of particular importance with regard to cultural space is the suggestion that "the occupation of public areas remains as much symbolic as physical" (Ferrell, 2001a, p. 14). Accordingly, crime prevention efforts commonly intersect with cultural values; values that are often expressed throughout public spaces.

Cultural criminologists suggest that much police work occurs within the context of contestations regarding cultural space. Culturally marginalized groups such as the homeless individuals, graffiti artists, street gang members, and street "cruisers," are often targeted by moral panic that lead to law enforcement action that further sanitizes areas of their presence (Amster, 2003; Ferrell, 1999; Goode & Ben-Yehuda, 2010). Efforts to engage in spatial crime prevention against such marginalized groups include alterations to public benches to prevent skateboarding, dimming the lighting in specific areas to discourage graffiti, removing homeless individuals from the streets, and criminalizing the wearing of particular gang colors and cruising-related driving habits. Criminalizing and related efforts to prevent such activities serves to restrict cultural activities and freedom of expression, and subsequently promotes the conflict criminologists' claims that powerful groups in society regularly and continuously use the law to impose their will against the less powerful (e.g., Lynch, Michalowski, & Groves, 2000). In other words, spatial crime prevention efforts that seek to infringe upon cultural space contribute to the ongoing conflict between powerful and less-powerful groups.

Determining the point at which spatial crime prevention efforts impose too far upon cultural space is often the subject of public debate. The United States is becoming increasingly diverse, and the onus is on representatives of the criminal justice system to appropriately recognize and respond to demographic and cultural changes (e.g., McNamara & Burns, 2009). In his discussion of identity, space, and social justice, particularly with regard to consumption, control, and cultural space, Ferrell notes that "As new cultural places are carved out by city planners and corporate developers, they serve to redesign city life along new lines of spatial exclusion, and to organize new forms of control against those deemed foreign to these spaces" (Ferrell, 2001b, p. 167). This statement, among other contributions, highlights the multi-faceted nature of spatial crime prevention.

Any discussion of spatial crime prevention warrants consideration of qualitative factors. For instance, criminalizing or contesting cultural space simply because authorities and/or other powerful groups may not understand, or willingly accept, harmless culture-based behaviors serves to promote particular interests and contributes to an increasingly sterile and generic society. Cultural spaces have been, and continue to be, infringed upon with justification that doing so attempts to protect or restore law and order. How to best balance the rights of cultural expression and crime prevention/fighting has challenged and continues to challenge lawmakers, politicians, and many others in society.

Geospatial Crime Prevention Efforts

Police personnel historically used simplified maps to track crime in their respective jurisdictions. Pin-mapping, as it is commonly called, was conducted with the intent to locate what have recently been termed "hot spots" of criminal activity. Pin-mapping has largely been replaced by technology-driven geospatial crime prevention efforts. Particularly, computers now provide notably sophisticated analyses of criminal behavior and other aspects of crime and justice. Among other benefits, such analyses contribute to enhanced crime prevention efforts. Computerized crime mapping, via GIS (Geographic Information Systems) applications, "can merge layers of information in a visual form so that the relationships between places, times, events and trends become more evident than they would from analyzing the raw data" (Dees, 2002, p. 43).

Several developments beginning in the mid-1980s contributed to police analysts increasingly utilizing computerized crime mapping. The advancements and accessibility of computer systems, the introduction and continued development of GIS software, and an enhanced focus on geographical factors with regard to crime prevention (particularly in accord with community policing efforts) contributed significantly to the widespread incorporation of technology-based crime mapping (Paulsen & Robinson, 2004). Virtually all U.S. major cities and many smaller jurisdictions actively use computerized crime mapping (Hickman & Reaves, 2006).

Geospatial crime mapping is used in policing, the courts, and in corrections. For instance, attorneys use computer-generated maps in presenting particular pieces of evidence, while community supervision officers may use maps to locate the homes of supervisees for the purposes of service area allocation. It is in policing, however, where geospatial mapping is most widely used. Specifically, mapping is used in four primary areas with regard to policing: patrol, investigation, community relations, and administration.

Patrol work is the backbone of policing. Departments are enhancing their patrol efforts by increasingly utilizing geospatial crime analyses to assess where patrol is most needed and determining the types of efforts needed in particular areas. Computerized maps generated by crime analysts typically focus on criminal intelligence, recent crime series, known offenders, calls for service, and information alerts (Paulsen & Robinson, 2004). To be sure, such information is vital for both responding to crimes and crime prevention efforts.

Crime mapping is also used during investigations of crimes. For instance, serial offense patterns become increasingly easier to understand, track, and respond to when visually presented to investigators. Investigators also use crime mapping to create and assess known suspect lists in relation to criminal events. For instance, identifying on a map the residences of known offenders in relation to the physical location of a crime may help investigators create a list of potential suspects.

Police administrators also use crime mapping, for example, with regard to crime reduction strategies. Problem-oriented policing efforts are facilitated through being able to visually assess problematic areas and the locations of criminal events, as administrators can more effectively respond and direct resources. Police administrators also use computerized mapping with regard to personnel issues, for instance as they pertain to shift-related requirements. Being able to visually assess crime at particular locations and times enables police administrators to determine the level of policing that may be required.

Finally, crime mapping assists police departments with regard to community relations. It is well established that enhanced police-community relations are vital to community policing efforts. Accordingly, many departments have reached out to the community in attempt to garner support and assistance. Along these lines, crime mapping enables police departments to better depict and explain their efforts to the public, for example by highlighting crime-prone areas, which enables citizens to become more aware of how they can protect themselves and others (see pp. 177–189 in Paulsen & Robinson, 2004, for elaboration of how computerized mapping has assisted law enforcement). Being able to visually assess where and what types of crimes predominantly occur, in visual form, has assisted many police departments. Subsequently, departments have continuously integrated crime mapping into their crime prevention practices, and it is expected that they will continue to do so.

Crime Prevention Efforts with Regard to Cyberspace

As evidenced in the discussion above, computers have enhanced police practices. Such enhancement, of course, is not strictly related to crime mapping. For instance, about 90% of police officers are employed by departments that provided in-field computerized access to vehicle and driving records (Reaves, 2015), and the introduction of CompStat (an abbreviation for "computer statistics" or "comparison statistics") has enhanced crime-fighting efforts in numerous departments. CompStat, a "multi-faceted system for managing police operations" (Schick, 2004, pp. 17–18) attempts to reduce crime via: (1) accurate and timely intelligence, (2) rapid deployment of personnel and resources, (3) effective tactics, and (4) relentless follow-up and assessment (Shane, 2004).

Intelligence-led policing initiatives strive to combine various policing applications to create proactive, agency-wide strategies for situational crime prevention (Ratcliffe, 2008). Originally developed in the United Kingdom and adopted by the United States in response to 9/11, intelligence-led policing uses data on offenders and crime areas, often across jurisdictions, to allocate resources for crime prevention efforts. Computer-generated data provide guidance for police departments to identify potential and current crime-prone areas, thus promoting more effective use of resources and police practices in general. While intelligence-led policing is often superficially applied, deeply integrated versions of the approach can lead to effective crime control (Ratcliffe, 2002). Computers have also provided significant and substantial challenges for policing, as new avenues for criminal behavior exist and continue to emerge. Of particular concern with the increasing prevalence of computer crime is identifying (and utilizing) methods by which these types of crime can be prevented.

Computers have undoubtedly added another dimension to our lives. Social interaction, economic transactions, and many other daily activities now occur regularly in cyberspace. To be sure, this shift in everyday life has notable implications for law enforcement. For instance, there has been a significant shift in the physical location of criminal events. Crimes that earlier occurred in public (e.g., theft, fraud) are increasingly occurring online, in private dwellings. This shift has particular implications for the study of spatial crime prevention.

Preventing crime via analyses of spatial factors has shifted from the streets to homes where computers are accessed. In other words, instead of analyzing neighborhoods, communities, or blocks, crime analysts are increasingly required to analyze URLs, IP addresses, email, and other related components of computer technology. This shift in focus requires reconsideration of traditional spatial crime prevention efforts. For instance, the physical co-presence of victim and offender that characterizes most conventional crimes is of little relevance to cybercrime. Analyses of victim behavior must consider the virtual environments accessed as part of cybercrime, instead of the physical environments they enter when victimized by street crime. Spatial analyses of crime and related crime prevention efforts must shift toward the offender and victim's computer, network, and/or Internet provider when confronting cybercrime.

Of particular importance with regard to spatial crime prevention and computer crime are the capability of law enforcement agencies to respond to cybercrime, and whether current spatial crime prevention approaches are viable for addressing this new form of crime. Research in these areas suggests that cybercrime is a distinct form of crime that is not receiving an appropriate level of response by law enforcement. For instance, earlier assessments of law enforcement preparedness to effectively address cybercrimes found somewhat discouraging results, as police departments seem to lack, among other things, the necessary resources to fight crimes such as Internet fraud (Burns, Whitworth, & Thompson, 2004).

Theorists have also addressed the uniqueness of cybercrime, particularly the inability of routine activity theory to explain this class of crime. Researcher Majid Yar stated that parts of routine activity theory's core concepts are applicable to cybercrime, however "there remain important differences between 'virtual' and 'terrestrial' worlds that limit the theory's usefulness. These differences ... give qualified support to the suggestion that 'cybercrime' does indeed represent the emergence of a new and distinctive form of crime" (Yar, 2005, p. 407). As noted, routine activity theory focuses on the convergence in time and space of a motivated offender, a suitable target, and a lack of guardianship. In Yar's view, "the cyber-spatial environment is chronically spatio-temporally *disorganized*" (emphasis in original, Yar, 2005, p. 424) and predicting the confluence of a cyber victim and offender is virtually impossible.

As Diamond and Bachman (2015) point out, however, routine activities research does not make attempts to pinpoint the convergence of these two actors, but focuses on the policy driven elements of the theory—suitable targets and capable guardianship—both of which find their equivalent in cybercrime.

Suitable targets for various cybercrimes will be those individuals who spend more time online, conduct more commercial business online, and frequent a larger range of websites. Capable guardianship that protects individuals from victimization may come in the form of encrypted passwords, firewalls, and network administrators and Internet citizens that recognize and report potential cybercrimes. While little research on the subject exists, the applicability of routine activities theory to cybercrime is supported with regard to financial fraud and online harassment (Holt & Bossler, 2008; Pratt, Holtfreter, & Reisig, 2010). Future research should continue to examine whether traditional environmental crime prevention theories are suitable for effectively addressing computer crimes, how spatial crime prevention applies to cybercrime, and the extent to which law enforcement agencies are interested and/or prepared to address cybercrime.

Spatial and Temporal Policing

Recent research on police practices has focused on the interaction of both time and space. Such research is long overdue, given the historical absence of such considerations in the research literature. In his ethnographic study of territoriality and the Los Angeles Police Department, Steve Herbert noted that "social action always occurs in place and thus is shaped by spatial contexts." Herbert added that "police officers so fundamentally embed their powers in the boundaries they create and enforce that analysis of their practices must attend to the means by which they make and mark space" (Herbert, 1997, pp. 20–21).

Robert Sampson is among the researchers who believe measurements of crime and justice would be enhanced through research investigating the relationships between time and space (Sampson, 1993). Similarly, Lawrence Sherman earlier suggested the need for enhanced research measurements, the identification and application of different theoretical models, and the observation of multivariate relations across various levels of analyses (Sherman, 1980). The increasing body of research examining time, space, police practices, and their interaction responds, in large part, to the calls of researchers such as Sampson and Sherman and has undoubtedly enhanced our understanding of policing. Such research includes the work of Phillips and Smith, who examined the impact of time and space variables using data generated from citizen complaints files. Based on their findings, Phillips and Smith stated: "time-space variables are important predictors of the use of major physical force by police against civilians" (Phillips & Smith, 2000, p. 480).

More recently, Crawford and Burns examined use-of-force reports from six police departments to assess the impact of particular factors across several levels of force. Specifically, their research was designed to assess how the interaction of time and space-related variables influence officer behavior. Among other findings, Crawford and Burns found that officers were significantly more likely to use police tactics and deadly force when working in locations known to be hazardous. Further, they found that officers were more likely to use restraints during arrests that occur in the street, yet notably more likely to use deadly force during arrests that occurred in a suspect's house (Crawford & Burns, 2008).

Ethnographic research on police practices in relation to time and space suggest that officers develop a sense of understanding and expectations with concern for the individuals with whom they interact in particular places and at specific times of the day (Brogden, Jefferson, & Walklate, 1988). Particularly, the location or area an officer is patrolling may affect police responses, as areas where troublesome individuals may frequent or reside will draw greater police scrutiny (Holdaway, 1983), and subsequent enhanced concern for crime prevention approaches.

Put simply, understanding the context and overall nature in which police work occurs is facilitated by examining time, space, and their interaction. Territorial awareness and police perception of offenses and offenders are largely impacted by both time and space (Van Maanen, 1978; Rubenstein, 1973), for instance, as individuals invading an officer's personal space or evading police interaction generate more punitive police responses than those who don't invade an officer's personal space or run from the police. Enhanced crime prevention practices, for instance through consideration of spatial and temporal factors, will undoubtedly contribute to more positive police-citizen relations, and more generally, a safer society.

Much of what police officers do involves crime prevention. For example, patrol work, making arrests, and conducting investigations are all aspects of crime prevention. Accordingly, understanding how spatial factors influence police practices sheds light on the present account of spatial crime prevention.

In Sum and Onward

Spatial crime prevention is multi-faceted to be sure. This chapter addressed traditional and non-traditional perspectives of spatial crime prevention efforts and approaches. The traditional spatial crime prevention approaches discussed in this chapter (i.e., routine activity theory, CPTED, situational crime prevention, and defensible space) each include a demonstrated concern for altering the physical environment for the sake of crime prevention. The non-traditional perspectives concerning spatial crime prevention (i.e., crime mapping; spatial crime prevention in cyberspace; consideration of time, space, and police practices; and crime prevention and cultural space) are less concerned with physically removing opportunities to commit crime than are the traditional perspectives. The non-traditional approaches discussed in this work more directly relate to considerations intertwined with spatial crime prevention; considerations that are certainly important, yet aren't typically discussed with regard to spatial crime prevention.

Examining traditional and non-traditional perspectives of spatial crime prevention provides a foundation of knowledge in the area and guidance for continued work in the area. In light of these traditional and non-traditional perspectives regarding spatial crime prevention, several directions for future work are offered. First, it is hoped that future research efforts involving spatial crime prevention consider multiple factors, not the least of which are the ability of technology to assist with crime prevention, the impacts such efforts will have on *all* individuals who may be affected, and consideration of the various ecological theories. Second, it is hoped that those who study police practices will further recognize the benefits of including spatial (and temporal) variables in their work. The continued advancement of police studies is dependent upon more thorough analyses incorporating a wider array of factors and variables. The evolving literature on policing makes a strong argument that police practices, including proactive policing efforts, are impacted by spatial factors. Finally, future research should closely consider the applicability of traditional spatial crime prevention approaches to computer crime. Put simply, criminologists and criminal justice researchers can no longer neglect the study of computer crimes. It is the responsibility of researchers to better understand how existing theories apply to emerging crimes. Such work could generate a need for altered theories, or new theories that better explain all types of criminal behavior.

Spatial crime prevention efforts should continue to produce innovative responses to a variety of social problems. Heroin injection clinics, for example, intend to reduce the harm associated with serious drug use by employing medical professionals to oversee the process (Johansen & Johansen, 2015). Mobile versions of these establishments targeting areas of dense heroin usage promise to increase heroin users' safety, and decrease their involvement in violent, crime-ridden areas—an assumption supported by research (Shannon, Rusch, Shoveller, Alexson, Gibson, & Tyndall, 2008). These clinics represent a controversial, yet inventive application of spatial crime prevention that should inspire future applications of the approach.

The idea of a crime-free society is comforting. Is it practical, however, to speculate that crime prevention efforts will completely eliminate crime? Probably not. Nevertheless, crime can be reduced. Doing so takes creativity, ingenuity, hard work, and perseverance, among other factors. Criminologists offer a multitude of theories explaining why crime occurs. There's also a significant body of work examining how crime can be prevented. Part of this body of work focuses on preventing crime through consideration and alteration of the physical environment. The challenge for future generations is to develop, refine/expand, and apply existing theories with consideration of our complicated and changing society. In sum, the incomplete yet promising study of how spatial factors contribute to crime and crime prevention efforts suggests that we can anticipate additional work in this area, with the hope of continuously advancing our understanding of all aspects of spatial crime prevention.

References

Amster, R. (2003). Patterns of exclusion: Sanitizing space, criminalizing homelessness. *Social Justice, 30*(1), 195–221.

Angel, S. (1968). *Discouraging crime through city planning*. Berkeley, CA: University of California Press.

Armitage, R., Monchuk, L., & Rogerson, M. (2011). It looks good, but what is it like to live there? Exploring the impact of innovative housing design on crime. *European Journal on Criminal Policy & Research, 17*, 29–54.

Brantingham, P. J., & Faust, F. L. (1976). A conceptual model of crime prevention. *Crime and Delinquency, 22*, 284–296.

Brezina, T. (2001). Assessing the rationality of criminal and delinquent behavior: A focus on actual utility. In A. R. Piquero & S. G. Tibbetts (Eds.), *Rational choice and criminal behavior: Recent research and future challenges* (pp. 241–264). London: Routledge.

Brogden, M., Jefferson, T., & Walklate, S. (1988). *Introducing policework*. London: Unwin Hyman.

Burgess, E. (1925). The growth of the city. In R. E. Park, E. W. Burgess, & R. D. McKenzie (Eds.), *The city* (pp. 47–62). Chicago, IL: University of Chicago Press.

Burns, R. G., Whitworth, K. H., & Thompson, C. Y. (2004). Assessing law enforcement preparedness to address internet fraud. *Journal of Criminal Justice, 32*(5), 477–493.

Clarke, R. V. (Ed.). (1992). *Situational crime prevention: Successful case studies*. New York: Harrow and Heston.

Cohen, L., & Felson, M. (1979). Social change in crime rate trends: A routine activity approach. *American Sociological Review, 44*, 588–608.

Cornish, D., & Clarke, R. (2003). Opportunities, precipitators, and criminal decisions: A reply to Worley's critique of situational crime prevention. In M. Smith & D. Cornish (Eds.), *Theory for practice in situational crime prevention* (pp. 41–96). Monsey, NY: Criminal Justice Press.

Crawford, C., & Burns, R. (2008). Police use of force: Assessing the impact of time and space. *Policing & Society, 18*(3), 322–335.

Crowe, T. D. (1991). *Crime prevention through environmental design*. Boston, MA: Butterworth-Heinemann.

Dees, T. (2002, August). Understanding GIS. *Law and Order*, pp. 42–46.

Diamond, B., & Bachman, M. (2015). Out of the beta phase: Obstacles, challenges, and promising paths in the study of cyber criminology. *International Journal of Cyber Criminology, 9*(1), 24–34.

Farrell, G. (2010). Situational crime prevention and its discontents: Rational choice and harm reduction versus 'cultural criminology'. *Social Policy & Administration, 44*(1), 40–66.

Feins, J. D., & Epstein, J. C. (1996). *Solving crime problems in residential neighborhoods: Comprehensive changes in design, management, and use*. Cambridge, MA: Abt. Associates.

Ferrell, J. (1999). Cultural criminology. *Annual Review of Sociology, 25*, 395–418.

Ferrell, J. (2001a). *Tearing down the streets: Adventures in urban anarchy*. New York: St. Martin's Press.

Ferrell, J. (2001b). Remapping the city: Public identity, cultural space, and social justice. *Contemporary Justice Review, 4*(2), 161–180.

Goode, E., & Ben-Yehuda, N. (2010). *Moral panic: The social construction of deviance*. West Sussex, UK: Wiley-Blackwell.

Guerette, R. T., & Bowers, K. J. (2009). Assessing the extent of crime displacement and diffusion of benefits: A review of situational crime prevention evaluations. *Criminology, 47*(4), 1331–1368.

Hayward, K. (2007). Situational crime prevention and its discontents: Rational choice theory versus the 'culture of now'. *Social Policy & Administration, 41*(3), 232–250.

Herbert, S. (1997). *Policing space: Territoriality and the Los Angeles Police Department*. Minneapolis, MN: University of Minnesota Press.

Hickman, M. J., & Reaves, B. A. (2006, May). *Law enforcement management and administrative statistics: Local police departments, 2003*. U.S. Department of Justice, Bureau of Justice Statistics, NCJ 210118.

Holdaway, S. (1983). *Inside the British police: A force at work*. Oxford: Basil Blackwell.

Holt, T. J., & Bossler, A. M. (2008). Examining the applicability of lifestyle-routine activities theory for cybercrime victimization. *Deviant Behavior, 30*(1), 1–25.

Jacobs, J. (1961). *The death and life of great American cities.* New York: Random House.

Jeffery, C. R. (1971). *Crime prevention through environmental design.* Beverly Hills, CA: Sage.

Jeffery, C. R. (1977). *Crime prevention through environmental design.* Beverly Hills, CA: Sage.

Johansen, B. S., & Johansen, K. S. (2015). Heroin: From drug to ambivalent medicine. On the introduction of medically prescribed heroin and the emergence of a new space for treatment. *Culture, Medicine & Psychiatry, 39,* 75–91.

Kushmuk, J., & Whittemore, S. L. (1981). *A reevaluation of the crime prevention through environmental design program in Portland, Oregon.* Washington, DC: National Institute of Justice.

Lab, S. P. (2000). *Crime prevention approaches, practices, and evaluations* (4th ed.). Cincinnati, OH: Anderson.

Lersch, K. M. (2007). *Space, time, and crime* (2nd ed.). Durham, NC: Carolina Academic Press.

Lynch, M. J., Michalowski, R., & Groves, W. B. (2000). *The new primer in radical criminology: Critical perspectives on crime, power & identity* (3rd ed.) Monsey, NY: Criminal Justice Press.

McNamara, R., & Burns, R. (2009). *Multiculturalism in the criminal justice system.* New York: McGraw-Hill.

National Crime Prevention Institute. (1986). *Understanding crime prevention.* Stoneham, MA: Butterworth.

Newman, O. (1972). *Defensible space.* New York: Macmillan.

Oliver, W. (2001). *Community-oriented policing: A systemic approach to policing* (2nd ed.). Upper Saddle River, NJ: Prentice Hall.

Paulsen, D. J., & Robinson, M. B. (2004). *Spatial aspects of crime: Theory and practice.* Boston, MA: Allyn and Bacon.

Phillips, T., & Smith, P. (2000). Police violence occasioning citizen complaint: An empirical analysis of time-space dynamics. *British Journal of Criminology, 4,* 480–496.

Pratt, T. C., Holtfreter, K., & Reisig, M. D. (2010). Routine online activity and internet fraud targeting: Extending the generality of routine activity theory. *Journal of Research in Crime and Delinquency, 47*(3), 267–296.

Ratcliffe, J. H. (2002). Intelligence-led policing and the problems of turning rhetoric into practice. *Policing and Society: An International Journal of Research and Policy, 12*(1), 53–66.

Ratcliffe, J. H. (2008). *Intelligence-led policing.* Portland, OR: Willan Publishing.

Reaves, B. (2015). *Local police departments, 2013: Equipment and technology.* U.S. Department of Justice, Bureau of Justice Statistics. NCJ 248767.

Rosenbaum, D. P., Lurigio, A. J., & Davis, R. C. (1998). *The prevention of crime: Social and situational strategies.* Belmont, CA: Wadsworth.

Rubenstein, J. (1973). *City police.* New York: Farrar, Straus, and Giroux.

Sampson, R. (1993). Linking time and place: Dynamic contextualism and the future of criminological inquiry. *Journal of Research in Crime and Delinquency, 30*, 426–444.

Schick, W. (2004, January). CompStat in the Los Angeles Police Department. *The Police Chief*, 17–23.

Shane, J. M. (2004, April). CompStat process. *FBI Law Enforcement Bulletin, 73*(4), 12–21.

Shannon, K., Rusch, M., Shoveller, J., Alexson, D., Gibson, K., & Tyndall, M. W. (2008). Mapping violence and policing as an environmental-structural barrier to health service and syringe availability among substance-using women in street-level sex work. *International Journal of Drug Policy, 19*(2), 140–147.

Shaw, C., & McKay, H. (1929). *Juvenile delinquency and urban areas.* Chicago, IL: University of Chicago Press.

Sherman, L. (1980). Causes of police behavior: The current state of quantitative research. *Journal of Research in Crime and Delinquency, 17*, 69–100.

Sherman, L. W., Gartin, P. R., & Buerger, M. (1989). Hot spots of predatory crime: Routine activities and the criminology of place. *Criminology, 27*(2), 27–55.

Simon, H. (1957). *Models of man: Mathematical models on rational human behavior in a social setting.* New York: John Wiley.

Sohn, D. (2016). Residential crimes and neighbourhood built environment: Assessing the effectiveness of crime prevention through environmental design (CPTED). *Cities, 52*, 86–93.

Springfield Police Department. CPTED Security Survey. Retrieved from http://ci.springfield.mo.us/spd/GeneralInfo/crimeprevtips/Home/CPTED.html.

Taylor, R. B., Gottfredson, S. D., & Brower, S. (1980). The defensibility of defensible space. In T. Hirschi & M. Gottfredson (Eds.), *Understanding crime* (pp. 17–36). Beverly Hills, CA: Sage.

Van Maanen, J. (1978). The asshole. In P. K. Manning & J. Van Maanen (Eds.), *Policing: A view from the street* (pp. 221–238). Santa Monica, CA: Goodyear Publishing.

Westinghouse Electric Corporation. (1976). *Crime prevention through environmental design: Residential demonstration plan.* Minneapolis, MN.

Wilson, S. (1990). Reduction of telephone vandalism: An Australian case study. *Security Journal, 1*, 149–154.

Wood, E. (1981). *Housing design: A social theory.* New York: Citizens' Housing and Planning Council.

Yar, M. (2005). The novelty of 'cybercrime': An assessment in light of routine activity theory. *European Journal of Criminology, 2*(4), 407–427.

A Few Closing Thoughts

I hope you have gained some insight from this journey through the spatial challenges that face law enforcement officers, departments, and citizens. Some of the topics that were discussed in *Spatial Policing* are not without controversy, notably the issues of race, deadly force, surveillance, and immigration. Each of the chapters of *Spatial Policing* offers fascinating reviews and interpretations that can serve as a starting point for the much-needed discussion of policy, prevention, and how space is marked and defined by police and government officials.

The study of space and location to explain crime and its control is not new, but its resurgence has been met with a great deal of excitement. I hope that as the authors shared their expertise and thoughts on some of the most complex spatial contexts in our society you expanded your awareness of how space impacts our lives and policing efforts. Far from solving these heated issues in criminal justice, my goal was to create a text that could serve as a starting point for understanding some of the issues surrounding the influence of space and place on crime and policing. Whether you are an interested citizen, a researcher, or senior-level law enforcement administrator, I do hope this book has encouraged you to take a closer look at theory, research, design, and history to gain a better appreciation of how space is made, used, and controlled by various groups.

If you are a student, I hope this text has helped you in some small way to sharpen your critical thinking skills. You may be the next senior-level administrator or community activist who is striving to make a change for the better in your space or particular place. Either way, as others turn to you for solutions you will find your thoughts and opinions can impact people's lives, sometimes for the better, other times not. Although few issues involving reducing crime, reforming the police, or creating a welcoming and all-inclusive public space are simple, I hope that the information presented in *Spatial Policing* provides a framework for understanding controversial policing actions and offers some possible solutions. In addition, I hope that when your colleagues, students, or fellow citizens turn to you for guidance your responses will be balanced and better informed.

About the Editor and Contributors

Charles E. Crawford holds a PhD in criminology from Florida State University and is a professor of sociology at Western Michigan University. He has published numerous refereed journal articles, book chapters, and reports on a wide variety of criminal justice topics. Some of his articles have appeared in the journals *Criminology*; *Police Quarterly*; *Crime Law and Social Change*; *Crime, Media, Culture*; *Police and Society*; and *Policing: An International Journal of Police Strategies & Management*. He is also the co-author of *Federal Law Enforcement: A Primer* (2nd edition), and co-editor of *Policing and Violence*.

Emmanuel P. Barthe is an associate professor of criminal justice at the University of Nevada, Reno. He holds a doctorate in criminal justice from the School of Criminal Justice at Rutgers. His research interests lie in the arena of policing, situational crime prevention, and spatial analysis. His publications include work on the impact of casinos and crime, the effect of different low-income housing on disorder patterns, and the legal ramifications of traffic checkpoints. He works closely with local law enforcement agencies and has served as an external evaluator for several projects, including a methamphetamine interdiction effort, a campaign to reduce commercial traffic accidents, and a BJA-funded Smart Policing grant covering prescription drug abuse.

Elizabeth P. Bradshaw is an associate professor of sociology at Central Michigan University. Much of her research focuses on state-corporate environmental crimes in the oil industry, criminogenic industry structures, use of surveillance by social movements, and resistance to crimes of the powerful.

Ronald G. Burns is department chair and professor of criminal justice at Texas Christian University (TCU). He has published over 75 articles in areas including policing, multiculturalism in the criminal justice system, the criminal justice system, and white-collar crime. He is the author, coauthor, or editor of eight books, including *Multiculturalism in the Criminal Justice System*; *Environmental Law, Crime and Justice* (2nd edition); *Federal Law Enforcement*; *Policing: A Modular Approach*; *Critical Issues in Criminal Justice*; *The Criminal Justice System*; *Environmental Crime: A Sourcebook*; and *Policing and Violence*. Dr. Burns graduated from Florida State University in 1997 and has been at TCU ever since.

Brie Diamond is an assistant professor of criminal justice at Texas Christian University. Her research interests include juvenile delinquency, corrections, program evaluation, and criminological theory with an emphasis on advanced statistical methodologies.

Jeff Ferrell is a professor of sociology at Texas Christian University and Visiting Professor of Criminology at the University of Kent, UK. He earned his PhD in sociology from the University of Texas at Austin. He is the author of *Crimes of Style*; *Tearing Down the Streets*; *Empire of Scrounge*; and, with Keith Hayward and Jock Young, *Cultural Criminology: An Invitation*. He is also the co-editor of the books *Cultural Criminology*; *Ethnography at the Edge*; *Making Trouble*; and *Cultural Criminology Unleashed*. Jeff Ferrell is the founding and current editor of the New York University Press book series *Alternative Criminology*, and one of the founding and current editors of the journal *Crime, Media, Culture: An International Journal*, winner of the Association of Learned and Professional Society Publishers' 2006 Charlesworth Award for Best New Journal. In 1998, he received the Critical Criminologist of the Year Award from the Division of Critical Criminology of the American Society of Criminology.

Gregory J. Howard is an associate professor of sociology at Western Michigan University. He earned a PhD from the School of Criminal Justice at the State University of New York at Albany. His current research is concerned with surveillance, mobility, and media.

Kim Michelle Lersch is a professor at the University of South Florida Polytechnic. Her primary area of research is police behavior, especially police deviance. Recent publications have appeared in *Journal of Criminal Justice*, *Policing & Society*, *Criminal Justice Review*, and *Policing: An International Journal of Police Strategies & Management*. She recently published the second edition of *Space, Time, and Crime* (Carolina Academic Press) and *Policing and Misconduct*.

Robert Hartmann McNamara is a professor of political science and criminal justice at the Citadel. He holds a PhD in sociology from Yale University. He has published numerous articles on a variety of topics and has been a consultant for state, federal, and private agencies. He is the author of dozens of books, including *Homelessness in America* (three volumes); *Juvenile Delinquency: A Student-Oriented Approach*; *Problem Children: Special Populations in Delinquency*, with Ryan Conlon; *Multiculturalism and the Criminal Justice System*, with Dr. Ronald Burns; *The Lost Population: Status Offenders in America*; *Boundary Dwellers: Homeless Women in Transitional Housing*, with Amy Hauser and Carrie Flagler; *Crossing the Line: Interracial Couples in the South*, with Maria Tempenis and Beth Walton; *The Times Square Hustler: Male Prostitution in New York City*; and *Police and Policing*, with Dr. Dennis Kenney. Dr. McNamara has also served as a Senior Research Fellow for the National Strategy Information Center, the Policy Lab, the Police Executive Research Forum, in Washington, DC, and the Pacific Institute for Research and Evaluation, in Baltimore, MD.

Ilse Aglaé Peña holds a bachelor of science and a master's degree in criminal justice. Her academic areas of interest include law and society, capital punishment, immigration law, and social justice. She has co-authored book chapters and refereed journal articles, and is currently working on a book entitled *Hispanic Soldiers: The Latino Legacy in the U.S. Armed Forces*. Vested in research, publication, and higher education, she will be pursing doctoral studies.

Frank Tridico is an assistant professor of criminal justice at Lake Superior State University and holds a PhD in sociology from Wayne State University. He helped design one of the earliest university courses on hate crimes in the United States, amalgamating primary field research with hate crime legislation, criminal cases, and statistical analysis. He has served as informal counsel to attorneys, law enforcement, and journalists with information pertaining to hate crimes, far-right groups, and legal issues. He is the author of several books and publications, including *The Social Construction of Reality* (2003); *How Sociologists Do Research* (2003), with Richard Fancy; *Contemporary Issues in Law and Society* (2004); *Law and Social Order* (2009); *Issues in Social Justice* (2009), with Joseph M. Pellerito and Jacob Armstrong; and *Hate Crimes* (2015).

Martin Guevara Urbina is a professor of criminal justice at Sul Ross State University. He holds a PhD in sociology from Western Michigan University. He is author, coauthor, or editor of over 60 scholarly publications on a wide range of topics, including *Hispanics and the American Criminal Justice System: A Critical Reader on the Latino Experience* (2017); *Latino Access to Higher Education: Ethnic Realities and New Directions for the Twenty-First Century* (2016); *Latino*

Police Officers in the United States: An Examination of Emerging Trends and Issues (2015); *Twenty-First Century Dynamics of Multiculturalism: Beyond Post-Racial America* (2014); *Ethnic Realities of Mexican Americans: From Colonialism to 21st Century Globalization* (2014); *Capital Punishment in America: Race and the Death Penalty Over Time* (2012); *Hispanics in the U.S. Criminal Justice System: The New American Demography* (2012); *A Comprehensive Study of Female Offenders: Life Before, During, and After Incarceration* (2008); and *Capital Punishment and Latino Offenders: Racial and Ethnic Differences in Death Sentences* (2003, 2011). His work has been published in national and international academic journals, to include *Justice Quarterly*; *Critical Criminology*; *Social Justice*; *Latino Studies*; and *Criminal Law Bulletin*.

Index